ALL MY LOVE, ELWOOD

ALL MY LOVE, ELWOOD

LETTERS FROM THE FRONT, EDITED BY RICHARD ELWOOD TURNER

DEEDS PUBLISHING | ATLANTA

Published by Deeds Publishing in Athens, GA
www.deedspublishing.com

Printed in The United States of America

Cover and interior design by Deeds Publishing

ISBN 978-1-961505-43-8

Books are available in quantity for promotional or premium use.
For information, email info@deedspublishing.com.

First Edition, 2025

10 9 8 7 6 5 4 3 2 1

Chapter/Section 1: Training

Enlistment date:	16 October 1942
Fort Niagara, New York	1 November 1942
Camp Stewart, Georgia	4 November 1942 – mid-Jan 1943
Camp Gordon Johnston Florida	17 January 1943 – early April 1943
Camp Stewart, Georgia	6 April 1943 – 30 May 1943
Camp Forrest, Tennessee (Tullahoma, Tennessee)	20 June 1943 – 1 September 1943

Chapter/Section 2: England

Leaves for England:	5 Sept 1943 – arrive 16 Sept 1943
England	17 Sept 1943 – 28 June 1944

Chapter/Sect 3: France, Belgium, Luxembourg, Germany 28 June 1944 – 19 August 1945

Discharge date 7 October 1945

This book is dedicated to the men and women who have fought for freedom and democracy around the world. May we all give thanks every day for their service and sacrifices.

Acknowledgements & Thanks

I've been blessed with the support, encouragement, and assistance of so many friends and family members over the years. Special thanks for making this book possible go to: my sister, Barbie Franks, who suggested, "You should turn this into a book!" Barbie encouraged me throughout the entire process, along with my brother Bob, sister Jenny, and family friend Lee Tornabene.

To my cousin John Jr. who exchanged letters with my dad throughout the war as a child and who now, at age 90, provided invaluable support to help me solve many puzzle pieces. To my cousin, Judy Norton, who was the subject of so many of my dad's letters, thanks for providing pictures, information, and funny stories about many of the characters. To my cousin Richard Hatcher, in Dorset, England, thank you for closing so many loops and getting me in contact with others in Sturminster Newton.

Thanks to Steve Case and Zilla Brown from the Museum of Sturminster Newton for providing key locations and timeframes. To Lisa Keith-Lucas of the Camp Gordon-Johnston Museum in Carrabelle Florida and to all the kind residents of Tullahoma, Tennessee who helped us visualize dad's time in Florida and Camp Forrest, Tennessee.

To my friend, Mark Moe, thanks for accompanying me on more than one journey to trace my dad's steps in France, Belgium, Luxembourg, and Germany. Our recent March 2025 visit to over fifty 4th ID locations in France and Belgium truly confirmed and answered so many truths outlined in dad's letters. While in Gerbeviller, we were helped by Leone, Edmund, and Mayor Noel Marquis. Thanks for your hospitality.

In Antwerp, thanks to Isabelle and Tim at the current day Meeting Center – The Old Bathhouse in Antwerp, Belgium, thanks for helping us walk the halls of the same building dad lived and worked in during July and August 1945. You are both so kind for giving us your time.

To Bob Babcock, my publisher, and past president and historian of the National 4th Infantry Division Association, I cannot thank you enough for clarifying just where on the battlefield my dad was and for walking me step-by-step through this process of writing and publishing a book.

To Michael Belis, historian for the 22nd Infantry Regiment Society, thanks for providing me so much invaluable information about dad's unit, the equipment his unit operated, and clarifying the meaning of some of my dad's awards.

And most of all thanks to my wife, Janice, our son, Bradley, and his wife, Kileigh, and our daughter, Angela and her husband, Kyle. Lastly, a big hug and thanks go to Brooke, Ace, Beckett and Brielle for giving Pa Pa the energy and reason for writing this book. Thanks for keeping me young. Please don't forget your Great Pa Pa, Elwood, and all those who served alongside, all those many years ago.

Introduction/Synopsis

The Wartime Adventures of U.S. Army Medic Elwood Almy Turner. "In case of my death, my body will be sent to you. Don't be scared. I said in case."

In the late 1990s, my aunt gave me 160 of my dad's letters dating from his entry into the Army in October 1942 and ending in postwar Europe in August 1945. The letters shocked me and revealed so much about my dad. They sharpened my regret that my dad and I never really talked much about his wartime experiences. There was an unspoken "I don't want to talk about it" aura with my dad. Now, as we approach the 80th anniversary of the end of World War II, I fully understand what my dad and other veterans endured.

Eight years after my dad's death in 1971, my job as a Department of the Army Civilian took me to Germany for a five- year assignment. My wife, Janice, and I traveled as much as we could while stationed in Europe and our son, Bradley, was born in Germany. We had no idea we journeyed some of the same roads and visited the same cities my father traveled while serving as a Medic for the 4th Infantry Division.

This book captures all 160 letters and traces Elwood's steps from New York, South Carolina, Florida, Tennessee, England, France, Belgium, Luxembourg, Germany and return to the United States. My passion is to preserve the legacy and selfless service of my father and his battle buddies for my family and others to enjoy. There is no better way to do this than to capture each letter in my dad's own words, by date, location and key points. Hear him describe in detail how he lived, where he went, what he saw and who he met along the way.

The list of "People and Places" on page 226 outlines all the geographical locations he traveled and some well-known international personalities he saw along the way, such as: General Bradley, Marlene Dietrich, and Harry Truman. Each Chapter ends with pictures taken over 80 years ago and many of the same locations in today's setting.

Elwood ("Dad"), the youngest of five children, was born on 3 February 1920, in Walworth, New York, to Almy and Almena Turner. His Mom died when Dad was only five years old. His father and two elder sisters, Esda and Eunice raised him. Dad's close family also included two other sisters, Lois and Margie. Almy instilled the importance of family, faith and hard work in my dad. Family was everything to him, as you will see by his frequent letter writing back home.

Dad was inducted into the Army on 16 October 1942. He was in-processed at Camp Niagara, New York and then sent to basic training at Camp Stewart, Georgia on 5 November 1942. He wrote home that he had safely arrived into the "Land of Cotton". He trained at Camp Gordon-Johnston, Florida in Feb/March/April 1943 before he returned to Camp Stewart, GA. Just prior to deployment to England, dad trained at Camp Forest (Tullahoma), Tennessee. Dad was ultimately trained as a dental technician and Medic after he rated very high on an IQ test.

Dad sailed for England on 5 September 1943 arriving on 16 September 1943. Dad's unit Battery A, 377th Anti-Aircraft Battalion was assigned to the 4th Infantry Division. He was ultimately stationed at Sturminster Newton (Stur), Dorset England from December 1943 until late June 1944.

Dad met 16-year-old Hazel Heather Hatcher in Stur at a dance. Hazel was born in April 1927 in a small town close to Stur, called Gillingham to parents Walter (Grandfi) and Susan (Grandma) Hatcher. During my childhood, Mom talked more about her wartime experiences than my dad. She told us of seeing German planes flying close overhead, close enough to see the pilot's faces. She talked of seeing plane crashes and body bags and keeping all the lights off at night to avoid becoming bombing raid targets.

Dad lived with the Mumford family while stationed in Stur. The Mumford family owned the city's Animal Infirmary and Dispensary. This book captures the only letters we have from the Mumford's to dad's family, revealing their love and admiration for him. From Ms. Mumford's letters, we learned that Dad was in the "last lot" to leave Sturminster Newton for Normandy on 28 June 1944.

Dad participated in the following battles and campaigns over the next 10 months: Normandy, Northern France, Ardennes, Central Europe, and Rhineland. Many of these battles and campaigns took place very close to where I lived while stationed in Germany in the early 1980s. Dad's letters and 4th ID situation reports provided me the details which facilitated my multiple trips back to Europe to trace his steps since I left Germany in 1984.

In March 2025, my good friend and fellow retired Department of the Army Civilian (34 years' service), Mark Moe, journeyed to France and Belgium to revisit over 50 sites highlighted in wartime records and dad's letters. Everywhere we journeyed, we met people who still celebrate their freedom and take time to honor those who fought for their freedom. This was so very encouraging to us.

At war's end, Dad was stationed Northeast of Nuremburg, Germany where he lived in Schnaittach, Germany for several months. Dad often wrote of the times he and his buddies would play ball and swim in the Olympic sized pool in Schnaittach. I was fortunate to see that same pool and town in 2019, 2021, and 2023.

Before returning to the States on 24 September 1945, Dad married Mom on 1 September 1945 at the St. Mary's Church in Sturminster Newton. This beautiful church dates to 1328. Over the many years, my family has visited this church and even saw original church records of the wedding with Mom and Dad's signatures.

Hazel left her Mom, Dad, and brother on 15 April 1946, three days after her 19th birthday for New York harbor. She traveled on the Saturnia, with all her earthly belongings in a 27"x18"x23" travelling trunk. That trunk is in my office to remind me daily of her sacrifice and love for my dad. She would not see her parents together again until they came to the States in 1952.

Join me as we retrace Elwood and Hazel's journey and experience the day-to-day life of a World War II Army medic as he served our nation alongside millions of others who, unbeknownst to them, belonged to the Greatest Generation.

From left: Almy Turner, Almena Turner, Elwood at age 5

Chapter/Section 1: Training

Enlistment date: 16 October 1942
Fort Niagara, New York   1 November 1942
Camp Stewart, Georgia   4 November 1942 – mid-Jan 1943
Camp Gordon Johnston Florida   17 January 1943 – early April 1943
Camp Stewart, Georgia   6 April 1943 – 30 May 1943
Camp Forrest, Tennessee (Tullahoma, Tennessee)   20 June 1943
– 1 September 1943

COLOR CODES

Black type = Dad's letters
Red type = 4th Infantry Division Situation Reports
Green type = Letters from Mrs. Mumford
Blue type = Letters from Mom (Hazel)

1 November 1942: Post card from Fort Niagara, New York. First post-card "Sunday 5 o'clock mailed from Youngstown, New York on 2 November. "Hi everybody, every card I've written today is about the same. I've got to buzz this off so I can go to the show. Sunday is our day off and we only have to get up at 6:45 a.m. instead of 5:45. We have until 6:25 to make our bed, mop the floor, get washed and dressed for assembly, then we march to breakfast. We march to dinner at 12 noon. We march to supper at 4 p.m. The morning seems long, so does the afternoon, because I'm usually tired from noon on. Thanks for the money belt. I wear it every minute I'm here.

Eunice, I am buying bonds here and they are payable to me, but the beneficiary will be David. Tell John they are to be divided between them, but I could only put one name on it. The bonds will be sent to you to keep for me… one every month and 3/4. Also, in case of my death, my body will be sent to you. Don't be scared. I said in case. You can tell Pop this when you see him. I'll write you a letter as soon as I get my permanent address, then you will be able to write me so until then, Elwood. P.S. Tell Lois to forward me Marjorie's address as soon as I'm located."

4 November 1942: Handwritten letter from Camp Stewart, Georgia: Dad's first letter: "Well, I'm in the land of cotton. It's dry and sandy. Warm in the daytime and cold and damp at night. God what a God forsaken place. (**NOTE:** Dad was born and raised in upstate New York. This is probably his first trip south and I can understand why he would be shocked culturally and by the climate.) 42 miles from the market city of Savannah. We are quarantined for a week which means we can't do a damn thing but remain in a restricted area. In the Army you have to wear your clothes, make your bed, anything you do has to be done the Army way or else you get K.P. When you're on K.P. you have to get up at 4:45 instead of 5:45 and work until 8 or 9 O'clock at night. I haven't been on it yet and I don't look forward to it. We left Fort Niagara at 2:10 and went to Niagara Falls. Hopped the train and went to Buffalo for supper. Mind you it takes lots of time to move for a bunch of yard birds. From Buffalo, after a 2 hour-wait we left to and thru Chicago to Cincinnati. Then we turned southward down through Kentucky, Tennessee, and almost to Florida-Georgia border to Atlanta. Then we moved eastward on to Camp Stewart. We arrived here at 11:30 Wednesday noon. We will stay here for our basic training, and I hope I'm shipped out of here after that. This land down here is swampy and there are cotton mouth snakes here and Alligators. I haven't seen any yet, but we have leggings to wear to protect us from the snakes. So far, we haven't got any arms of any kind. I guess they are to come yet. I asked to get in the Air Corps or

Cavalry, so they put me in the Coast Artillery. That's what you get for being drafted. I imagine that's why I don't like it here. Oh well, there is a chance to be transferred after our basic training, so I won't give up yet. In my clothing (Barracks Bag) I've got: 1. Raincoat; 2. Overcoat; 3. Off Duty (O.D) Blouse (2 of these); 4. Field Jacket; 5. 2 pairs O.D. pants for cold weather, 2 pair for hot weather; 6. 2 shirts; 7. 2 suits of Fatigues, (a form of overhauls for everyday); 8. 2 pairs of shoes (Big ones) 9 D. size; 9. 5 pairs of socks (2 dress and 3 work socks); 10. 3 handkerchiefs; 11. 2 suits of long underwear and 2 pairs of short underwear; 12. 2 sweat shirts; 13 1 pair lettings; 14. 3 ties; 15. 1 fatigue hat, 1 overseas hat for winter and 1 for summer; 16. 3 towels; 17. Shaving brush, cream and razor; 18.. Canteen; 19. Mess kit; 20 Army manual

"There might be more, but I can't think right now. I've got to mail all these things with indelible ink sometime with my last initial and the last 4 numbers of my serial no. ex-T.7801. Eunice all my letters are somewhat different so if you would show this to the rest and them to you, you'll be able to learn everything I've been doing so far. It's easier for me that way. Here's my return address below so make sure to write me back: Pvt. Elwood A. Turner, Btry A. 377th C.A. (Bn) (AA) Camp Stewart, Georgia, U.S.A. Army" He then explains the Army acronyms: Btry = Battery; CA = Coast Artillery; B. N. = Battalion; (AA) = Anti-aircraft.

7 November 1942: Post card from Camp Stewart Georgia, Medical Detachment 377th, Sep C.A. Bn. (AA). First Post Card from Camp Stewart, Georgia. Dad was assigned to the Medical Detachment because of his "good marks on my I9." (**NOTE:** Today, and since 1986, the I-9 form, or Employment Eligibility Verification form, is used by employers to verify the identity and employment authorization of new employees. From Dad's comment about "my I9" it must have been some Army aptitude test taken soon after enlistment). Dad was one of only three out of 150 or 160 men selected for the Medical Detachment. The "fellas" in the unit call him "Doc" He plays the guitar for the others along with a

guy who plays "a mouth organ". He says, "I think we are going across."
(**NOTE:** Dad would not leave for England until September 1943. He
had a lot of training to complete!) Most of the fellas in his unit were
from the West and Mid-west. Dad says, "Boy, you should hear their
drawl… "Sho-nuff". He ends with "Use the address on the front of this
card and pass the word on. Elwood." (**NOTE:** This sets the tone for the
next nearly three years. His family, all four sisters, his dad, girlfriends and
his church family would write him frequently, and he would reply to all
the letters. I'm confident that the time they took to write Dad helped
keep him sane.)

8 November 1942: Post card from Hotel Savannah, Savannah, Georgia.
Dad starts: "Here I sit on a nice soft bed with a pen in one hand and a
drink in the other. Two other fellows and I got a weekend pass and came
here to Savannah." He was very pleased to already be getting mail! He
asks Uncle Johnny to take care of his car. Either sell it or whatever. He
did not care. "If you want the radio, take it. Be good and I'll write later,
Uncle Elwood."

19 November 1942: Letter from Camp Stewart, Georgia: "Well, so far,
I've written 3 letters and I'm getting tired. But I must write to you all.
Notice my southern accent? I just finished writing Margie, Esda, Lois
and Pop. I'm busy every minute because of our basic training being only
2 weeks. Our battery is considered to have more training than the other
fellows who have had eight weeks, so you have an idea of how fast we
are being pushed. About 95% of us all had high IQs, so they expect us
to learn faster." Dad had gone thru a "gas drill" which he explains with
great detail: "1st we walked through war gases to know how to detect
the different ones by odor and reaction on the body. We walked, without
gas masks, through the following gases: phosgene, chloropicrin, lucite,
and mustard.

(**NOTE:** Phosgene is also commonly stated as white phosphorus.

ALL MY LOVE, ELWOOD

Chloropicrin was used in World War I and in the Ukraine invasion. The "lucite" Dad referred to is probably lewisite which is a chemical warfare agent which causes blisters.)

"The 1st two are lung irritants and the latter two are both lung and skin irritants. For instance, lucite gas forms blisters on the bare skin or clothes, providing you come in contact with the liquid form. In such a case you aren't supposed to open the blisters for it will make more if it runs onto the skin not affected. It is also a lung irritant, and it smells like geraniums. It is considered as one of the most poisonous. If you get two breaths of any of these, you are a goner.

"Next, we walked through a dense smoke screen and put on our masks in it. With our gas masks on, we went through the tear gas chamber, but before we could get out, we had to remove the masks and walk across the room and out. This gas made me cry and for a few seconds. I couldn't even see which way the door was. After that, we reversed the process by walking in without a mask and we had to put it on inside. Boy, I got mine on in nothing flat.

"After I got it on, I had to blow the contaminated air out and then everything was all right. The mask is good for 40-45 hours in such an area. It's a good thing to have and I'm not kidding.

"There was only one casualty, and he was sent to the hospital. The gases bothered him because of his stomach. He hasn't eaten in 4 or 5 days because he's homesick. I'll bet he goes nuts and I think it's his parent's fault. He's scared already and keeps saying he wants to die.

"I don't especially like a lot of things, but in the Army, there is only one way of doing things and that is the Army way. That's the way I'm doing it and it's not so bad. Saturday, we start firing the rifles. Before we go out on the range though, we all are taught the Army way of shooting and when we get out there, we are expected to hit the bull's eye every time. We'll find out next week.

"If you or anyone wants to send me anything you can send candy of some sort and cookies. I couldn't use any jam here because we get that in the mess hall. I didn't put this last sentence in the other letters. I forgot. So, you can tell anyone you want. I think most of the letters are particularly the same except for that. Lots of love to you all, Uncle Elwood."

26 November 1942: Post card from Camp Stewart to his nephews, John Jr. and David Elwood: "I didn't rate so bad today. For dinner I had a full breast of a turkey, mashed potatoes, cranberry sauce, celery, cabbage salad, tomatoes, gravy, coffee, pumpkin pie and ice cream. I had a double order of potatoes and salad. It was really the best meal I've had since I've been in the army.

"I got your letter Eunice and thank you so much for the dollar. It made me happy because I just got $10 that Lois sent me. I owe a guy $10, and I get paid Monday so, I should get along all right. I haven't got time to write to anyone else, so, you can tell Lois here to pay for stamps out of my money because I don't want anyone to feel that they are obligated in any way. There is no reason why they should. I'll write after I come back from maneuvers. Love, Elwood."

30 November 1942 "Monday noon the 30th, pay day": Handwritten letter from Camp Stewart, Georgia: "My basic training is over and this morning I wrote a letter to Papy, Esda, and Lois. I just finished Lois's letter, and they called me out to go to school. We had two lectures this morning and I've got to go back again this p.m. We had a lecture on upper respiratory diseases and artificial respiration.

"Well, I spent last weekend in Jesup, Georgia and had a date Sunday afternoon with a cute southern gal. I took her to the show and the two fellows I went with didn't get a date, so they went along too. We didn't' get into Jesup until 9 p.m. Saturday night and it took us two hours to find a room. In that town, one has to be off the street at 12 o'clock, so, consequently we didn't do much.

"Sunday, I went to a brand-new Baptist church in Jesup and everyone was glad to see us there. The church is about the size of West Wal-

16

worth's Baptist church only its' brand new. After church one of the choir members cheerfully invited us out to dinner. We all had fried chicken dinners. Boy do they really know how to fry chicken down here.

"After dinner o'clock I had to pick up my date for the show. Then we got the bus for camp. They have changed our reveille to 5 o'clock now and it certainly makes the morning drag. I got a brush cut Friday night and boy it isn't any longer than ¼ inch in front and it tapers down to about 1/32 of an inch in the back. It really is a honey. It is much more convenient with all this dust down here. Now when I wash my hair my scalp shines like the buttons on my uniform.

"I weighed myself for the 1st time since I've been in the Army, and I have gained 11 pounds. I weigh 149 pounds now. Thanksgiving, I got a dollar from you, a pound of Fanny Farmers from Esda, and two dozen chocolate cookies with nuts in them and frosting on them from Mrs. Bellis. I wrote her a card one Thursday and she ups and sends me some cookies! They are really good.

"Bonnie promised to send me some chocolate chip cookies, but I haven't gotten them yet. I suppose she is busy keeping her dates. At least it certainly looks like it. I only got 4 letters from you so far. Oh well, everybody seems to want a picture of me in my uniform, but I haven't got a camera. If you can get one some place, I can use it for a while, and I'll send it back.

"As I've told the rest of the family concerning Marjorie, I think it's her privilege to get married whenever she so desires. I can see Jimmie's side of it because I am in the Army too. Even though I haven't got anyone in mind to marry, I can still realize the importance of it. It's about time they got married anyway.

"If you read Pappy's letter, you can find out some of the things I've been doing in the past week. I'm trying to tell you all a little something. Oh. Boyce joined the Army because they reclassified him to 1A. I feel sorry for him. I don't know what I can get you for Xmas and I doubt if I can get the kids anything they want down here. If I get a chance to go to some big city, maybe I can at least get the kids something. I'm going to try to. I guess I'll still have some money left in the bank so, help yourself to a X-mas present.

"Tell John Jr. I like his letters and want him to keep on writing. I also miss the kids a lot. I'm sorry but I don't think I'll be able to make it home for X-mas. Maybe I can make it home for my birthday.

"Well, I got to go to school cause it's 1 pm. I'll write later. Oh, if you want to send me anything, I need cigarettes. Don't forget to lend me a camera. Love, Elwood."

7 December 1942: Handwritten 4-page letter from Camp Stewart, Georgia: This letter gives a great detailed account of the type injuries that can be sustained in an anti-aircraft artillery unit, and it also shows the great empathy dad had for his patients.

"Well, here I am writing more letters. I wrote 10 letters last Monday and they were all answered, and more too this past weekend. I got a letter from that fellow from Ontario.

"It sounds to me as if you could get more money. However, this fellow wants the radio and I kind of wanted you and Johnny to have it. If you got it tuned up a little, it will be a pretty good radio. Here's what you do. Sell the car for more if you can but take the radio out. Unless you can make enough more with the radio in it so that you could buy one for the extra amount of money. I'll sign the registration and send it with this letter if I can find a notary public.

"I bought the kids an Army sweatshirt with "My Uncle is in the Army." I hope they'll fit alright. Tell them that the sweatshirts will be their X-mas gift unless I can find something else before X-mas.

"I got a letter from the War Department in Washington and the Chief Officer of the Signal Corps recommended my transfer to the Signal Corps to work in V-mail. I think I am going to take it because of two things: I'll be stationed at Camp Edison, New Jersey for a while and it will be closer to NY City. (Only about 400 miles from home). The

V-mail is foreign service, but I'll probably have to go across soon anyway. Another thing, I'll be a technician Sergeant at $77 a month. I'll let you know more about that later.

"Well, I've been going to school all day long up until Friday. Friday morning I had to get up at 4:30 because our 377th Battalion started on another overnight convoy. We got out in the Georgia jungles about 26 miles and camped. Each battery camping in a different section of a certain area. On this convoy, two medical men were situated with each battery. I was with "Battery A." About an hour after we were situated, one of the gun crew men got his right foot run over by a big 40 M.M. Anti-aircraft gun. It turned out to be a constriction or something. The other medical man and myself had to pick him up and put him in a jeep. Of course, we had to check for shock and find out whether it was a fracture or not. We took him to the Doctor stationed at the Headquarters Command Post (CP).

"Then we went back to the CP of Battery A where we were stationed and about an hour later, we got a phone call from another gun crew that a fellow had his foot crushed by a 40 M.M. gun. We got him to our CP and laid him down. His shoe was split open in 2 places, so we didn't touch his foot. We knew right off the bat that he had fractures in his foot because the entire weight of the 40 mm gun (5,500 lbs.) fell on it with his foot up right like this. (He draws a picture)

"We called the ambulance and while we were waiting, I took his pulse and kept his mind off his foot. He was still conscious and when the Doctor came, the Doc took off his shoe and sock. I'm telling you that poor kid was in agony. I tried to hold him steady, and it seemed as though it was my foot that was crushed. I found out that they are both coming along fine. I also took a steel sliver out of the battery commander's finger. I fixed a couple of fellows up with pills for a cold and fever. I put a bandage on a cut for the cook and after that he gave me a steak sandwich every time I wanted one. I had five steak sandwiches and three steaks with my dinner. Boy were they good. I was eating all day long and

I weigh 155 pounds now. We were like guests. All we did was inspect the cleanliness of the kitchen, the garbage pit, and the latrine trench. And of course, take care of the sick. We came back to camp Saturday night about 6 p.m.

"I got a saw buck from Lois and some cookies and fudge from Bonnie. Her mother made them. I guess Bonnie can't find time to do such things. Some laugh, eh? I haven't written to her so much lately and I got two letters from her today. I also have been getting some nice letters from Jane Dunk. She is in Texas now on a vacation or rest. She has written about as much as Bonnie and I only kissed the girl once. Maybe I got a chance with her. Eh" (This letter had 4 "P.S.'s")

"PS 1: Hey, John Jr. when are you going to write me another letter? Tell me how you and David are getting along. Also tell your daddy I hope he get $20 a ton for his cabbage.

"PS 2: "I just went to see my first lieutenant (Doctor Blum) and he's going to see about notarizing my signature on the registration. So, I'll hold this letter up."

"PS 3: "Tell Arnold I got his card, and I enjoyed it. I would like to answer it, but I haven't got time now."

"PS 4: I think I got rid of my cold. I only cough occasionally now.

Wednesday the 9th: "I just got my signature notarized by a civilian this a.m. I tried to do it Monday and I couldn't because I had to go to a fatigue conference where the General, Colonels, etc., commented on our last field problem. Tuesday, I went on a 25-mile hike, and it rained all day too. It took all day. Boy you should see my left heel. I got 2 beautiful big blisters about the size of half dollar. I made it, though.

"This morning after I helped the doctor take care of sick call, which there were 75 fellows, I soaked my feet, and the doc put adhesive tape on my left heel. I'm limping around like an old man. I got some bed slippers from Esda and Doug today. They're nice. I'll write later, Chow time, Elwood."

11 December 1942: Typed letter from Camp Stewart, Georgia: His commanding officer, Capt. Hoffman, had seen him type, so he asked Dad to come to his office to type a letter. "I got rather nervous, but I did it alright. If you notice the letterhead, that is the way I had to make the letters. "Medical Detachment, 377th Coast Artillery Battalion (AA), Camp Stewart, Georgia."

(**NOTE:** Dad helped many soldiers with various health problems and is nervous when he has to do something new to treat a soldier.) "I swabbed about ten sore throats for the first time. Some fun! Each day I do something new and different. Boy you should see me shake when I do something different." The doctor has been treating Dad's blisters he got on the 25-mile hike. Dad's unit went on another "bivouac, an overnight convoy."

"In the medics, however, one doesn't have as many details such as going out on the range every day and guard duty. I keep reminding myself how easy I have it compared to the other fellows. I like this better than working at Kodak, except the fact that I can't see you all." Dad had received packages from Esda and Doug (slippers). "Boy, they came in handy this week because of my blisters. In fact, I've got them on now.

"I'm going to ask the Capt. if there is a possible chance to come home for Marjorie's wedding. He's such a pleasant man. Personally, I don't think he will let me come. I've only been in the army six weeks, and one is supposed to be in the service at least three months before he can have a furlough. So, you see, my dears, it looks rather impossible. Don't you think?

"I've got to get to work now so I'll bid my adieu and wish you all a "Merry Christmas and Happy New Year" signed Elwood Turner, PVT. First Aid Man."

(**NOTE:** Dad continued in a handwritten note on the back of this typed letter. Interesting stuff.) "Dear Soaks, how do you like my typing? Not bad, eh? I hope you got my last letter okay. I'm sorry it was held up so long, but it was the best I could do. (**NOTE:** If I learned anything from Dad, it was what he just said, "always do the best you can do.")

"Don't forget, use your better judgement on the car business. I know if John Sr. is selling it, he'll get as much as it's worth (no cracks). I've heard about him buying tires, etc. and I fully realize his ability as a buyer and salesman (Ha Ha). Some boys are in the infirmary getting short arm inspections now and they're making an awful lot of noise, I can't concentrate."

(**NOTE:** The term "short arm inspection" originated in World War One with American and Australian troops using the term. It is a medical inspection of a man's private area for signs of sexually transmitted diseases and other medical problems.) "Another fellow in the medics and I are trying to get out of the habit of swearing and each time either one swears, the other one takes a swing at him. He's a big fellow and I'm not swearing so much anymore. I got some film, and I borrowed a camera, so, as soon as the weather permits, I'll have some pictures taken of me and I'll sent them home. Lots of love to everybody, Elwood." (**NOTE:** I don't EVER remember Dad swearing in front of us kids. He was very conscious of trying to better himself. If he ever heard one of his kids say anything that sounded bad, we were corrected immediately.)

14 December 1942: Typed and written letter from Camp Stewart: "Dear Eunice, John, John Jr. and David: "I received your package today and it was swell. You didn't have to send so much. I didn't expect all of that. So far, I've got a lot for Christmas, I think. One other fellow got a package today and it did have some cookies in it for a while.

"Did David and John get the sweatshirts yet? I bought a small football for them in Jesup, and I forgot it and left it in the hotel room. Darn it. If I find another one, I'll send it later. I had my picture taken on Saturday night and I'm going to send it to Pappy as soon as it is finished. It cost two dollars and a half, so I'll only send one home now. As soon as I get enough money, I'll send some more. I'll send some snaps also.

(**NOTE:** Regarding the "snaps" (pictures) Dad mentions, I'm confident those were the pictures we have of Dad standing in the woods by some barracks with a rifle and some protective gear.)

"I feel rather guilty not giving you people any presents now that I've got some from you. I'll try to call for Christmas. Pappy didn't tell me how much that last call cost, so I don't know how much it does cost. I suppose you realize by now that I won't be able to be home for Christmas. I asked Capt. Hoffman, and he said I had to be in the Army longer before I could possibly get one. The only exception would be in case of serious illness or death in my relations.

"I started to type this letter, but I had to stop so that it could be used for business. I guess that's all for now, so I'll go and eat. Thanks again. By the way, what's the cloth used for? I can't figure it out. The only thing I thought it was used for was a shoe rag."

17 December 1942: Handwritten letter from Camp Stewart, Georgia: "I am sending you some snap shots in this envelope. You'll no doubt notice the bulge in the envelope. I also was in a terrible hurry, but I want to get them sent out before Christmas. I'm sending 7 snapshots and they'll be like the ones I'm sending to the rest of the family. Also, I'm sending Pappy 2 portraits I had taken in Hinesville. They were rather expensive so all I can send is two. In other words, I'm broke again. I owe $15 that I borrowed to get the pictures and film, and I also went to Jesup again with my buddy John Foley. I didn't have the money, but he teased me to go and of course he had to foot the bills. I'm getting rather nervous about paying him back because I might have to go to New Jersey by the 1st of the year.

"So now you see why I haven't the money to send more. I figured that they would be home for Christmas day, even though I won't be able to be there. The snapshots I'm sending aren't going to be marked on the back like Lois' and Esda's are, but you can see things and get what I mean by writing on the back of them.

"I got your letter today and tell John Jr. that I enjoyed his letter an awful lot. I laughed out loud when I read the part about him going skiing and falling in a few times. Oh yes, tell him that he can have my skates and different things like that that he can use. I thought I told you that you could go ahead and take my radio. You seemed to be uncertain about it.

"Bonnie has been writing more often and much sweeter letters lately so I feel a lot better about that. Eunice, will you and John go to a florist and send Bonnie (2613 Titus Ave) a dozen red roses on Christmas day. Take the money from my account but be sure to send them. (Good ones). Also, while you're at it, you can buy some flowers for your table Christmas day, (on me). Please, please make sure you do this."

He closes with: "I'm glad to hear you're going to be Margie's maid of honor. I'll bet you'll both look swell. Lots of love and thank you again for the wonderful Christmas presents. Elwood. P.S. Let me know if the kids get those sweatshirts."

26 December 1942: Letter from Camp Stewart, Georgia: "Did you all have a merry Christmas. From the way you described the wedding, it sounds as if you had a lot of fun. I got a letter from Marjorie today and she said she was quite nervous. I bet Jimmie was more nervous than she was. Thank you for seeing that Bonnie got the flowers okay. I tried to call for Christmas, but the lines were so full I would have had to wait 5 or 6 hours. Even then I might not have been able to get you, so I'll let it go until I know when you are all going to be together again. It'll have to be on a quiet day though and not a holiday.

"I didn't get up until 11 a.m. X-mas morn and sponged breakfast off of my friend the cook. I drank some beer while I was waiting for dinner and on the dinner table. We had a water glass full of wine. We had turkey and all the trimmings with pumpkin pie for dessert and candies after that. I found out that I couldn't get you on the phone. I wrote a letter to pappy and took a nap. I went to the show X-mas night and completed my holiday chewing the fat with my Captain (Capt. Hoffman) at the infirmary. We exchanged our opinions on all the states and cities we had been to. He's from Albany, New York so we seem to have a lot in common when we talk about New York.

"Saturday, I spent the whole day out on the rifle range firing the new M1 rifles. I only did 128 out of a possible 220. I have a stye on my eye, so I'll use that as an excuse. I qualified but I don't know what for. Tell your husband he ought to shoot the new M1. They are the smoothest rifle there is made. I fired 16 shots in a minute, and you should hear the noise when 50 guns are firing 16 shots in a minute. It takes two days for my ears to stop ringing due to the continuous noise. It's a lot of fun though. Captain Hoffman told us the Japs don't pay attention to the red cross, so in other words, we are getting rifle practice in case we go to the Pacific war zone. (**NOTE:** Similar to the reference above on profanity, after dad had a family and became responsible for raising children, he never allowed us kids to use derogatory terms for any race, gender or nationality. In wartime, this was the term for one of their enemies, so I didn't edit.)

"It means we'll be armed with either rifles, pistols, or sub machine guns. The Germans haven't yet bombed any hospitals or shot at any medical men to our knowledge, so it looks like things are going to happen pretty soon. (**NOTE:** Dad thought he would be going to Europe soon, but he'd have to wait eight more months.)

"Oh well, if we go west, all I hope is I can kill as many Japs as I can save American lives." (**NOTE:** Pearl Harbor had happened a little over a year prior.) "The medical men are going to have double duty from now on. I'm starting to get anxious to get in the midst of things, anything to get out of this hole in the ground.

"Tell Arnold that I got his card and I enjoy hearing from him. I have to laugh at the way he mentions "the boss" (Uncle Johnny). I also got a Christmas card from Aunt Nora and Uncle Allen. They both promised to write to me later on. I think that's about all the news I have on hand right now but if I've missed something, you'll find it in Esda's or Lois' letter. Love Elwood.

"P.S. I had a few other snapshots taken and I sent them and the negatives to Lois. If you want some of those, you'll have to have them made up because the photography isn't so hot in the south as it is in Rochester. The rifle I was talking about is in the picture."

He gives a special note to David and John Jr.: "I'm glad you liked the sweatshirts and, in the near future, I'll send you both something else. John Jr. You certainly are helping Uncle Sam to win this war by doing all the things you have written and told me about. I hope you feel better by now. David, you be a good boy and tell your mother to get you kids a lot of grapefruit to eat so you won't get any colds. Tell her to feed you a lot of orange juice too. Vitamin C is essential to prevent colds. I hope you both had a merry Christmas and want you to write and tell me what you got for Christmas. Lots of love, Uncle Elwood."

7 January 1943: Letter from Camp Stewart: Handwritten on Camp Stewart stationary. "Dear Eunice, John, John Jr. and David Elwood: Boy that's some starter. Well, this afternoon I took for myself a nice long nap. I worked at the Dental Clinic this morning from 7:30-11:45. I just got back from a field problem (Exercise) Wednesday a.m. at 7:30. First of all, I spent last Sunday out on the range firing the rifle again. I had to get up at 4 a.m. Sunday morning so we'd be out on the range before daylight. I bettered my score to a marksman. My score was 175 out of a possible 220. Now I'm qualified for a sharpshooter so if I'm armed, I'll feel pretty safe if I came in contact with any Japs.

"I went to the show Sunday night to see White Cargo and I had to get up at 3 a.m. Monday to go on the field problem. It was cold again, naturally, and I had to ride 50-miles in the back end of a supply truck. I managed to keep as warm as I could and also got a little more sleep. We reached our destination about 7:30 and it was an old deserted farmhouse. I slept in one open air room Monday night. I woke up at 4 a.m.

colder than the devil. I went over to the kitchen to warm up and my feet didn't thaw out till about 1 p.m. I bandaged up a couple of smashed fingers that morning and in the afternoon, I got a honey of a patient. He said he had cramps, and he had chills. I figured he needed a laxative, but the Doctor thought he might have appendicitis. So, I got a "Peep" and had someone drive me over to the "doc". (**NOTE:** Peep was the common term for a Jeep used by Armored units, since the primary role for jeeps in those formations was reconnaissance. The job of a "peep" was to "peep" at the enemy and then call in more support.)

"I had quite a ride. We had the peep going 60 miles an hour with the top down and the windshield was broken. The driver knew it was my first ride in a peep, so he took me through a ditch, over logs and through big water holes. We went through a water hole and the water came up over the hood of the peep. Do you get an idea what the swamps are like? They compare somewhat with the Montezuma near Syracuse, only of course, a great deal larger. (**NOTE:** The Montezuma National Wildlife Refuge is near Syracuse, New York. The natural ecology of this area is cedar swamps and salt marshes. Syracuse is a wetland, and a lot of it was drained for development).

"When we took the doctor back, he looked at this fellow and he didn't have appendicitis. He told me to keep an eye on him and report any changes. I had to tell him to keep his overcoat on and to keep as warm as possible, because he was so dumb. He kept telling me he thought we was going to die and all he had was a bad cold. I think I had a cold as bad as he did but now, I am feeling fine and he's in the hospital. We got back Wednesday a.m. at 7:30 and we had to get up at 2 a.m."

Dad talks about pictures of Margie's wedding and then talks about future movement of his unit. "Today I found out for sure that our battalion is leaving Camp Stewart to points further south. I think I know exactly where we're going, but I can't tell you. We couldn't turn our dirty sheets, and pillow slips in tonight because we are going to leave either next Monday or Tuesday. So don't write many more letters until you get my new address. Please tell Esda and I'll tell Lois in her letter. I doubt now if I'll be able to get a furlough the 1st week of February. I'll try anyway, but I doubt it very much. I still haven't heard about my transfer to New Jersey, and I want to try going to Officer's school. I've been waiting to hear from my transfer before I applied to "O.C.S." (Officer Candidate School). I found out that it'll cost me around $250 to get started in as an officer because an officer has to buy all his clothes, meals, and everything. I wish I knew what I was going to do.

"I just looked out the window and all the fellows are hustling around getting their helmets, washing dirty clothes, and in general we'll be busy as hell until we're moved. I'm getting rather anxious and excited now myself." Dad closes with, "Lots of love and keep your chins up. P.S. According to the paper, the gas situation is quite bad, eh? I'll let you know my new address as soon as I can."

17 January 1943: Post card from Camp Carrabelle, Florida on a Tallahassee post card. "I just got back to the service club from having my pants and blouse pressed. It rained hard last night when we came into town and my uniform lost its creases. I had a pretty good time last night trying to get acquainted with these beautiful women here. Of all the places I've been in down south, this is tops. I'll write you a letter very soon to tell you more, Love Elwood."

1 February 1943: First handwritten letter from Camp Gordon-Johnston, Florida: "I'm sorry that I haven't written before to thank you for the dollar. You were a life saver. As soon as I got it, I let a yell out of me and headed to the Post Exchange and got me some cigarettes. I've been bumming them for 2 or 3 days and so I bought 3 packs out of your dollar, and I had a quarter left for Kleenex and a bar of candy. I ran out of cigarettes yesterday and Lois sent me a dollar in the nick of time for some more.

"Esda sent me a box of candy and I passed it around once leaving me about 3 or 4 pieces. Lois sent me a box of Fanny Farmers this afternoon and all I got left of a lb. is 5 pieces. I passed that around too. Its' funny every time a fellow gets a package there are about 20 fellows standing around your bed waiting for you to open up your package. I hope these guys get a birthday pretty soon. (**NOTE**: Dad shared with others, and he taught his kids to share with others, even if it leaves you with a few pieces out of a big box of candy for yourself. Thanks dad.)

"Eunice, that poem you copied on the back of my birthday card was wonderful… even though it brought tears in my eyes. The fellows looked at me kinda funny. I guess they were wondering what was the matter. It seemed so real, and I enjoyed it. Pappy might come down to see me. Not bad, eh?

"Today it was about 90 degrees above or more. We went on a 15-mile hike and double timed the last five miles. I sweat, oh how I sweat. I had to take my glasses off so I could see because every time I perspire a lot, my glasses steam up. We started at 0830 and ended up by 2 p.m. with an hour for lunch. We carried our lunch in our packs and all we had was 3 sandwiches and an apple and an orange. I got a couple extra oranges from the cook, and I had 5 bars of candy along. I ate everything up, naturally." Dad closes with discussing the boys' pictures. Dad closes with "Give my regard to Arnold, Mrs. DeRoos and Uncle Ike. Thanks again for the birthday card and the dollar, Be good, Love Elwood."

12 February 1943: (Handwritten letter on Army stationary). "Dear Eunice and Family: I bet you thought I forgot your birthday. I didn't but I did forget to get you a birthday card while I was in Tallahassee. I'd try to send you something, but I only got $27 left, and we won't get paid until the 15th of April. Also, if they start giving furloughs, I have to have enough money to buy a round-trip ticket home or I can't come. I'll think about you anyway. How's that. Enough?

"I'm glad to hear that Margie is going home for a week or so to help move our furniture. I'm sure you all like to have her come home every once in a while. It would be great if I could come home the same week, but I can't count on it. If I come from here, I might be able to make good time. I'd have to take a 3 ½ hour bus ride to Jacksonville, and a train from there to New York City. The Seaboard Liner, I guess. All together it would probably take me about 40-48 hours. I'm about 12 or 13 hundred miles from home from here. Oh well, it's all a dream, I guess.

"I sent a package home to pappy with some more of my old letters, a group picture of the Med Det, my watch, and some of those dog biscuits we had to eat on our field problem. Try them! You won't like them, I know. I don't even think your dog would eat them.

"Today I have to give a lecture on first aid to the battalion and I've got to talk for an hour. I'm not so used to making speeches, but I guess I can do it. The latest rumor is that we are going to stay here for training purposes due to the fact that we were so outstanding in our work down here. We are considered the best C.A. outfit yet to have had this training and they praised us highly. They might hurry us across too, so it's hard to tell, just where we're going. I still hope it's north. I asked about going to O.C.S. school and our commanding officer said that I could try. As yet, I haven't made out an application for it because I don't know whether I'll make it or not. I could try I suppose. I'm rather dull on my math and physics and social studies. My I.Q. mark is 110, my mechanical test is 118 and the Radio test 101. I am the highest in the Medical Detachment in the Mechanical and Radio tests and third high in I. Q.

"The mumps are still running strong and they have one ward filled up in the hospital already. The fellows that are coming down with them now have to sleep out in the woods until they get room in the hospital. Here I go out to lecture. I'll write later, Love Elwood. P.S. Did I get my income tax blank yet? I'd better make it out, don't you think? If I did get one, send it to me." (**NOTE:** I believe the income tax blank was a way dad could apply, as a soldier, to have no income tax taken out of his check.)

22 February 1943: Post card from Camp Gordon-Johnston Amphibious Training Center: "Has the snow covered up my "Jitney" yet. (**NOTE:** Dad was referring to his 1936 Chevy which he must have used to carry his two nephews around in. In the early 1900s, *jitney* was slang for *nickel*, but it wasn't long before the term was applied to a new mode of public transportation that only cost a nickel. When they were introduced in American cities at the beginning of the century, vehicular jitneys could be any automobiles that carried passengers over a set route for a cheap fare, but eventually the term was applied specifically to small buses— and, nowadays, to the motor shuttles used by airlines and hotels).

"I bet it'll take a month to start it up again. It should start to warm up, up there, shouldn't it? I hope it warms up when and if I get a furlough. Last week the coldest day we had was about 23 degrees above. It warmed up quite a bit though. Eunice, after the 1st of March, I should have 2 war bonds. You should receive them, not me. It probably takes time to make them up. Let me know when you get one. Love Elwood." (**NOTE:** The front of the postcard shows a soldier saluting an officer walking by on the sidewalk as the soldier swept a doorway and after the officer walks by the soldier brushes dust on the officer!)

27 February 1943: Letter from Camp Gordon Johnston on Camp Carrabelle stationary: "My dear family, Today I had a break, we got a cold spell down here and today is one of our special training days (swimming). Yesterday we had special training also, but the water was wonderful. I was the last one to come out when they blew the whistle. Next Monday is the last day of special training. Tuesday and Wednesday we have off to get ready for our divisional problem; Thursday, Friday and Saturday we will be out in the ocean someplace. After our training here, I think we are going to Louisiana. It's only a rumor so don't count on it. It seems every time I move, I go farther away from home, doesn't it?

"As I started to tell you, today I'm in charge of the infirmary. This morning, I was busy until 9 a.m. assisting the doctor on sick call. After sick call I cleaned up the infirmary and shaved. Lieutenant Guiliano (the dentist) waited for me, and I rode up to the main P.X. (Post Exchange) with him in a 36 Chevrolet, like mine. It seemed funny to ride in a car again and especially one like mine. He and I fooled around up there for about an hour. There was a pretty blonde working behind the soda fountain, so I spent most of my time drinking milk shakes and chewing the fat with her.

"I would like to go to Tallahassee tonight to have my watch fixed (have my new wristwatch band put on). I don't know if they'll let me go because we are supposed to be quarantined to the area. (Mumps). We have a new commanding officer (Doctor) again. The last one had heart trouble. I've got to ask him (new doctor).

"I received your letter today Pappy and I'm glad to hear that you're getting plenty rest. Keep it up. Don't work too hard and keep that flag flying that Eunice got for you. Maybe I'll get a chance to come home and see you in the near future. I also received your letter Eunice and if you keep talking about those porter house steaks, I'll be going AWOL. Ha. Ha. They do sound good. We only get coffee once a week and I haven't seen any butter in 2 months. Not that I give a darn. We get ice cream once a month too, so don't let anyone tell you the Army is getting everything. I think they're sending all that stuff to other countries."

He addresses chit chat with Lois and Esda and closes with: "I hope you're all feeling okay and David, I hope you get rid of your cold soon. I'll bet you and John Jr. will be big boys by the time I get to see you. Be good and say hello to your Daddy and Arnold for me. Lots of love, Elwood." (**NOTE:** On the back of the envelope, "Elixir of Turpin hydrate with codeine" was written in pencil. This medicine is used to treat coughs and other conditions of the respiratory tract, i.e. bronchitis, pneumonia).

8 March 1943: Letter from Camp Gordon Johnston written on a Monday. (Provides great detail into the life of a soldier in training during very bad weather.) (A long 12 pages handwritten letter): "As I sit here and write to you, I thank the Lord that I'm able to. I guess I'm just lucky or something. Last weekend (6-7 March 1943) we had our divisional problem (exercise) and we had one of the worst electrical storms I've ever seen. It was awful in every sense of the word. Saturday there were 17 boats (D-day landing craft) lost at sea and one bomber crashed in the sea. An officer of the paratroops is still missing too. The latest news that was broadcast over the radio was only 13 dead, but probably there will be several more found today and tomorrow. Boy those little boats we have don't stand a chance with those huge swells of the sea. Especially at night and during an electric storm. I was fortunate enough to be on the biggest boat about ½ the size of the coble boat. (**NOTE:** A Coble is a type of open fishing boat mostly used on the Northeast coast of England. It has a distinctive shape, flat-bottomed and high-bowed, and is built to cope with the particular conditions in this area. Dad probably should not have put this detail in his letters, as in about 15 months during the invasion of Normandy, these same type boats were used).

"We lost a lot of rifles and equipment amounting to about four of five hundred thousand dollars. It sounds fantastic, doesn't it? Well, it was just like a bad dream. To start off from the beginning, I'll cover the mild part that I had over the weekend. Wednesday night I went to bed early because I had to get up at 3:30 Thursday morning. The other fellow going with me, Larry and myself overslept an hour; thus, we missed the convoy we were supposed to be on. Our ambulance driver got up and took us up to the town of Carrabelle where we caught the convoy. It was colder than all hell and it was about 5 a.m. when we caught up with our outfit. We found our positions and I spent the rest of the night doing calisthenics trying to keep warm.

"After the sun came up, I got warm and had some hot coffee, which helped. We spent all day Thursday, up until 8 p.m. right near Carrabelle out in the woods someplace. At dinner time, I ran into Stan Marshall of Rochester. He used to go to John Marshall High. He recognized me, even with my glasses on. He is in the Medical Detachment in the 112th Infantry. He knows Jimmy and Margie.

"At 8 p.m. we got march order to load the boats: There were more Generals, Colonels, Majors around from all over. They were taking flash pictures all the time we were loading up. We got loaded up around 9 p.m. and I fixed myself a bed on the back end of a truck. I slept with a life preserver on, and it served as a pillow, and it also kept me warm. I slept pretty good except that I woke up two or three times and the boat was rolling over the swells and it was cold. The sky was pretty but there're wasn't any moon out and it was darker than some of these negros down here. I'm glad I don't get seasick, even though it seemed I was riding on a roller coaster.

"I went back asleep and slept until 7 a.m. We were about a half mile from shore then. We were ordered to prepare for landing. We landed about 8 a.m. And the infantry had already landed before us and captured a beach head from the enemy troops. So, all we had to do was land and set our guns up. I didn't do much until after I had my K-ration breakfast. (a can of ham and cooked eggs, coffee power for a cup full, a stick of gum, 4 cigarettes, a fruit bar of raisins, and prunes and all kinds of tasty fruits, dates, etc. all compressed in a bar form. 3 lumps of sugar and 2 packages of dog biscuits some of which I'll send home for you to sample).

"After I ate my cold breakfast, I walked around to the gun positions to see if anyone got injured or supposedly shot. I had to bandage up 10 or 12 skinned knuckles and fingers and gave out a lot of pills for colds and so forth. Then, I got a ride back to the battery C.P. (command post) which I was assigned to for the problem. There I stayed by the switch board in case of any casualties I would be able to go in and peep to the fellow's care. I didn't get called at all, but the Btry Commander got sick, and I had to go to the field hospital for an ambulance in a peep. You see they simulated enemy aircraft with our own planes, and we got gas thrown at us that morning.

"This Btry commander and a sergeant got too much of it and it made them nauseated, and they threw up all morning. I got the ambulance and had him evacuated to the hospital. That's about all the medical work I did. Then came Friday night, the curse of the entire problem. I went to sleep on the ground all rolled up in my blankets under a bush about 5 p.m. I was awakened about 10 o'clock Saturday morning by rain drops and a flash of lightening. I covered myself up with my shelter half and went back to sleep. About an hour later I woke up and I was soaked to the skin. Miserable! Gad!

"There was about a 30 mile an hour gale and the small trees were bent down to the ground. Every time it lightened; I could see soldiers bucking the wind trying to hang on to their equipment. I got up and put on my raincoat, which was as wet on the inside as it was on the outside. I folded my blankets up in my shelter half and started to walk across to the switch board so I could keep company with the operators when a sharp strike of lightening hit a barrage balloon, (valued at $4,000) and it went up in flame like a firecracker. The hydrogen gas in it ignited so fast it looked like a skyrocket. The lightening hit the cable holding the balloon and a flame shot up the cable like a skyrocket and "pop".

"The barrage balloon is used as anti-aircraft and it's shaped like a zeppelin, only smaller. During the night 16 of them were hit and they were right over our heads.

"Well, I went over to the switch board and crawled in under a tent. I had a cigarette after I stopped shivering, and I took a nap in there until it rained harder, and I go wetter from the water running in the bottom of the tent. Then I got up and stood out in the rain until daybreak, wetter than hell and colder than a bitch. I said a prayer one minute and cussed the next. What a night. No wonder those small boats capsized because the sea was ugly, and the waves came in over the roadway about four feet inland.

"Finally, daybreak came, and some engineers started a fire, so I went over and partially dried out. Then I made my breakfast. Well, I got half-way through with eating and the planes came over again and threw some more tear gas on us. I whipped my mask on, and I helped one fellow who didn't have his gas mask nearby. I told him to wet his handkerchief and burry his nose in the sand. I covered him up with a comforter and it didn't bother him. That a.m. at 10 we got march order and came back to Camp at 1 p.m. I cleaned up my equipment and 7 p.m. Saturday night I started hitch hiking to Tallahassee.

"Another fellow, Matty and myself walked about 4 miles and we got a ride in a ¾ ton truck into Crawfordville. We went into a general store there and had 2 bottles of beer, when suddenly 4 women drove up and came in. (Two in formal) I asked them where the dance was and eventually, I got us a ride into Tallahassee. That isn't all. They took us out to a night club and we danced and drank until 2 o'clock. We also had a chicken dinner. Boy, I had a lot of fun. The girls are pretty as the devil in Tallahassee. They took us to the house where I stayed before, and I wake the lady up and she gave us a bed with inner spring mattress on it. Oh, it was all like a dream.

"I slept until 12 o'clock Sunday and we went downtown to have dinner. I had a sizzling sirloin steak the size of a meat platter, 2 orders of French fries, coffee and about 10 slices of bread. For dessert I had egg custard pie, they didn't have any more pie, or I'd have eaten two pieces. I'm telling you I enjoyed it so much after dinner we were supposed to meet 2 of these girls and go to the show. We saw too many women around so we gave them the air. We ended up going to the show alone. Ha. Ha.

"We saw "Arabian Nights" Good! After the show we got a cab and went out to the chicken house for another chicken dinner and more beer. It was good too. Then we took a cab back to town and at 9 p.m. had spaghetti and meat balls and pie for dessert. It must have cost me $10 for meals alone. Anyway, I spent about $17 altogether but I sure enjoyed all of it.

"At eleven p.m. we got a ride back to camp on a convoy. Well, it's taken me all morning to write this, so I'll end up pretty soon. I weighed myself and I weigh 162 now so even after all of this tiresome training, I gained 4 more lbs.

"I got my eye prescription from Kodak today along with a letter from Lois. Oh, I also got the cookies you sent Lois and they're awful good, my dear sister. Thank you. Pappy, I should be getting my bonus from Kodak soon and maybe they'll send it to you because I had my last check signed over to you. You know what to do with it. Put it in the bank and let me know how much it is. It should be over $140 or $150 anyway.

"We will be leaving this camp this week sometime, so I'll be sending my watch home to be fixed and some more of my old letters. My watch has to be repaired, cleaned, and I want them to put my new band on. I hope you're all fine and healthy and I'll try to call you up if I end up near home. I wish I knew where we're going.

"There goes a mad rush out to the chow line, so I've got to go too, naturally. If I've forgotten anything I'll write tomorrow or Wednesday. Bye now, Love, Elwood.

"P.S. Keep on writing! My mail will be forwarded on to me. P.S. Thanks for the stationary Margie. I like it. P.S. After chow I had another chicken dinner, mashed potatoes, gravy, beans, grape aid, and peaches. Not bad!" A sad last P.S. was crammed into the top of the first page: "P.S. We just had a final word on the dead soldiers. There was only 14." (**NOTE:** When Dad says "only" I am sure everyone thought it was much, much worse. In fact, the final death toll the Army later released was 14).

30 March 1943: Post card from Camp Gordon-Johnston, Florida, the Amphibious Training Center: He writes to his nephews John and David and calls them, "My little Dutchmen."

"It's been a long time since I've written you but don't think I've forgotten you. I don't get much of a chance to get any place to buy you something or I would send you something. I carry your picture in my billfold but by now you must be bigger than you were in the picture.

"Today I went on a 5-mile hike, and we had to make it in 1 hour, but we ended up by making it in 55 minutes. John Jr., you would have had a hard time keeping up to us on your bike. You will be seeing her pretty soon, wont' you? Maybe I'll get to see you pretty soon too. Be good and say hello to Mommy, Daddy, Arnold and the dogs for me. Love Uncle Elwood."

1 April 1943: Letter from Camp Gordon-Johnston, Florida "April Fool's Day": "My dear Eunice: I received your letter yesterday and I'm sorry to know that you hadn't received a letter from me in two weeks. I'm sure you must have received one by now. I sent the kids a post card the other day. I ran out of stamps temporarily, but I'll try to get some soon and maybe the letters will come sooner.

"Well, I see you sold my car! It sounds okay with me. I mean the price. Ask Pappy what he thinks about the price? I think it'll be okay if he pays $50 down and the rest per month and you can give the money to Pappy to put in the bank for me, Okay? The registration is already signed by me and Johnny should have it, right?

"I suppose by the time you get this letter your husband will have reached the age of 33. He's only 10 years older than I am, isn't he? And your age is creeping up to almost 30. Wow, time certainly flies by, doesn't it? It doesn't seem long ago that we moved off the farm and you were only 18. I bet you had a nice birthday dinner for Johnnie and with Margie there. I bet you had a good time.

"I got a letter from Ezzy and Margie yesterday too and Ezzy was so pleased that Margie was home again for a while. If I come home, will have another big party at your house like we had before I left, how's that? Agreed upon? You and David take care of your colds and don't work too hard on your house cleaning, maybe you can still find someone to help you.

"Happy Birthday", Johnnie and thank you for taking care of my car. Take some money from the car sale and buy yourself a good quart of Whiskey for your birthday and your commission. Love, Elwood."

6 April 1943: Post card from Camp Stewart, Georgia: "I'm working now at the dental clinic in Camp Stewart and I'm trying to write you in between patients. I wrote a letter yesterday to Lois telling her about my new home in the woods so you can read that letter to find out the particulars. Is your and David's cold better? I hope so. What did you do about my car, is it sold yet? I'm going to try to call you some noon between 12 and 1 o'clock. Maybe today. Be good and careful, Love Uncle Elwood."

19 April 1943: Handwritten Letter dated 19 April on stationary but postmarked 30 April from Camp Stewart, Georgia: "Last night we went on another field problem (**NOTE:** Dad referred to training exercises as "field problems") and I didn't get to bed until 1 o'clock this morning. We didn't have reveille this morning, but I got up at 7:30 for breakfast. This morning, I had two fried eggs (cooked to order), bacon, hot sliced apples, cereal and coffee. It was really good because of the eggs just being fried. Usually, the eggs are cooked an hour before we get them. We had lamb for dinner yesterday and lamb stew every time we get it. It tastes like they forgot to cut the wool off the damn thing. We call it goat meat and run around after chow "Baa-ing away." We've had more damn goat meat in the army than anything else. I'm getting so I can't even stand the smell. If I ever get in civilian life again, I'll kill the guy who mentions the damn word to me. Well, I got that off my mind for a while.

"Instead of giving a lecture yesterday, I helped the lieutenant give it. I answered their questions and gave a demonstration. Yesterday morning our doctors had to give physical examinations for insurance policies, and I took part in that too with 2 or 3 other fellows. I had to take the blood count (pulse readings) and record them on the insurance papers. It was different so I enjoyed doing it. We also saw a training film yesterday

39

morning, "Next of Kin." It showed how a loose word given by the soldier causes so much disaster to the fellows who had to make an attack over there. In fact, it gave several instances of soldiers writing home and telling his parents and girlfriend where he thought he was going next and the German spies found out all the information they wanted through his letters. Thus, in the end the Germans were waiting for the attack, and they wiped out 80% of their men.

"Those are our odds if we go across. It doesn't sound so pleasant does it. Well, if we make a surprise attack, the loss of lives will be cut in half. It's those kinds of movies that makes one stop and think. It would be good if everyone could see them and I'm sure it would make them realize the danger in loose talk. I've been writing letters home before now and saying things I probably shouldn't have, so I felt kind of self-conscious. I don't think anything I've said has gotten in the wrong hands, so I feel more relieved.

"Lois, I received your letter yesterday and the question you asked is like this. Eunice will be the one my body would be shipped to if I were to be killed. Her name is on my dog tags. I've forgotten if Pappy would know first, but don't let that bother you because a German or Jap bullet isn't good enough to kill me, I'm an "American".

"I also got Pappy's letter, and I must say, Pappy, you are getting pretty good at writing letters. I'm glad to see Kodak is giving out a bonus, but I won't get much because they lowered the amount. I'll write later. Love Elwood."

21 April 1943: Typewritten letter from Camp Stewart, Georgia: "My dear family: I just finished writing Pappy a card, so now I'll write to everybody, including Pappy.

"How is the weather back home? Is the good old spring finally giving forth? I sure would like to be coming home to see you pretty damn soon. I bet we won't get our furloughs until we get across. It would be just my luck, don't you think? As I told Pappy in the card I just wrote, I've been alone for three days while the rest of the battalion were on a field problem. There were a few fellows that stayed back also, and we had a nice quiet time here. Last night twelve of us drank four cases of beer that the lieutenant in charge bought for us. It tasted pretty good. (**NOTE:** You have probably noted the references to drinking in my dad's letters. You will see more later in his letters. Just like the swearing and slang words for our enemies he used as a young man, when dad became responsible for little ones in his house, he never had even a bottle of beer in the house. He never drank around us kids).

"You should have seen the pretty nurse that cleaned my teeth for me the other day, she did a good job even though I was staring at her all the time. She kept smiling at me, but she is married, damn it. I didn't get any letters in three days except for one from Janet Hummel and the trig book you sent Ezzy. I'll study up on the trig anyway, just to be doing something.

"Janet sent me a picture in her letter, and she is cute. You should see the envelope that her letters come in. She paints a greeting on the envelope, and it is clever. She also writes a very interesting letter. You'd think we knew each other before, the way we correspond.

"Ezzy, I received the socks you knitted, and they are pretty neat. I looked for a dropped stitch, but I couldn't find any. Ha. Ha. I'm going to save them for a real cold day, but I don't think I'll wear them to bed. Talking about sleeping, the other day a fellow found a poisonous snake in a bed! I'm going to have a hard time going to sleep nights now, I think. Back home it was that rat and down here it is the snakes. Boy oh boy, what a life.

"Eunice, I hope that David and John liked the cards I sent them, because I couldn't find them anything else to send. I'm sorry to hear about the colt breaking its leg because it was such a nice animal. I should still have the movies of him back home some place, shouldn't I? I'll get them out when I come home, and we'll have a picture show.

"I hope you can go down to New York to see Marjorie over Easter,

Lois. Esda mentioned something about coming down to see me, but I don't think we will be here very long now. In fact, I don't think it'll be over a week or two. I could find you a place to stay, Ezzy, but I might be gone before you got down here. I'd like to see you though." (**NOTE:** Dad thought he was going to deploy sooner than what actually happened. He would not leave for another 5 months).

"Well Marjorie, I knew I had to write you a letter pretty soon so I made a carbon copy for you because I'm kinda tired tonight. Be good and careful and I'll write more later. Love Elwood."

25 April 1943: Typed letter from Camp Stewart, Georgia on Easter Sunday: His first long paragraph spoke to the importance of Easter to the Turner family over the years. "My dear family: I was walking down to the latrine this morning, and someone told me that today was Easter. My, was I surprised! I always remember Easter time as our family went to church at Lake Avenue, when we all walked up to church all dressed up. Remember Marjorie always made up her own style Easter bonnet every year and Dad or Pappy as I call him, always had me shave his neck before we went to church, and he used to be so mad if we weren't ready to go to church on time. Esda always wore lavender every Easter and usually stunk with some new cologne of some kind.

"Once in a while, Jack would break down and bring Lois over to church on Easter and usually they had to wait for us because Ezzy and Marjorie would get up late because they stayed up too late the night before with Doug and "Worry Wort"(Uncle Jimmy) and all the time poor Eunice way out in the country (**NOTE:** Eunice lived way out of town on their farm on Salt Road) and had been using all her time getting John and David all dressed up and washed and getting Johnny to wash the car before they went to church, and usually he just about did it in time to get shaved and cleaned up. If he got mad, he would yell at her and say, "You take the kids to church and I'll stay home and get dinner."

"Eunice usually won the argument, and it ended up she was putting her powder and rouge and hat on in the car on the way. I was always ready even though I forgot to clean my fingernails several times and I ended up cleaning them in church. Yes, Easter Sunday was a big Sunday for the Turner family, but I'd rather go through it all again this year rather than being down here in the woods not even knowing whether it's Easter or New Years." Dad then says something to each of his sisters and Pappy. He was going to a show with Larry. He thanked Lois for some cookies and peanut butter. Then, "CHOW TIME"

"Well, I just had chow, and we had ham for dinner with sweet potatoes, asparagus, and lemonade. It wasn't too good, but it filled me up." He ends with: "I also had a chance to go to church. This morning after I started this letter, I took time out and got cleaned up to go to church. We had a field service right out here in the woods. It was awful good and there were quite a few there. A lot of officers had their wives with them and one of our officers sang a couple of songs. Boy, was he ever good. The Chaplin's wife and he sang together. They sounded better than Nelson Eddy and Jeanette McDonald.

"I don't know whether I told you or not but I went to church last Sunday when I was in Glenville, too. I have to finish this letter so I can get it mailed before I go to the show. The convoy goes in at one o'clock and I haven't got much time left."

14 May 1943: Letter from Camp Stewart, Georgia: "My dear family: Today I received a letter from Lois, Esda, Pappy, and Janet. Boy, I certainly hit the jack pot, didn't I? It made me feel just as blue as all of you seemed to be when I found out how much you were looking forward to my furlough. I'm sorry I got you all excited and made so many plans and then I couldn't even make them all come true. I just wanted to be sure if I did get one that I would make the right connections. It's been six and half months since I've been home so naturally, I was a little excited in getting there. If we don't get any furloughs in the next month, I doubt if we will ever get any at all.

"The way the allies are fighting over in Africa, I doubt if the war will last long now and maybe I'll be getting a nice long furlough after the duration. The war will last about three years after Hitler surrenders. All in all, it shouldn't take any more than four or five years. Let's see, I'll be about twenty-eight or twenty-nine by then. I know you won't agree with me, Pappy, but I hope it ends sooner too." (**NOTE:** Dad was more pessimistic than he needed to be regarding the length of the war. In fact, the war in Germany ended a month after Hitler died and Dad was 25 when he got home, not 28.)

"Do you remember reading about Major General Bradley in the newspaper this last week? About the great work he did in North Africa. I'm sure you have if you have been reading the paper. Well, he is the highest-ranking officer I have seen in person. When we were in Florida on the day we had that street fighting course, he pulled up in a jeep with three other generals and he spoke to the group of men I was with. At the time he announced that he was our commanding officer of the Seventh Corps., which we are now in. Since then, he has replaced another general over in Africa and it looks as if he is doing all right for himself. I should have asked him for a match or something, eh? Ha. Ha."

"There is another dance tonight but I'm not going to this one. I just shaved and cleaned up so I could write this letter. I might have to work tomorrow afternoon at the dental clinic and the rest of the battalion has tomorrow afternoon off. I got gypped out of a corporal rating and I still have to work harder than the fellows that got them. The dentist is trying to get the rating for me but so far, he hasn't gotten very far. He says I'll get the next one, but there won't be another opening until one of them gets busted or gets a transfer.

"I'm going on a strike pretty soon. I've got a clean record so far but from now on the sparks are going to fly. I may even go over the hill for the experience. I like the work pretty good though, so that's why I haven't squawked much. It's clean work for one thing."

"I guess Bonnie and I are kinda washed up because she doesn't write anymore. She probably dates a lot of those sailors that are taking over Rochester. I don't blame her for going out, but the least she can do is write once in a while. I don't miss her letters so much anymore, though.

"I gave my check to one of our officers to keep for me so that I wouldn't spend some of it. It's still in check form too. I only have a few bucks left in cash and that means that I have to stay in this weekend and next, but I don't mind because I went out the last two weekends in a row. I hope you are alright everybody and healthy and happy. Don't work too hard, Pappy, will you? I enjoyed your letter very much, Pappy. Will you write me another one pretty soon? Will you send this letter to Marjorie?

"My shoulders are tired from typing because I haven't typed lately and they are too tired to type another letter to Marjorie. Thank you. I'll write more over the weekend so I can get to bed early tonight. Lots of Love, Elwood. P.S. Here's a picture I had taken some time ago and I just found it tonight. Maybe Majorie would like to have it."

28 May 1943: Short handwritten letter from Camp Stewart, Georgia: "If the flies will let me alone for a few minutes, I'll try to write this letter. I'm sitting in the front seat of the ambulance at the present time out in the sun. It's getting hotter all the time, it seems. Last night I worked from 3 till 11 p.m. and today I worked from 8 till 3 p.m. I still have half a barracks bag of dirty clothes to wash, and I'll have to be packing all my belongings Sunday. (**NOTE:** Dad was going to Tennessee shortly.) I've gotten used to sleeping on the ground again, but this morning I saw a huge black beetle or bug of some kind get out from under the covers when I did. I sure hope we can sleep in barracks for a short while again." Dad had taken some pictures with friends Frank and Larry from their pup tent. Dad ends the letter: "That's all the news I've got for now, but I'll write soon. Be good and careful. Lots of love, Elwood. PS Chow time."

30 May 1943: Post card from Camp Stewart, Georgia on a post card from Hinesville, Georgia: Dad said, "I've been back now a week already and I still would like to be home and have a party like the one we had at Grahams. Today I got packed and washed my clothes, so I'd be ready to move out of this hole next Tuesday sometime. I also got more tan today during the process. (**NOTE:** Dad was headed to Camp Forrest in Tennessee.) Write later, Love Elwood." (**NOTE:** Dad had a one week pass back to Rochester in Mid-May of 1943, around 17-24 May. He had been in the Army for six months now. Judy Norton confirmed that the pictures taken during his leave were taken at Aunt Nora's backyard in Rochester, New York.)

20 June 1943: Letter from Nashville, Tennessee APO 402: This is a typed and handwritten letter with the stationary heading "Tennessee Maneuvers, somewhere in Tennessee" The letter starts off weird. "Today is Saturday all day. So, what! When I went to the horse barn to get the mail, someone typed "so what" on my letter." There must have been a fire at Eunice and Johnny's farm that was quickly put out, because Dad praises Eunice for being a good fireman. Dad talks about three medical cabinets. One has a typewriter and the other two are filing cabinets. (**NOTE:** This is why Dad could type most of his letters. He was in a medical unit, and they took those containers overseas.)

"FLASH, FLASH, FLASH. Two of our men just came over to the medical tent armed with rifles to arrest two of our men. They are pretty well oiled up and one of the fellows popped off too much. There were restricted to the area, and they broke restrictions. They are laying around here laughing and wise cracking and making it worse for themselves. They will get court marshalled and those things go on their records. They can only go to chow and to the latrine, but only if the guard goes right behind them. One of the fellows is a good guy and I think it's a shame that he should get in so much trouble because one fellow is always getting into trouble. Oh well.

"I had some money yesterday but today is another day." Dad had won

46

$50 playing cards. Dad and a buddy went to Nashville. "They certainly soak the hell out of a soldier when he tries to buy something. Steak dinners cost me two dollars for a T-bone. Matty and I bought a pint of liquor last night and we had two pretty girls from Arkansas, and we had a party in one of Nashville's' hot spots. We were with the girls from four o'clock until nine and then we had to go back to the trucks in time to catch the convoy back to this cow pasture. A good time was had by all.

"Nashville sure is a good place to have a good time. There were plenty of girls for all the soldiers around here. There were two girls at a place we were at that were trying to make us and we already had two with us. There were plenty of other soldiers around without girls, but they couldn't get those two girls to dance with them even. This guy is jabbering so much that I can't think of anything to write." Then he talks about the future. "I think I'll be here in Tennessee for a while yet and I think we are going on maneuvers for another three month or less." (**NOTE:** Dad was almost spot on as he was later sent to England in early September 1943).

Dad closes the letter in handwriting. "I weighed myself in Nashville and I weigh 165 according to those scales. I thought I'd lost weight, but I guess I haven't. I'm getting nowhere with this letter because there is so much jabbering going on. Everyone is on edge and quarreling. I've got to take a walk, I can't stand this, ye gads! Be good and careful. Lots of love, Elwood."

28 June 1943: Letter from Camp Forrest, Tennessee: This letter is mostly about his sisters and asking and answering questions. Starts out: "Today is a hell of a day in Tennessee!!!! (copying Farm and Home Hour). (**NOTE:** There was a popular radio program in the 1940s out of Chicago with the name Farm and Home Hour. It was heard Monday-Saturday as a 30-minute program!)

They go on many hikes for hours at a time. "They are trying to make Boy Scouts out of us, I presume. I have a bad case of athlete's foot, and my left foot seems to bother me a little bit. We gave tetanus shots this A.M." A lot of Dad's stuff was stored under his tent, but rain came, and he dug a trench around his tent. "I started digging a small ditch around it, it started to come down in torrents. You can bet your next bond I got soaked. I salvaged my raincoat, and I haven't got a new one as yet, to replace it.

"Oh yes, I finally got rid of my G.I.'s Thank the Lord." Pappy got an easier job, and Dad was glad to hear it. He tells Ezzy and Doug he was sorry to hear Aunt Lucy died. (**NOTE:** First and only mention of Aunt Lucy. Believe she was on Doug's side of family.) He coaches Ezzy not to get so upset over Margie and Mrs. Graham. Don't make it harder on yourself. (**NOTE:** More than likely Ezzy didn't like Uncle Jimmy's mother.)

Dad gives Ezzy good advice: "Rest assured she means well, the same as you do. I'm sure Mrs. Graham is the same way." Dad closes with: "How's little David Elwood? Still got your uniform, David? Be good boys, won't you? Well, I'm all run out of conversation for now. Be good and be careful! Lots of Love, Elwood."

26 July 1943: (**NOTE:** It was over a month since Dad wrote, unless I'm missing letters.) Typed letter from Camp Forrest, Tennessee: Colonel Ackerman came out to check some of the men's teeth and when Dad went to greet him, the Colonel told a Major, "I came out to help Lt. Giuliano's very capable assistant (meaning me, of course). Ha. Ha. It made me feel good to have him say it in front of our Major." Dad really appreciated the compliment in front of the Major. (**NOTE:** Another key lesson day passed on to us kids: don't hold onto a compliment. Share compliments as quickly as possible. Encourage others.)

Dad mentions who is in charge for the captain when the captain is on furlough, Dad thinks is a much nicer guy. "He just walked into our aid tent and asked me a question and I told him I was telling you people how good I thought he was." Dad says, "How do you like the news about

Italy being on the verge of collapsing. Mussolini has resigned and the Italian people are pleading for peace. I'm beginning to think the Second Army will be an army of occupation. Maybe I'll be in Italy pretty soon.

"By the way, the reason I told you that I thought I was going across was so that you wouldn't be surprised. I think we will, and I figured if I told you now, you would expect it. Comprenez-vous? ("understand".) This morning at reveille they asked us if we had enough insurance and if we wanted to make out a will."

Dad later asks Lois if she thought a having a will was a good idea. "I really haven't very much to give away upon my death except for my insurance money and a little money that I have in the bank." Dad talks about buying more $50 bonds and says, "Maybe I can save up enough money while I'm in the Army, I will have enough money to get married so that I could have a wife down here with me to spend free time with." He talks about going into town for a few beers. He says, "Some guys sit around and do nothing at all and be happy but I'm not that well contented. I've got to go out and be doing something. I guess that's why I'm kinda anxious to go across and get my mind occupied to the fullest extent. Because when a guy is dodging bullets, his mind is pretty well filled up and I don't mean maybe."

He forgot all their phone numbers and said he would get them all next time they talked. Says he didn't think Margie would be able to come down and see him. (**NOTE:** In fact, Margie visited him in less than a week!) He mentions seeing her in New York City. Hints he wants more cookies from Esda. Writes this to Lois: "Lois, what do you think I should do about making out a will? Do you think I should? You know my financial status; don't you think it would be better if I didn't. All of you people could decide what to do."

He ends with a request from his dad, Pappy for "a dagger with a blade about six- or seven-inches longs and send it to me, I'd appreciate it. I'd want a good one because if I don't get a gun issued to me, I want the next best thing…. a lot of fellas are getting them, and I'd feel a little more at ease if I had one." He received a letter from Earl and needs to write Boyce. He ends with: "Be good and be careful. I love you all, Elwood."

1 August 1943: Post card from Chattanooga, Tennessee on a Rock City Gardens Lookout Mountain Tennessee post card. Aunt Margie was visiting Dad when he was stationed at Camp Forrest, Tennessee. They just made a phone call to Rochester. "Boy, it sure was good to talk to you all again. It seems as if you were only in the next room. I guess I did most of the talking and Margie didn't get much of a chance to talk to you. Now we are going out to dinner and probably we'll go to a show after dinner. Tomorrow we might go swimming at Wander's Park and then go to "Look Out' M.T. Inn for dinner. Shortly after that Margie will have to get her train to Va. I'll write a long letter when I get back. Love Marge and Elwood."

11 August 1943: Typed letter from Camp Forrest, Tennessee: "I'm getting rather reluctant in my letter writing and I'll tell you why. I've been playing ball every night and most every other night after the game I go to a show and take a shower. Last night I played in the outfield and threw my arm out of place on a throw to the plate."

Tells his sisters: "I hope I didn't say anything in my last few letters that none of you didn't like. Probably you are all very busy, eh?" Dad asks his Pappy to "What I'd like to have you do when you go over to Lake Avenue Baptist Church, is to find out if I still owe them any money on any pledges I made before I came in the Army, if so, I want you to see that it is paid up. I get that on my mind every now and then and I feel guilty to think I haven't paid them up as yet." (**NOTE:** Dad always worried about paying his bills. Another lesson for his kids: if you make a commitment, live up to it.)

He closes with: "I'm going to cut this letter short for two reasons, one being that it's getting too dark to see and the other is my arm is starting to bother me too much. I'm a little worried about you all because I haven't heard in five days, so be good and be careful and I'll probably get a letter from Lois and Marjorie tomorrow or the next day. I should write to Marjorie tonight, but I guess I'll have to wait until tomorrow. Boy, it's really dark now. Good night, everybody, Elwood. P.S. Did you get that box I sent home yet?"

25 August 1943: Handwritten letter from Tennessee: (**NOTE:** This is his last letter to his family before he sailed for England.) "My dear family, In the near future, you'll be receiving cards concerning my where-abouts. Please be calm, cool, and collective about everything. Starting Friday, all the letters I write will have to be censored, thus you won't be able to know anything about me except my health and my attitude about things you won't know about.

"By now, you must realize my future journey and you will be in-formed by the government whether or not I get to my destination okay and also my new address. Right now, I'm in good health and I'm quite anxious to do my duty that I'm required to do. I'm not scared in the least and I want you people back home to feel just as self-assured as I do, about being able to come home again. Don't worry about me but maybe you'd better say a prayer for me, huh?

"Today I received a letter from Boyce, and he is some type of an engineer in the big "B17" flying fortress over in England at the present time. He seems quite happy, and he likes England a lot. He also is in good health. Wouldn't it be swell if I could meet up with him sometime on my journey? (**NOTE:** Dad more than likely expected to be in En-gland. Later he and Boyce met up in London for rest and relaxation.)

"I received your card today, Pappy, peanut butter and candy you sent, Ezzy. Everything was swell. I enjoyed it very much. Thank you. I also received your letter today. I don't think you'd better send any more stuff until I reach my new destination. I'll have enough to carry as it is. Thank you just the same.

"Lois, I don't know yet what I'll do about taking a little extra money along with me as yet but if I need any, I'll try to wire you. So far as I know, we won't get paid this month and I might need some for a few extra cigarettes or something. **Listen to this, all of you!!! I'll try to write to you again before we leave here, but if for some reason I can't, I won't be able to write, phone, or wire while enroute. Remember that so you'll know that I can't write to you when you think I should. Attention everybody!! Please, please, Will item #1**: You Pappy, keep my $2,000 endowment policy up to date by paying the required $11.58 every 3 months. Also, let me know if this hasn't been done. **Item #2:** Will someone please make sure my debt to Lake Avenue Baptist Church is paid up and also please let me know when it is. My income tax can wait till I return from duty. If there is anything else that needs doing for me, will you please see that it's taken care of and let me know of any such thing.

"I'll probably make out a will sometime before I leave the U.S., but in case I can't, I think there will be no misunderstandings about what I want done. I mentioned it in one of my last few letters. My clothes of course would go to Pappy, and he can give away any of them he wants to. Upon my death, my insurance money will go to Pappy. Lois is the co-beneficiary on the $10,000 policy and I think Marjorie is the co-beneficiary on the $2,000 policy. Pappy of course being the beneficiary on this policy. From there on Pappy will be the one to decide who gets the money after he passes away, and I hope never.

"Pappy, of course, will make out a will sharing everything with his four daughters, if I'm not mistaken. He is to use his own discretion. All of this I've been telling you is probably unnecessary, but just in case things turn out for the worse. Okay? Well, I have to write Marjorie and Boyce and Earl now, so I'll bid my farewell until the next time. Everybody be good and be careful! Lots and Lots of Love, Elwood."

1 September 1943: Change of address card from Camp Forrest, Tennessee: Dad sent a card to Eunice with his new Army Post Office (APO) address. (**NOTE:** This is the last correspondence from Camp Forrest, Tennessee before dad sailed for England.)

Clockwise from top left: Dad using a bayonet at Camp Stewart, Happy Warrior, Looking for airplanes with a gas mask on, CPL Elwood Turner at Camp Forrest, TN

From left: Dad at Camp Stewart, Dad with John Jr. and David Elwood Furlough (1943), Dad with Pappy Furlough (1943, Rochester, NY)

Dad with sisters Esda, Margie, Lois and Pappy Furlough (1943)

Business Section of Hinesville, Georgia, Near Camp Stewart

Chapter/Section 2: England

Leaves for England: 5 Sept 1943 – Arrive 16 Sept 1943

England: 17 Sept 1943 – 28 June 1944

17 September 1943: Handwritten V-Mail from England: (**NOTE:** V-mail, Victory Mail, was a new way soldiers could correspond. They are very small, 4 x 5 ½ inch notes.) Dad's first correspondence from England after arriving on 16 September 1943 begins with: "Hi there, ole chaps. It's a beautiful day in England. I arrived safely and am feeling quite well. The terrain I've seen so far is beautiful; the grass is such a pretty green; the trees (a lot of chestnuts) are pretty and the shrubbery and flowers are gorgeous. It's the most beautiful land I've seen so far. Everything is so fresh looking it reminds me of spring back home.

"It rains quite often over here, so I imagine that accounts for being so green. The cities are nice, they are so clean looking, and I always did like English architecture. Most every house in a city has a lawn and some flowers and shrubs around it. It's an antique place but the beauty of it all counteracts everything else. I wish you could see England." (**NOTE:** This is a PERFECT description of what I remember of England).

He ends this short note with: "I'm glad that I was able to come here, I just hope I can stay here awhile." Dad would stay until 28 June 1944. His exact arrival date to the town Hazel lived, Sturminster Newton, is not certain, for many reasons, but I believe it was December 1943.)

24 September 1943: Handwritten V-mail note from England: Dad opens with: "Here I am again coming to you from England." Dad had received a lot of mail and said, "It did me a lot of good to hear from you again." Dad thanked Pappy and his sisters for taking care of the things he asked them to take care of before he left the U.S. (paying the Church and keeping his life insurance paid up).

He adds: "If you can get my watch fixed and if you could send it to me, I wish you would." He thanks them again for a dollar they sent him. (**NOTE:** It is very interesting that a single dollar meant so much to Dad.) "I'm sorry to hear that David and John had such a bad spill. A few little knocks won't hurt them now and then, but tell them to be careful for me." (**NOTE:** We heard "be careful" many times as kids! Every single time we left the house for anything, dad would say, "be careful".)

He tells Esda: "Janet wrote and bawled me out for not writing to you enough." Dad thanks them for writing and says he will try to do better, but he says: "It's hard to tell what I'll be doing day to day, though. Be good and be careful. Love to all and be careful. Love to all, Elwood." (**NOTE:** More than likely, Dad is in a town close to Sturminster Newton. He still does not mention Mom or the people he stayed with, the Mumfords.)

3 October 1943: Handwritten V-mail from England: He had received 12 letters and was trying to answer them all! Janet and Bonnie were still writing along with all his sisters. He says, "Pretty good haul, huh? I can't believe John is in fourth grade already. He certainly is doing fine. I'd love to see David in school. They must be careful riding back and forth to school on their bikes.

"You asked me what I wanted for X-mas, Eunice and Esda, but I was one jump ahead of you. You may send the knife, Eunice, if you wish to. I'm glad that you are going to send me some woolen socks, Ezzy, I could use them over here. The weather warrants heavy clothing over here now. I am wearing my long johns right now. At night I have 4 blankets and my overcoat over my bed, and I still get cold. I'm getting used to it though. I must leave you now so I can write to Margie. Be good and be careful. Love all, Elwood."

October 11, 1943: Typed written V-mail from England: (**NOTE:** The typewriter we heard about before he left the U.S. must have arrived.) "It's early in the morning and my fingers are stiff and cold but I want to get this letter off this morning if I can. Using the typewriter gives me more space to write in. We had a lousy breakfast this morning, as usual, but I guess they can't do any better because 99% of our food comes in a can. (**NOTE:** This means he was still not in Stur with his English family. He was alongside many troops eating in a big mess hall.) "Every day, I make a resolution not to have this or that when I have a home of my own. I hope I have the money to make them good.

"You and Johnny sound awfully busy to me. I hope you're not over doing it. You people back home sure are taking good care of Pappy for me. Pappy, you've got a nice set up eating Sunday dinner with your daughters every week. I wish I could do the same.

"Did I tell you about the Sunday I went to the Church of England? It was the largest church in the town I was in, so I went there. Their services are the same as the Christ church back home. Bonnie and I used to go there during Lent week and on Christmas Eve. Well, the church I went to here wasn't heated and I practically froze but I enjoyed it nevertheless. (**NOTE:** Stur has a Church of England church and another church, but I'm confident he was not in Stur yet.)

"If and when I get to London, I hope to attend the services in their largest cathedral." (**NOTE:** Dad did in fact make it to London and went to Westminster Abbey and St. Paul's Cathedral). "So far, I haven't been doing much visiting and I'm not expecting to do very much, even thought I'd like to.

"Esda, I got four letters from you yesterday and one from Bonnie. I think I have received all my back mail by now, excepting the money that Lois sent. I'm beginning to think that that letter got sunk in the ocean someplace. I haven't had a chance to visit any art galleries yet, but I plan on doing so. Some questions you asked me I can't answer. (**NOTE:** He could not be specific of what town he was in, and he never mentioned Stur in his notes while in England.)

"I guess you'll have to wait until I get home. However, I don't want you or the rest to worry too much. When you send me the addresses of those people you mentioned, I'll try to get in touch with them. I got my week's ration yesterday and I've eaten the candy up already, so I'm waiting patiently for the Fanny Farmers. I hope they don't melt on the way. Ha. Ha.

"It's getting close to fifteenth and so far, I haven't been able to get anything to send you people for Christmas. I just got paid last Saturday, but I can't buy anything over here unless I have a ration book. I'll go to the Red Cross and see what they can do for me. If I don't prove success-ful, I want you to know that I wanted to send you all at least something. Maybe I still can, I hope. My fingers are still cold and every five minutes I have to defrost them.

"The latest news I have about my work is that I will be working with the dentist, assist on sick call every morning at the aid station, and do whatever else comes my way. I got my morning paper, "Stars and Stripes" and a Yank magazine. I'll digest some of the news, if I get time. It sounds pretty good, doesn't it? Love to all, Elwood." (**NOTE:** U.S. Military to this day publishes the Stars and Stripes. That's the paper I read while stationed in Germany. The news Dad refers to is the good progress of the allies in Italy and Northern Africa.)

29 October 1943: Typed V-mail from England censored in two places. "It is late in the afternoon and it's dreary as the devil. Even the radio is playing a very dreary song. They play quite a few classics over the radio during the daytime. It sounds like the radio back home on Sunday af-ternoon. This afternoon we quit work early to read our mail. You people back home are certainly writing a lot and I'm glad for it.

"It's about time they started sending you my bonds, Eunice. Have you received any since I've been over here. I've been over here almost (2 months was censored out) now you should be getting another fifty dollar one pretty soon, shouldn't you? I do know that I have only received partial pay for the last three months and the reason why I'm getting partial pay this coming month is because of the increase in my allotment that I made (next several words were censored). (**NOTE:** He was promoted to a Tech 5).

"Esda, your garden was a great help to you again this year, wasn't it? You would enjoy seeing some of these Limey's gardens over here. They still have flowers in their gardens, and I imagine they have them all year round. In a month or so I'm going to try to find some of your relatives now that I know what country they came from. Majorie wrote to Lillian, and she is going to write me. Maybe she can tell me more about where I can locate them. Chow time! Lots of love, Elwood."

4 November 1943: Written V-mail from England: Dad had received many letters from back home. He thanks Uncle Jimmy for writing and asks his nephews to write. "I had quite an experience today. I cleaned four fellow's teeth this afternoon.

"Eunice, you asked about my eyes in your letter. They still are the same; I still have granulated eye lids, but they aren't so bad as they were. I wish I could get them cleared up. My eyes still aren't corrected, and I've worn these damn glasses better than a year now. Such is life without a wife. It doesn't look as if I'll ever get married if I have to stay in the Army very long. Ha. Ha. Be good and be careful. Lots of love, Elwood."

15 November 1943: Postcard from London, England. Dad was on a furlough to London, England. (**NOTE:** It has been six months since Dad went on furlough in May 1943 to Rochester.) First postcard shows the Tower of London and Tower Bridge: "Dear Eunice and Family, this is the view I got when I was on the top of St. Paul's Cathedral. The Tower Bridge is in the distance. Love to all, Elwood."

The postmark on the second post card could not be read, but the ink and timing was the same. The Houses of Parliament postcard was to "Dear Ezzy and Doug, Notice 'Big Ben' in this picture. I just saw this building at a distance. They do have tours through it, but there wasn't any the day I was there. Lots of love, Elwood."

17 November 1943: Typed V-mail from England: "I can't understand why you haven't received a letter from me in two weeks. I'm sure I meant to write to you as often as anyone else. It won't happen again, I promise. I haven't been writing to Majorie as much as I should have, but I'm catching up on my writing right now.

"Now that Johnny is through with election and most of his harvesting is done, he'll probably be around the house more, eh? It's remarkable how he does so many different things and does as much as he does. He's a damn good man, if you ask me.

"The other day I received the package you sent and even though I'm dying to open it, I haven't opened it so far. As soon as I open it, I'll write more about it. I got a package from Earl that I opened, thinking it was candy, but instead it was a set of face powder, after shaving lotion, and a bottle of brilliantine. It's very nice.

"I opened two more packages that Esda sent me because I know what was in them. She sent me two pounds of Fanny Farmers and they are all gone. The other box had my watch in it with gum, lifesavers, soap, socks, handkerchiefs, and Kleenex. I wrote her a letter, but I forgot to mention the handkerchiefs. I'll bet she doesn't like that. You tell her they're just what I needed. I also got a package from Lois that I haven't opened yet.

"It seems strange getting Christmas packages at this time of the year. I hope I'm home for Christmas of 1944. I hope little David and John have a nice Christmas this year. Where are you people going to have Christmas dinner this year? Are you all going to be together? Be good and be careful. Thanks again for the packages. Lots of love, Elwood."

22 November 1943: V-mail dated 23 November 1943 from England: Dad refers to his mom's birthday, 22 November: "Today is the 22nd of November and if I'm not mistaken, it's our mother's birthday. I thought about her quite a bit today and I was trying to imagine how it would be if she were still with us. I wonder how she would react to my being in the Army and my being over here. I suppose she would feel the same way as any other mother of a soldier.

"Our entire life would have been 100% happier if she had lived, wouldn't it? I read and I know about the great men of the past and know a few of their birthday dates and Mother's birthday rates among the best of them, in my mind. I wonder if she knows how much we miss her?

"They say stuff a cold and starve a fever, and I'm trying my best to stuff the damn thing. I eat like a hog, or I should say as much as a hog. I'm getting a big gut, and I don't have enough exercise to keep me in trim. When I was in Florida, I really did myself justice… when I came on furlough last May, I was in the best health I've ever been in, in my life. I still weigh 165, but the fat exceeds the muscle a little. I feel good though.

"My birthday comes next February the 3rd doesn't it? How about sending me a few more pounds of Fanny Farmers and Hershey's? That is if you are going to send me something. Ha. Ha. Boy I'm an optimist, aren't I?"

Then he goes on to say he broke his watch crystal playing ping pong. "If I ever get to London again, I'm going to try to get it fixed there." He ends with: "Well, I haven't had a letter in about a week, but they say there is going to be a lot of mail tomorrow. I'll probably get one from one of you, I hope. Be good and be careful. Lots of love, Elwood." (**NOTE:** This just goes to show the importance of mail to dad and how he longed to hear from his family, every day. Yet another lesson: stay connected with your family always. Life is short.)

Note about December 1943: It is not clear by reading Dad's letter which day in December his unit entered Sturminster Newton, but it was a day in December. I confirmed this by reading Dad's letters below, and by reading a copy of The Sturminster Tymes newspaper, recorded below. Sturminster Newton, England, was a very small market village in 1943. My dad would have met Hazel, my mom, within days of arriving in Sturminster, especially if his office was on Church Street.

(NOTE about Dad's Unit in STUR and two letters to a Sturminster Newspaper in 1997: A July 1997 Sturminster Newton newspaper, "The Sturminster Tymes", published a letter from Jack Tubert, of Massachusetts, who said the 377th arrived in Stur in September 1943. Jack said the townspeople were not friendly with him when he returned to be a part of the 50th anniversary of D-day in 1994. Here is part of Jack's letter to the editor of the Sturminster Tymes: "I write because I was stationed in Sturminster with Battery C, 377th Anti-Aircraft Battalion. We lived in the Mason Hall-next to the Church. (**NOTE:** This is directly across the street from Hazel's house on Church Street.) I think we were on Church Street, just off the town center. Maybe it was Penny Street.

The 377th Battery C was in Sturminster from September 1943 until about June 9th or 10th—three or four days after the Normandy Invasion began. We left for Portsmouth Harbor (69 miles from Stur) for a boat ride to Normandy, arriving D-Day +11, June 17, 1944. In Normandy, the 377th rejoined the 12th Regiment of the 4th Infantry Division for a journey across Europe, earning five battle stars. Many died, but the lights went on again-all over the world.

After three years I write to ask why there is no marker in Sturminster to acknowledge that we were there? Portsmouth and Weymouth have markers! I returned for the 50th anniversary of the Normandy Invasion, and I took time to travel from Bournemouth to Sturminster (Dorset County had more that 3 million Yanks training in 1943-1944)

(**NOTE:** Jack is not correct here. During the entire war for all of England, over two million servicemembers were in England, not three million in little Dorset County alone.) Reaching Stur was a shock. It was a town that had slept for 50 years. Nothing seemed changed, except the civilian automobiles, and nothing was the same. Only colder…the people. No one I talked to could recall the 377th or that any invasion army unit had ever lived there. Yet we were there 9 months.

At least two of our soldiers married Sturminster girls. One couple would not live in Rochester, New York, I think. (**NOTE:** This couple was Elwood and Hazel Turner). We gave up three years of our young lives, close to one year in your town. Yet, no one remembers. Could they not at least have put a brass plate on the door of the Mason Hall? It could say "Battery C, 377th U.S. Army-was billeted here from September 1943 to June 1944 leaving to participate in the Normandy Invasion."

Vicar John C. Day of St. Mary's (**NOTE:** The Church Mom and Dad got married in) was the only civil person I remember. He did not know anything about a U.S. unit being in the town during the war years. He did present me a Tourist Guide, and a copy of your June 1944 "The Bridge" #295. Men at the Royal British Legion (**NOTE:** Grandfi, family friend, Lee Tornabene, Bob, and I have been in the British Legion several times over the years. The patrons' love and admiration for Americans and their sacrifice were evident every single time we visited.)

The 50th anniversary edition of "The Bridge" made no mention of the 377th. Maybe there is word at the town library. No one I spoke to mentioned a town library or I'd have looked there. I would appreciate your printing a small item in "The Bridge" asking anyone with memories of the 377th being there to write to me: Jack Tubert, Post Office Box 2691, Worcester, Massachusetts 01613 U.S.A. (**NOTE:** I wrote to Jack in the 1990s and never heard anything from him. He was probably 19-22 years old in 1943 but would have been in his 70s in 1997).

A few months after July 1997, a Catherine Snook responded to Jack's letter and said Dad's unit didn't arrive in Stur until December 1943, which matches better what Dad says in his letter. Here is Catherine Snook's letter: "From reading the letter in the Tymes, I felt compelled to research further into the history surrounding Jack Tuber and the American Battery Unit No 377, stationed in Sturminster for nine months during World War 2. To me, as a fifteen-year-old, I found it very difficult to comprehend how the soldiers must have felt, not a lot older than myself, being shipped off to a foreign country, not knowing what they were to encounter, not knowing whether they would survive the war or ever see their families again. It was a huge sacrifice they made without a doubt.

They arrived in December 1943 and departed in June 1944 after D-Day. Jim Hatcher (our Uncle Jim) was a teenager living in Sturminster at the time of the War and recalls some of the soldiers. There was a Mexican named Delian with an Italian called Dejulio, both were billeted in what is now Market Cross Kitchen. This was where offenders were locked up, although at night the boys from the town would creep in and play cards with them!

The dining halls were in the Swan assembly room and the delicatessen beneath it was used as a kitchen with stairs from there to the dining hall. Also, there was a dining hall in what is now Buy-Lo's Car Park. The medical room was at 25 Church Street and the P.X. (Post Exchange) or NAAFI as it was known by the English, was in the Masonic Hall where the Americans could get supplies, e.g. gum.

There were some humorous stories told to me about the "Yanks", one of whom was a North American Indian. He couldn't get to sleep in the White Hart because the other soldiers would not turn the lights out, so he ate the light bulbs! This very same soldier also had to get some athlete's foot ointment and being illiterate, he didn't understand the instructions, so he drank it!

In his letter, Mr. Tubert also mentioned that two Sturminster girls were wed to American soldiers, and I was able to locate the brother of one of them. Her name was Hazel Hatcher who was billeted with the vet, Mr. Mumford in Rixon. Before coming to England, he worked for Kodak in Rochester, New York and after the war, he and Hazel returned there to live. However, many Americans stationed in Sturminster never returned home and died in action. It must have been an emotional time for Jack Tubert when he visited Sturminster for the 50th Anniversary.

I can't imagine how it must have felt to return to a place bearing such memories of war and the friends he had lost. I think an appropriate gesture to commemorate the sacrifice made by these young Americans in the form of a plaque situated in the memorial gardens would be well suited. Thank you to contributions made by Mr. Hatcher, Mr. Anderson, and Mr. Rose. Catherine Snook."

Bottom Line: I believe Dad arrived Sturminster in December 1943. If Dad had been on Church Street right next door to Mom's house, they would have met. I believe he landed in Southampton, or Portsmouth, England, a short drive to Sturminster Newton. This is why the allies chose towns like Sturminster Newton which were very close to ports going to France. There was a picture in Dad's belongings of Dorchester, England. Dorchester is only 36 miles from Stur and could easily have been a place the troops initially went when they arrived in England.

2 December 1943: Handwritten V-mail from England. "Today, as usual, it's raining and it's terribly gloomy. I still have my cold to contend with and it seems I just can't get rid of this cough. I've been taking medicine, but that doesn't help. This damn weather isn't fit for man or beast. Last night I went out on a pass and had a few beers and later I went to a dance.

"Well, Eunice, so far, I haven't opened the package you sent me, but I think I will tonight because I think it contains a cigarette lighter, and I need one bad. I run out of matches too often. It's almost time for me to go to work, so I'll leave you now. I hope you are all well and that you're not working too hard. Be careful, Lots of Love, Elwood."

5 December 1943: Handwritten V-mail from England. Still coughing from the cold. "I wish I had a quart of Canadian Club or 4 Roses. I'd get cured or drunk, one of the two, probably both. That's great about paying off $500 on your mortgage. You two are really doing a swell job paying off that mortgage. I bet you wish it was the last payment. I hope next year you can do better. If it's within your power, I know you will. I wish I could handle my money and deficits as well as you two do. I'm always in the hole.

"Bob Hope is on the radio now. Don't forget to wind your watch and be good. Lots of love, Elwood."

15 December 1943: Handwritten V-mail from England. "Well, I finally opened the package you sent me, and it was swell. The big bar of chocolate was swell, and was I glad to get those Kleenex. I am wearing a pair of the socks now, they're swell. I found the cigarette lighter, and it works well. I was offered a pound for it but didn't take it. I need a new toothbrush too. The Chinese checker game will help pass a few lonely hours and I've already started reading "Claudia". Thank you very much for everything. I've received nine packages so far and they've all been swell. In fact, I have a half of a barracks bag full of Christmas boxes. All the eatables are consumed, darn it. (**NOTE:** This means he was not yet at the house he lived in Stur at the Mumfords, but he could have been in Stur at one of the big halls, but I seriously doubt it. Stur is so small, he for sure would have run into Hazel and noticed her).

"I should have a few letters tonight when the mail comes in. I hope everything back home is running smoothly and that the kids are getting along alright. Be careful and have a nice Christmas. Write soon. Lots of love, Elwood."

During mid-December 1943: Letter written to Lake Avenue Baptist Church and published on 23 Jan 1944 in their Sunday program. "Dear Pastor and friends of Lake Avenue: Every day I anxiously await letters from home and lately I have been receiving the church calendar. To me, the church calendar is like a letter containing the weekly news about my church. As I read it, I feel as if I were actually sitting in Lake Avenue Church. I'm also interested in the changes of addresses of the men in service and the activities of the congregation. Thank you all so much. Your letter, Dr. Watkins, was most welcome and I shall cherish it highly. I, too, pray that we'll all be home soon and I'm quite sure that with faith in our Lord, our prayers will be answered. (**NOTE:** Another lesson dad taught us, Matthew 22:37: "Love the Lord your God with all your heart and with all your soul and with all your mind." By his actions as my earthly father, he taught us that our priorities should be: God, family, job, hobbies. He loved his local church.)

"I've had the privilege of visiting Westminster Abbey, St. Paul's Cathedral, and attending several churches in England while on pass, and I received many hours of enjoyment in so doing. May you and the members of Lake Avenue have a most joyous Christmas and may 1944 bring forth a peaceful world."

24 December 1943: Handwritten V-mail from England. "I'm glad Johnny got a good price for his cabbage. Even Pappy mentioned it in his letter. He takes an interest in Johnny's crops." He still had a few packages left he had not opened yet, "so Christmas morning will be like the ones back home." He ends with, "I'm going to have it nice for Christmas this year, but I still would rather be home with you. Be careful. Lots of love, Elwood." (**NOTE:** This could indicate he was with the Mumford's or at least having Christmas with an English family. Christmas in 1943 fell on a Saturday.)

28 December 1943: Handwritten V-mail from England. "I realize it's been a long time since I've written but I've had such a wonderful X-mas and I've been on the go every night for a week. I went to a dance Christmas Eve and to one last night with HAZEL. (**NOTE:** This is the first mention of Hazel. Dad met Mom during Christmastime and probably on 27 December it got a bit more serious.) "There's a dance New Year's Eve, but I think I will be in London with Boyce, I hope. I've been invited to a party New Year's Eve with the family that I had Christmas dinner with, but I had to refuse them. They are awfully nice to me. I'll tell you more about them when I come home." (**NOTE:** I believe the family is the Mumford's and not the Hatcher's.)

"I received the lovely X-mas card you sent, and the two bucks will come in handy. I thank you. Gee it's good to see that good old money again. I kissed the right girl, and I didn't get pie-eyed. I'm waiting anxiously for the Fanny Farmers and again I want to thank you for sending me that wonderful X-mas package, everything was so useful. I'm sending some pictures to Pappy that I had taken over here. Lots of love, Elwood."

3 January 1944: Handwritten V-mail from England. The V-mail opens: "Well now that the holidays are over, I bet you are thankful because it usually is so much work for you. I hope you, John, and the kids had a good time over the holidays. I suppose your old man had a quart or two around the house. Ha. Ha. I could really go for a nice shot of scotch right now while I'm trying to catch up on my letter writing. I got too far behind over the holidays, and I suppose you've noticed. I've been going to parties, dances, and I also got to see Hazel quite often lately. The last two weeks remind me of home because I've been on the go so much.

"Did you and the kids get the X-mas package on time? Marjorie did my X-mas shopping for you this year and she did a very good job, I think. I don't see how she managed to have any money left of what I sent her to get something for herself. I must bid adieu now because I have to write to Pappy, Lois, Bonnie, Janet, Earl, and Boyce yet tonight. Be careful and as soon as those Fanny Farmers candies come, I'll have a piece for you. Lots of love, Elwood."

13 January 1944: Handwritten V-mail from England. "This morning, I have a few minutes before I have to start work and I'll attempt to fill out this page at least. I just had a cup of coffee and some jam tarts for breakfast, and I got everything ready in my office to start work.

"The other day I received letters from Margie, Lois, Esda, and you telling me all about what a wonderful Christmas dinner you had. I'm awful glad that you liked the red roses and the centerpiece. I thought they would remind you of me around Christmas day. I see that they worked wonders, but I'm terribly sorry that yours, Esda's and Lois's Christmas packages didn't get there before Christmas. I wanted you to be surprised when they came so that you'd be more thrilled about it. Margie and I went in together on the kids trench coats. Imagine she told you. I'm glad they liked them okay. I'll leave you now and get to work. Be careful. Lots of love, Elwood."

20 January 1944: Handwritten V-Mail from England: "I'm pleased to hear you had a pleasant New Years Eve and the rum and cake sure sounds marvelous, even though I don't care for rum.

"You told me about you having roast chicken for dinner one Sunday, so I'll tell you about the lovely chicken dinner I had at Hazel's house last Sunday. In fact, I'm at Hazel's house tonight writing this letter on the kitchen table." (**NOTE:** We were in that same kitchen when we visited England in 1963 and probably ate at the same table.) Dad never finishes telling them about the details of the chicken dinner.

"I don't know what you and Pop mean about my wanting a third interest in your farm, but if you're thinking that I would be able to get out of the army, I think you are wrong. In fact, I don't think I could that way. If you're thinking of a different angle about needing some money or something, of course it's all right with me. I couldn't figure it out so maybe in your next letter you can be more specific. Okay? Be careful! Cheerio until the next time. Lots of love, Elwood."

26 January 1944: 4th Infantry Division (4ID) Command Post was in Tiverton (Collepriest House), England. Tiverton is in Southwest England, a town in Devon, England, 65 miles west of Sturminster Newton. Dad was not yet assigned to the 4ID. Many pre-D-day training exercises took place in Devon. (**NOTE:** I am now adding 4th Infantry Division Command Post locations to provide context to the letters. In the end, this critical bit of information allowed me to trace my dad's steps in France, Belgium, Luxembourg, and Germany.)

26 January 1944: Typed V-mail from England: "Yesterday I received the box of Fanny Farmers and they are gone already, as usual. Boy were they ever good!! Thank you so much for sending them to me. Can you people get things like that without coupons, or do they have them rationed by now? How about butter and coffee nowadays? Are they still rationed? Over here one has to have a coupon for practically everything one buys. We in the army can't get anything in a store that you need coupons for, but we really don't need anything other than what we can get in our canteen.

"We had a wonderful dinner this noon for a change, we had pork chops, mashed potatoes, corn, spinach, bread with apple butter, and lemonade." (**NOTE:** The chow hall was in the basement of the Swan Hotel/Pub in downtown Stur, less than a five-minute walk from Hazel's house.) "We don't get fresh eggs at all, but I get one every once in a while at Hazels' house. They have a few chickens. Lately, we get canned fruit cocktail, canned peaches, canned pears or apricots with ever meal as dessert, and I don't mind it at all. As long as they feed me good, I haven't got much to bitch about. I'm in good health but I still have a nasty cough, and I can't seem to get rid of it.

"Last night Hazel and I went to the dance from ten o'clock til 11:30 and we came home for tea and beer. I had some beer there that I didn't finish drinking before I went. I think I got about twenty Christmas cards this year and about half of them came about a month late. I'm still getting a few. The time is passing quickly, and I have to fall out for retreat in a few minutes. I hope you are all in good health and that you're happy. Are the boy's behaving themselves lately? I've forgotten completely if David is going to school this year or not. That's the way you get after being away from home so long. 15 months almost. Cheerio with love, Elwood." (**NOTE:** Dad was counting the months!)

2 February 1944: Handwritten V-mail from England. "No, my dear sister, I'm not in the guard house yet. But I'm keeping my fingers crossed. (**NOTE:** Eunice must have teased Dad about going to the military brig.) My furlough starts tonight at midnight, and it ends on the 9th. I'm going to meet Boyce next Monday night in London and we are going out and tie one on. I'll only be with him a day and a night and the rest of my time, I'm going to try and locate some of our relatives. If I have the money, I'm going to try to locate some of Bonnie's relatives also. You see I had to borrow six pounds so that I could go someplace and that means next month and the rest of this month, when I come back, I'll be broke.

"I'm having a birthday cake and a birthday dinner at Hazel's house, so things don't look too bad, eh?" To Eunice: "I hope the dentist does a good job on your tooth. I've seen crowns made, but we don't make many of them in the Army. I'm glad you and Johnny are able to have your house fixed up. You two have done a lot to that place. Lots of love, Elwood."

10 February 1944: Handwritten V-mail from England: Dad talked about his furlough to London, and we don't have the full story here, but this is what was on this one-page V-mail: Dad had received pictures from home. Dad says his nephews "got an awful lot for Christmas but I'm sure they deserve it."

Details of his London furlough are sketchy: "I left off by leaving Bonnie's cousin's wife and going back to London. I had a nice visit there and we talked all about Bonnie's family and she told me where I could find Mrs. Bonfield's brother. I wrote a two-page letter to Pappy telling him about what I did Sunday. Monday I slept late as usual, till about 11 a.m. I went to Madame Tussaud's Wax Museum. It was wonderful. After that I ate and went to the theater. I saw '*Larson Desert Mysteries*.'

Monday night I went out to a dance and drank a few beers. I also had a few good shots of whiskey. Tuesday, I left London and got home about 5:30. I got back here. {**NOTE:** Dad calls it home. He took the train probably out of Waterloo Station in London and the train would have stopped in Sturminster. The distance is only 120 miles.) Dad closes with: "Will you please see that Marjorie gets to read this continuous letter, so I won't have to re-write it all. Thanks a lot. Much love, Elwood."

14 February 1944: Handwritten V-mail from England: "When you wrote about that farm deal, I didn't know what you had in mind at first, that's why I wrote back the way I did. I got the check for $12.50 okay, and I believe I can use it okay. I can't send you Hazel's address for military reasons. I believe she'll be able to write to you though and then you can answer her letter, Okay??

"Yes, Eunice, your young brother isn't so young anymore. Boy, I hate getting old. It doesn't seem to me that you'll be 30 next March and Esda has hit 40. They say life begins at 40. (**NOTE:** Dad had just turned 24.) "Margie sent me a Christmas present. I got a billfold with a five spot, a fountain pen, and some peppermint patties and Clark bars. The bill fold is really nice. So was the five spot. I have to take some medicine for my cold now and go home to bed. Cheerio for now and be careful. All my love, Elwood."

19 February 1944: V-Mail note from England. "Thank you for the lovely birthday card and Valentine. I received both a birthday card and a valentine from all my sisters, and I've received most of them in the last three days. It's fun getting a lot of mail, but it's hard as hell to answer it all. I also got a birthday card from Bonnie's mother, but so far nothing from Bonnie. That's a good one, isn't it?

"I'm glad you liked the letter I wrote to Dr. Watkins. It took me long enough to write it. I got the church calendar that it was in also." (**NOTE:** See above letter published in the Lake Avenue Church News on 23 January 1944. Dr. Watkins was the Pastor of Lake Avenue Baptist Church.) 'This army ruined my memory. I even forgot how old Bonnie is and the date of her birthday. I wrote and asked her when it is. I'm writing about four different women now and it's a job trying to keep them straight.' Dad still had his cold and ended the note with this: "It snowed for a while today and it was the first snow I've seen for two years. All my love, Elwood."

19 February 1944: Handwritten letter from Hazel Hatcher (mom) from 'Marley' 2 Church Street Sturminster Newton to Eunice: "It is giving me lots of pleasure to write to you, as Elwood has told me that you would like me to write. He has come to my home quite a lot and it has given us all great pleasure in welcoming him and we are all great friends. I only wish he was staying here until the war ends. (**NOTE:** Dad stayed a little over four months before he left for France). We do our best to look after him well, but despite it all he seems to get nasty colds, due I think to our damp climate; I don't blame late hours. I hear quite a lot about your two lovely boys John and David Elwood. And with their photos I can see they are just cute. Should imagine they will be like their Uncle Elwood.

"I have a brother Jimmy thirteen years old and he chases your boys for their gum. You will be delighted to know Elwood is very happy, the extra bright spot of the day is when the mail arrives from home. It was unfortunate that Elwood could not meet Boyce on his eight-day leave. We are trying to arrange for him to come here. This is a very difficult letter to write, but I'm sure you will understand the circumstances. My family joins me in sending their very kindest regards to you all, and we think all the photos are lovely. Yours sincerely, Hazel Hatcher."

29 February 1944: V-Mail note on Leap Year 1944 to Mrs. John De Roos: "Happy Birthday!!! I got you a birthday card the other day, but I haven't mailed it as yet. You'll think it's a small package when you get it, but it isn't anything but a card. I thought I better tell you so you wouldn't be disappointed.

"If your dentist did a good job on your tooth, I wouldn't say that it costs too much. I asked Captain Kantrowitz. (**NOTE:** This is the first mention of Captain Kantrowitz. Dad's office was at 25 Church Street. Right down the road from Hazel!) about it and he explained it to me. I also had to be a dental patient last Saturday when I had a tooth filled. I'm glad it's over because I don't care too much about being worked on by the dentist. He did a good job on it.

"Yes, I'm still buying bonds, but it takes three months to complete one. You said I had about two hundred dollars' worth in one of your letters, didn't you? Or am I making that figure kind of high?

"When I was in London, I was in the American bar, but I don't know if it was the American Eagle Club or not. The next time I go, I'll try to locate it. If I ever get enough money together again to go anyplace. I'm glad Pappy is sending some more money. I'll sure need it to get my rations every week. I always have tea and tarts every day, and I believe I spend about a buck a day in the tea shop. (**NOTE:** The tea shop was Pop Cluettes. (See picture at end of chapter.)

"It's kinda cold today and I still have my cough. My cold had started to clear up but now I think it'll get worse again if this damn weather doesn't clear up. I've had a damn cough ever since I've been over here and the only way I can get rid of it is to go back to Rochester. The people in America can't appreciate the fact that America is the best place in the world until you leave the place for a while. I've got to do some work now and I'll have to finish as quick as possible. Be good and take care of yourselves. All my love, Elwood."

10 March 1944: Handwritten V-mail from England. "Boyce wrote to Hazel and said he was coming the 10th, which will be tomorrow night sometime. I'm going to meet the train at the station so if he comes, I won't miss him. He will come in between 5 am and 9:30 pm. He and I will sleep at Hazel's house while he's here.

"I'm glad David and the John's are in good health too. I hope you can do something for little John about that twitching.

"The last couple days I didn't get any mail, and it seems funny about Bonnie not even writing or sending me a birthday card. Her mother did. It's chow time now and I'm really hungry. Be careful. All my love, Uncle Elwood."

14 March 1944: Handwritten V-mail from England: "After breakfast Sunday morning, we had a few bottles of beer, and then we headed for a pub. It was a beautiful day, and Norm brought his camera along. We took some pictures and when they're developed, I'll send a set of them home. We got pictures of the Hatcher family, the Mumford family, and I believe there is one of Hazel and me. There's one of Boyce and me too.

"We drank beer until 2 p.m. again and went home to Hazel's for dinner. (Wonderful dinner). After dinner we went for a long walk with the Hatchers, and it did us good." (**NOTE:** I am positive they would have walked the same walk Grandfi took us on often.) "The weather was just like a spring day back home. We had tea upon our return and did exactly the same thing Sunday night as we did Saturday night, only we didn't have quite so much to drink. We were dead tired when we went to bed at 12 o'clock. This morning Boyce and Norm left on the 8: 10 train and I saw them off. (**NOTE:** This means Norm came with Boyce to visit from a nearby Airbase. It's impossible to tell which U.S. Airbase Boyce was from because the U.S. was forming more bases at this time and using several older British airbases. From an earlier letter from Dad, we know Boyce worked on the B-17 Flying Fortress Bombers. A well-known airbase in England where B-17s were stationed is in the County of Suffolk England. The airfield was known as Framlingham Station 153, about two hours, 15 minutes from London.)

He closes: "I'll write a little bit more about Boyce. He's going to write Pappy and I'm going to write his wife and mother. Love, Elwood."

18 March 1944: Handwritten V-mail from England. The letter is dated the 18th but Dad starts out: "Today is the 17th— "Happy Birthday" ... It's a beautiful day over here and I hope you have just so pretty a day as it is here. Spring is in the air but it's still a little chilly around here. I'd love to be home now. I think I miss home more in the spring of the year than any other time." Dad likes the way Eunice is arranging their house and wishes the boys well. Dad had just heard the Jimmy Dorsey band on the radio. "English bands are positively no good. This country is so far behind times, it's pitiful. America, I love you."

Dad ends with: "Happy St. Patrick's Day and Happy Birthday, again. Say hello to your old man for me. Cheers All my love, Elwood."

27 March 1944: Handwritten V-mail from England: "The clock just struck 7 and the sun is just about out of sight. Hazel is washing dishes and when she is finished, she's going to make me a piece of toast and jam. (**NOTE:** Dad is either sitting in the kitchen or living room at Hazel's house. We probably heard the same clock in 1963 as Dad heard.) "I've eaten practically all Mrs. Hatcher's jam supply up and she'll have a job getting sugar enough to make more, so if you could manage to send me a few jars, about 12 of your strawberry and pineapple jam I'd really appreciate it. Can you put it in a big tin of some kind, then there wouldn't be any danger of breaking the jars." (**NOTE:** Dad underlined the kind of jam he wanted. Sugar was rationed in England, so that's why Grandma Hatcher would probably not be able to make more jam.)

"I just received that lovely Easter card with the five dollars attached and it came in real handy. It's only about four days to payday so I made out just right with those five dollars. Thank you, a lot.

"Mrs. Mumford received your letter before Lois and Esda's, and she let me read them. They were all very nice. It seemed funny reading letters from you that were written to someone else. Esda's letter was the only one censored. Nothing was crossed out. I'll write tomorrow again and answer your two letters. Love, Elwood." (**NOTE:** Sometimes we only think that letters originating from overseas were censored, however, many were censored coming from the U.S.)

30 March 1944: Handwritten V-mail from England: Dad had just cleaned up his office preparing for the next day. It was chow time, but he had to make his dental appointments for the next day. As Dad was writing, Hazel was expecting him to come by. There was a show in the mess hall, but Dad didn't plan to go. "Seats are on benches and it's hard on the bottom and the back. Last week, I had to sit way down in front, and I had a stiff neck and a sore back. Tonight, I'll take some beer over to Hazel's house and read my newspaper (nice set -up). I still like my beer now and then." Dad mentions the name on Mom's house, "Marley." Dad ends the letter by saying he forgot David's birthday date. "I'll look up in my old letters from you and find it." (**NOTE:** I thought all along Dad tossed old letters, but this indicates he held onto them for a while. I am sure he could not take them later to France.) "I hope I'm not too late. Give him a kiss for me on his birthday in case I am too late. Love, Elwood."

6 April 1944: Handwritten V-mail from England: "Am so glad you had such a nice time for your birthday and while I'm talking about birthdays, I want John Sr. to look for a Shetland pony for the kids. It'll be their birthday present from me. I wrote and told Pappy to get the money for Johnny, so now all you've got to do is get the pony and cart, if needed, and you send the bill to Pappy. They are at the right age now to enjoy it, and I believe John Donald could manage it by now, don't you? I've want-ed someday to give the boys a pony, so don't disappoint me. I could get one for nothing over here, but I'm afraid it'll be impossible to ship it to

America." (**NOTE:** See pictures at end of this chapter. Another lesson dad taught us all, "never give-up". Dad's persistence paid off.)

"I suppose now that spring is here, your old man will have to get out and do a little work after laying around and drinking beer all winter. Ha. I must write to Margie now. Cheerio with love, Elwood."

12 April 1944: Handwritten V-mail from England to Aunt Esda and Uncle Doug: (all prior letters were to Aunt Eunice and Uncle Johnny) "First of all, I want to thank you for the big box of gum, life savers, and candy. It arrived two days before Easter, and it was devoured by Easter. I gave a lot away to my friends to show my appreciation for what they do for me. I don't believe you could send Mrs. Hatcher and Mrs. Mumford any packages, but I told them what you said, and they thank you for thinking of them. I hope you can get the oranges for me.

"I wrote Pappy Monday and told him in detail what I did, so I'll just make a few remarks about it in your letter. Had I gone to church the way I should have, I could probably tell you more. I didn't get up till late, but the church bells woke me up and it put me in the thought about when we used to walk out of Lake Avenue and get in the car to go home. Remember how well we could hear the church bells when we were driving home? I didn't see many purple hats, but I bet you had a purple one and Doug wore a purple tie, right? I made you something for your birthday and I'll send it soon." (**NOTE:** We heard the same church bells in Sturminster Newton while we visited our Grandparents and stayed on Church Street).

12 April 1944: Handwritten V-mail from England to Eunice and Johnny: He hopes Aunt Eunice's trip with Johnny to Pennsylvania was fun. He couldn't believe they left the two boys behind. "So, your old man is 34-years old. Happy Birthday, Johnny. The next time I go pubbing I'll have a double brandy and drink to you, if I can get the brandy. Hazel's birthday is tomorrow. I just dictated a letter to Hazel because I'm getting tired of writing. It was to Gooche (Boyce). I didn't go to church on Easter Sunday because I didn't get up on time. I managed to get a few beers from 12 until 2 p.m., which wasn't too bad. I thought about you all and imagined the funny shaped hats you probably were wearing. Ha. Ha. I remember what a hard time I had trying to see the altar when we went to Lake Avenue because of all the women and their Easter bonnets. I made you something for your birthday and it'll be in the mail soon. Love Elwood."

17 April 1944: Typed V-mail from England (which was censored) to Eunice and family: "It's past nine o'clock and I still have to write to Majorie. It took me two hours to write two letters and I'm getting tired. I still have a cold in my head, but I've had that ever since I've been in England. We've been having rather nice weather lately except for an occasional two-day rain." Dad told them about two shots they had to have. (**NOTE:** This V-mail was censored. The type of shots was blacked out because that could tell the enemy where they may be headed.)

"Mr. and Mrs. Hatcher just came in and we are going to have a cup of tea in a few minutes, then I'll have to go home and go to bed. I'm going to be in a GI musical show this coming Thursday night. We're putting on two shows that night, and until then we have to practice every afternoon and every evening. We are going to have a party after the show, just for the members in the cast. I'm supposed to sing the opening number, but I'm a little scared. If I had a few drinks before I sang, I might do alright." Dad asks for the status of getting the pony and ends with this: "I've had my tea and now I have to take the typewriter back and go home to bed. Good night, Elwood."

22 April 1944: Handwritten V-mail from England: "It's a beautiful day out today and after I finish this and a letter to Margie, I'm going home and take a bath. Tonight, I'm going to a beer party being held for the members of the cast in our show. It went off real good considering the short time we had to rehearse. We put two shows on Thursday and two on Friday night. I had a lot of fun, but it tires you out.

"I bet your house looks very nice now that you've had it fixed up some. You and Johnny are doing wonderfully well on the farm. John's a good man to have done so much. I hope someday you two can sit back and enjoy your good work and not have to work so hard for what you get.

"I asked for a lot of your jam, but you know how well I can eat a can of your jam. Mrs. Hatcher's having a hell of a time getting jams, so I'll have some when I'm there. Eunice, I sent your birthday present okay with Esda's and Lois's to Esda. Hope you like it. Love to all, Elwood." (**NOTE:** The Turner clan was very, very close. Just one example of their closeness, Dad wrote them multiple times each week and sent presents to all sisters from overseas.)

1 May 1944: Handwritten V-mails from England. "Another Sunday has come, and in a few hours, it will have gone. Today I had dinner with Hazel, a wonderful dinner. I like Mrs. Hatcher's cooking. We get paid this afternoon and I'm letting Mrs. Hatcher hold most of my money, so I won't spend too much. I gave her ten pounds to hold for me last month and every time I needed money, I had to get it from her. I managed to spend it all. I only drew 6 pounds 13 shilling payday, but last month I won a hundred or some odd bucks and I had a little extra. I still have $44 loaned out and I have $38 cash for this coming month of May." (**NOTE:** The $100 Dad won either playing poker or betting on something, is worth over $1,785 today.)

"Tomorrow night I have to go to practice again for the show. We're giving another performance next Thursday and Friday nights in the surrounding towns.

"Well now, I've written to all of my family this week and I know you all think I should write more, but with summertime it's hard to sit down long enough. All my love, Elwood."

7 May 1944: Handwritten V-mail from England. "I thought I was going to have a cup of tea before I wrote this, but the place doesn't open till 1000, and I still have a few minutes before it opens. (**NOTE:** Dad penned this V-mail in the main square of Sturminster Newton at Pop Cluettes, which was a tea shop, torn down in 1963. There is a picture at the end of this chapter). Dad talks again about the pony: "I figured the pony would cost around a hundred dollars, between seventy-five and a hundred. I've seen quite a few ponies around here. They're real cheap over here. The cost doesn't matter, as long as the kids enjoy it and they're careful." He still has his cold and says: "I wish I could completely get rid of my cold. I think I've got to quit something, maybe it's cigarettes. I only smoke a pack a day, that's all I ever smoke." (**NOTE:** I sure wish Dad had quit smoking right there and then. When he died in 1971, he was smoking three packs a day).

7 May 1944: Handwritten letter from Mr. Mumford to Eunice written on 'The Animal Infirmary and Dispensary,' Sturminster Newton, Dorset letterhead. "I am afraid I am rather late answering your kind letter, but the real reason for the delay is we intended taking some snaps of us all, including Ellwood in our garden, but unfortunately, we could not get film. However, I have now got one, but as Ellwood has gone away for a few days on what he calls a problem, I shall wait to take the snaps until he returns but decided to drop you a line in the meantime. All my family are taking a day off tomorrow and we are going up to Bath in Somerset to a big dog show. Ellwood was coming with us, but this problem came along, and we shall have to go without him. He was very disappointed, but it couldn't be helped. He loves dogs and it would have been a great joy to him to have seen it.

'The yanks gave a concert here a few days ago and I believe it was a great affair. Ellwood took part in it, but he was disguised so well my kiddies could not pick him out, neither did they recognize his voice. I was not able to see it but the whole thing went down well. It would be very nice to think that Ellwood would be here for the duration, but I suppose one day he will be moved, and we shall miss him very much.

"I hope you received your silver bangles (a rigid bracelet) he sent you. He was very proud to bring them home for us to see and it gave him a lot of pleasure in the making of them. Keep smiling, it's a long road that has no turning and we can all see the bend in the distance. Very sincerely yours, Winfred Mumford."

(**NOTE:** This letter gives us a lot of insight into Dad, i.e. he loves dogs and performed in front of crowds on many occasions when he was in the Army. Dad told them he was going on a "problem" and that is what the Army now calls "exercise". The 4th Infantry Division did conduct exercises in late April called "Exercise Tiger" using live ammo. Earlier exercises were also conducted in December 1943 in the South Hams area of Devon, England, 77 miles from Stur. Note how Mr. Mumford spells Dad's name "Ellwood")

9 May 1944: Cursive handwritten letter from England, his first air mail letter. (**NOTE:** The air mail cost for a stamp was six cents.) "Am glad to hear the kids like the pony and I can hardly wait to see a picture of it. That was more than I expected it would be but then, I don't know the prices on many things back home. I'm sorry there was a dispute on everybody's minds about it, but in my mind there isn't. I've made up my mind to buy them one, so I'm going to do it. Lois said she didn't think I ought to spend so much money, that I should have it for when I get home.

"In fact, they all said or implied that. It seems she doesn't want to draw the money out, so I'll send you so much every month. How's that? I'll wait till I get an answer to these letters today before I send any because she may change her mind. It all depends. I'd like to pay for it all, but if Johnny thinks he wants to go in halves with me, it's okay. At least that's what you said in your letter, that I could give as much as I wanted. I hope everything turns out okay.

"I'd like to have seen the boy's faces when they got it. I bet they were surprised, or did you tell them before? Tell them they must be careful with it and take good care of their saddle, harness, etc. Johnny Sr. will probably see to that. Tell them to keep him in good shape so they can take me for a ride when I get home." (**NOTE:** We have pictures of Dad in a wagon with the pony showing he lived up to this wish.)

"Today so far, I've written three long letters, had a haircut, shaved, cleaned one of our officer's teeth, treated two men for trench mouth, and cleaned up my office." (**NOTE:** Trench mouth is a severe gum infection caused by a buildup of bacteria in the mouth. It's characterized by painful, bleeding gums and ulcers in the gums.) "I washed my field jacket and leggings also. It's now chow time and after supper, I'm going to take a shower and swash my hair.

"Hazel and I are getting along quite well, but nothing is serious. Whatever I tell her to do, she does. She does all my mending and all that sort of stuff. She even gives me money for beer if I'm broke and then I'll go out and leave her all alone for a couple of hours. Not a bad woman – eh? I don't ask her to do that, though. She is very nice. Hope you liked your bracelet, okay? All my love, Elwood."

14 May 1944: Handwritten V-mail from England: "Today is your day of honor being Mother's Day. I hope you had a nice time and the old man no doubt cooked dinner for you today and did the dishes, or did he? I suppose you went to church today. I didn't go, but I heard parts of a service as I was writing to Ezzy early this afternoon. They held an open-air service right near here. I've written to everyone except Margie today and I'm going to write to her when I get back from a bike ride with Hazel. I would have had it written if I didn't fall off to sleep this afternoon.

"I'm glad you've taken pictures of the pony and the kids already. I'll be anxiously waiting to see it. I also hope everything is straightened out by now about it. I had a picture taken with Captain Kantrowitz Friday afternoon. I'll send it home as soon as I get it. Also, Mrs. Mumford took some pictures of her kids and me Saturday. I'll send one of them home too. (**NOTE:** Brad and I made a picture in the exact spot this picture was taken on Church Street, Sturminster Newton.) Dad ends with: "The sun is going under a cloud and I'm going now for a ride. All my love, Elwood."

15 May 1944: 4th ID Command Post was in South Brent, England. South Brent is a large village on the southern edge of Dartmoor, England, in the valley of the river Avon. (92 miles southwest of Sturminster Newton)

17 May 1944: Handwritten note on stationary from England: Dad talks about going to a show with Hazel's brother Jim. He sent some "snaps" to Pappy of Mrs. Mumford's children and Dad. Dad's cold continues and he has taken a lot of different medicines, to no avail. He ends with: "Hazel and her mother went to a play and I'm waiting for them to come back to get me something to eat. We're just good friends, nothing serious. Hope you'll excuse the paper; it's the best I could find. Good night and all my love, Elwood."

25 May 1944: Handwritten V-mail from England: "I received both your V-mail and the air mail with the pictures of the pony. It's a real pretty pony. Does he have any spots on his body or is he all white except his head? It looks all white except his head. John looked very happy on his back. I'm glad that they're taking such good care of it. Pappy looked swell all decked out. Your house looks very nice. I'm afraid I won't know your place when I get home, you've redecorated so much. In all, the pictures are excellent.

"I told Hazel you were going to answer her letters as soon as you had time and I told Michael and Mary hello for John and David. Mrs. Mumford thought that would be very nice of you to mention that. (**NOTE:** Michael and Mary Mumford were the Mumford kids. During my visits to Sturminster over the years, we visited Mary. To be frank, I didn't know or was not able to appreciate all they did for Dad. During one visit, Mary gave me 300 pounds to give to Mom). He ends with: "I'm glad that you like the bracelet I made, and I hope you can get it completed alright. Give my best to your old man and the kids. Lots of love, Elwood."

29 May 1944: Handwritten note from England: "Lois said that Pappy would endorse my allotment checks to you in payment of the pony. I'm glad that's all off my mind. I made up my mind and I wanted to do it.

"I'd like to have heard Bonnie over the radio, but "USAY" couldn't broadcast to England. I'll tell her you heard her. I'm sending some negative of the pictures I sent to Pappy to Lois and if you want a set, tell Lois and she'll have some made for you, okay? Hazel is keeping one negative to have a few made for she and her mother. I'll send it later.

"Yesterday, the Hatcher's and I went on a picnic, and we went swimming, the first time for me this year! We sunbathed and had a real peaceful day of it. I helped Mrs. Hatcher do my laundry before we went. I have another brush cut for the summer and it's rather short. but comfortable. Is John going to get one this year? Mrs. Mumford says I look like Gandhi. Hazel still lets me come to see her, so it can't be that bad. It's 9 p.m. and time for tea. Hazel wants to go for a walk, and I still have to write Margie. Good night and all my love, Elwood."

5 June 1944: Handwritten V-mail from England: "So far, I haven't received your jam, but I'm hoping it comes soon. I got a jar of peanut butter from Ezzy and some nice candy and peanuts yesterday. Lois is sending me some more popcorn and candies. Bonnie is supposed to be sending me a camera. I'm not doing bad, eh? I'm glad you helped fix up Mother's grave also. I was wondering about it. Last night Mr. Mumford, Michael, Mary, and I went to a gymkhana (**NOTE:** competitive games on horseback), horse racing and jumping. I didn't have much money, so I didn't do any betting. This morning, I had breakfast in bed, fried egg on toast and tea. I had my dinner at Mrs. Mumford's too. I had some strawberries from their garden this morning. They were really good. It is time for tea now. Bye – All my love, Elwood." (**NOTE:** I always heard Mrs. Mumford treated our dad great and here was just one example! Breakfast in bed!!!)

(**NOTE:** Command post (CP) locations are now in France. My friend, Mark Moe, and I visited over 50 CP locations in France and Belgium during our March 2025 trip. We visited CP locations in Normandy, even though my dad was not yet deployed, to remember and honor those who served.)

6 June 1944: There were three different 4th ID Command Posts (CPS) on D-Day. First CP was on Utah Beach of Normandy in the Manche region of France. The second CP was on Road U5, Manche region of France, and the third CP was in the town of Audouville-la-Hubert, in Manche region of France.

8 June 1944: 4th ID Command Post was in Beuzeville-au-Plain, Manche region of France

9 Jun 1944: Handwritten V-mail from England: "Yesterday I received the jam you sent and already one jar is gone. It seems good to taste your homemade strawberry jam again. I took it over to the Hatchers because I'm there every night for supper (9 p.m.). They all like it very much and they said that when I come back to visit them after the war, they'll have the jars filled with whiskey for me. Ha. Ha. The Hatchers have said several times that they're going to Rochester after the war to have a cup of tea with Pappy Turner. I hope they can. You'll like them.

"I suppose you too have been sitting next to the radio lately as I have. The news is wonderful, I think, and I hope it continues being good. (**NOTE:** This was written 3 days after the Normandy Invasion.) Dad says: "I don't believe it'll be too long now, so don't worry about me. Thank you for sending me the jam. I'm really enjoying it. All my love, Elwood."

10 June 1944: 4th ID Command Post was in Le Bissson, Manche region of France.

14 June 1944: 377th Anti-aircraft Artillery (AAA) is assigned to the 4th ID. (Reference: Shelby Stanton's US Army Order of Battle WWII.) (**NOTE:** The 377th would remain assigned to the 4th until 23 March 1945 and then reassigned to the 4th from 6 April – 9 May 1945.)

15 June 1944: Typed V-mail from England to Eunice and John and boys: Dad had received mail from home and says: "I suppose by now you have heard from me, and you'll probably get two or three together. I imagine it gave you cause to worry a little at first because I'd worry if I hadn't heard from you in a long time. I told Mrs. Mumford that you received her letter okay. She's been writing Margie this week and sending some pictures of their house so you can see where I stayed. I've had some strawberries out of Mrs. Mumford's Garden last week. I finished the jam you sent. It was awful good. Thanks again.

"You have quite a collection now with the pony, lamb, cats and dogs. I figured it out and it will take six months and a half, I believe, to finish paying for the pony. I think I'll be in the army that long, if not longer, darn it. According to the news every day, things don't look too bad." Bonnie had moved to Palm Beach Florida and was not happy there. Dad ends with: "Cheerio with all my love, Elwood."

20 June 1944: 4th ID Command Post was in two locations: First in Bois de Montebourg, Manche region of France and second at La Tardiverie, Manche, France.

20 June 1944: Typed V-mail from England addressed to: "Dear soles" "I

slept at Hazel's last night and this morning I had bacon, eggs, and potatoes for breakfast. We don't have any dental appointments this morning
or any his afternoon, but I do have to work around the aid station. Yesterday, I was on charge of quarters. Being Sunday, Hazel was home, and
I managed to get a few hours off to go for a bicycle ride in the afternoon
with her. (**NOTE:** The aid station was right there on Church Street). I
had dinner at her house yesterday also. I'll have to start paying them rent
pretty soon. Last Saturday I went up to Mumford's for tea and I went
out with Mr. Mumford on a call. He had to look at a sick cow. I've gone
out with him several times since I've been here. He let me drive his car
one time. Their cars over here are a little bit bigger than a baby Austin,
but there are a few people who have American made cars.

"According to the papers this morning, allies are doing wonderfully
on all fronts. I wonder how long it'll take for the Germans to find out
they're licked? I hope they discover it soon.

"I just went over to Pop Cluettes for tea and cake. It's very convenient." (**NOTE:** Boy was Pop Cluettes "convenient". It was a two-min-
ute walk from Hazel's. Pop Cluettes was torn down in 1963; however,
the building it was attached to is now the town museum). "Well, I've
managed to fill the page alright. I hope you are all well and happy. All
my love, Elwood."

23 June 1944: Typed V-E letter from England addressed again to "Dear
soles" "I don't know whether my last letter got photographed because I
made carbon copies or not, so I'll try it again. I still haven't heard from
you so that's why I'm writing the same to everyone. I hope we get some
mail tonight. Last Tuesday afternoon I went out with the Hatcher family and helped them rake hay and helped stack it up. We worked from
three thirty until ten thirty and by the time we were finished, I was ready
to fold up. I got about ten blisters on my hands and two sore feet, so you
can see I'm not used to hard work.

"It did me a lot of good though, because I gained seven pounds since then. My weight has been dropping and gaining every now and then. I weigh 166 lbs. to date. I had my shirt off all afternoon, and I had a better tan. I had to soak my feet before I went to bed and the next morning, they were as good as before.

"Last night Hazel, her brother (Jim) and I went to the movies and saw "*Hit Parade of 1943*." It wasn't a bad picture and the only reason I went was because it was an American film. The British films are stinko. I wouldn't go across the street to see one."

He listened to Bob Hope on the radio. He closes with: "I surely hope I get a few letters from home today so I can have something to write about. I hope you are all alright and that you've received all my mail. Be good and I'll write again soon. All my love, Elwood."

24 June 1944: 4th ID Command Post was in Bois du Coudray, Marche, France.

27 June 1944: Typed V-mail from England Tuesday. (DAD'S LAST V-mail from England before he went to France, the very next day): (**NOTE:** This was Mom and Dad's last day together for over a year, but they had some good times over the past four days and nights.) "Here I am again trying the same old stunt of carbon copies. I sure hope you can manage to read them alright. Two weeks have gone by and still not any mail from home. They just went after the mail, but no doubt there probably won't be any again. The weather today is cloudy and damp, but the rain came too late, according to the farmers around here. All their crops are very poor, and their fields are brown instead of green. I helped Jim Hatcher rake and draw some more hay yesterday, but this time I didn't work as hard. He only had two acres this time. (**NOTE:** In 1972 and 1975, I helped Grandfi rake hay, and it was very hard work.) "Last Saturday night (which was a 24 June 1944) Hazel and I went to the show and saw "Shanty Town" and a cowboy picture. They weren't bad. Last Friday night we went to the dance after I managed to have a few beers and today when I went to chow, by the way we had chicken, some fellow at the same table complimented me on my dancing.

"Well, I told him it was probably my double because I couldn't dance very well, but he went on to describe Hazel, so it must have been me. What took me by surprise was when he told me he used to be a professional dancer in Arizona. He seemed sincere, too. If I wasn't broke, I could have at least pitched him a six-penny or a shilling but as it was, I exchanged the compliment because funny enough I had noticed how well he could dance." Dad had listened to Jack Benny and Guy Lombardo on the radio. He ends: "That's all that's new for the time being. Be good and take care of yourselves. All my love, Elwood." (**NOTE:** Dad was very good about keeping it secret they were about to deploy. I'm sure he could tell he was going sometime soon, but he did not suspect the next day or two.)

From left: Dad and Capt. Kantrowitz at 25 Church Street Sturminster Newton (May 1944), Dad at Pop Cluettes Tea Shop with the Cluettes Sturminster Newton, Dad with Mrs. Mumford and Mary Mumford England

Elwood and John Jr. and David Elwood with Prince

From left: Grandma Grandfi Uncle Jim on Church Street Sturminster Newton, Hazel 1944 or 1945

From left: Grandma and Grandfi Hatcher at the garden on Church Street,
Rick with Grandfi and Grandma Hatcher (1976)

From left: St. Mary's Church in Sturminster Newton — Mom and Dad's wedding
(1 September 1945), Rick and son Brad at 25 Church Street
Sturminster Newton (July 2001)

From left: St. Mary's Church where Elwood and Hazel were married (1945), Sturminster Newton Town Square

Chapter 3: France, Belgium, Luxembourg, Germany

28 June 1944 – 19 August 1945
Discharge date – 7 October 1945

28 June 1944: 4th ID Command Post was in Chateau de Tourlaville, Manche, France.

30 June 1944: 4th ID Command Post was in Gourbesville, at a rest area, Manche, France.

2 July 1944: Dad's first V-mail from "Somewhere in France". (**NOTE:** It was typed so his unit must have deployed with all their gear.) "Dear Peoples, I'm somewhere in France now and a wee bit tired. My first night here I had to dig in, and by the looks of things, I'll be digging most of the time I'm here. It was raining when I dug in so, consequently, I had to sleep with wet clothes on. It wasn't any fun, but you can't be choosy over here. I managed to get to sleep about two p.m. and glad to get up at six thirty for breakfast.

"Today I had to set up my dental equipment and helped pitch a tent. After that I managed to shave and take a sponge bath and change clothes. It was the first time I had my clothes and shoes off for four days and nights after living with the Mumford's and Hazel for (**NOTE:** The next two words were censored and I believe it reflected how long they were in England), sleeping in feather beds. I don't mind telling you it's hard to get used to.

"Once I'm used to sleeping on the ground, it'll be better. My mail was held up three weeks and it was all waiting for me when I arrived here. I had twenty-three letters, a newspaper, and a few church bulletins. I'm glad that you're all ok back home. I've just copied the letter I wrote to Pappy in ink, and I've written to Esda in ink, but I got tired of repeating myself, so I got the typewriter out. I don't know how much time I'll have to write letters, but I will try to write as often as I can.

"I wish all of you would write to Hazel and her mother also Mrs. Mumford and thank them for what they have done for me while I was in Sturminster Newton. Pappy has Hazel's address. When I left there, it was like leaving home. They had been so wonderful to me. If you can send them a package of Fanny Farmers or anything you think they would like, please do…." All my love, Elwood." (**NOTE:** This is the first time since September 1943 that Dad mentions in the clear the name of the town, Sturminster Newton, he was in most of his time in England).

5 July 1944: 4th ID Command Post was in an assembly area near Groult, Manche, France.

5 July 1944: Dad's second V-mail from France. "It's early morning and a slight bit chilly for July. It rains so much here, I guess that's the reason. While the sun it out, it isn't bad. The night before last, I slept very good, but last night was something like the first night here. If I have a chance this afternoon, I'm going to take a nap." Dad had written the previous letter and said "everything is about the same. I left a big box of my old letters at Hazel's house and everything that I couldn't take with me. After the war, she's going to send them to me. I guess I'll have to burn all my old letters now. I miss that gal a helluva lot. She's young, but she's got good common sense. Boyce and I took some pictures of her when he was here, but so far, I haven't heard from Boyce since February, and he has the pictures. I don't know what's the matter with him for not writing."

He says the French countryside is "similar in landscape to any other country. I have noticed some poppies growing in the wheat fields while riding along. So far, I haven't talked to any French people and, if I did, I'd have a job understanding them. I'm anxious to talk to one of them to see how much French I do know. We were issued some pamphlets about the French people with several common French sayings for us to learn. I know most of the grammar, but I've forgotten a lot of the words for food, clothing, etc. I imagine I'll learn a lot more by talking with a few Frenchmen.

"Most of the people have evacuated these areas while the fighting is going on and they come back after the war is over. I thought the English people had it bad, but the French have it worse than any. Their fields are all dug up and their houses blown to bits. I'm awful glad America is far-away."

Dad mentions a farmhouse nearby with a lot of cider. He said it tastes pretty good, and he mentions Cognac which he had not tried. "When we left England, our money was changed from pounds to Francs. A franc is equal to two cents. I have about six hundred and fifty francs now, but no place to spend it. I'll try to send some home if I can accumulate a little more. All the money is in paper form and backed by the U.S. It started raining again, per usual, but now I have my tent up. I have a lot of dirty clothes to wash out soon. These I have on could stand up on their own. They're beginning to stink worse than the German graveyard I went by yesterday." He had been busy helping Captain Kantrowitz pull teeth. "Some fellows don't take very good care of their teeth and as a result they get trench mouth. I get my mail every day now, if I have any to get. I usually get one or two a day. Be good and I'll try to write in a couple days. All my love, Elwood."

6 July 1944: 4th ID Command Post was in Cantepie, Manche, France

NEW 7 July 1944: Letter from Mrs. Mumford to Eunice, from Sturminster Newton, England: (NOTE: This gives some very good insight into the exact day Dad left England and how the town supported the troops as they left. This is the first letter Mrs. Mumford sent to Eunice trying to allay their concerns about Dad.) "Dear Mrs. De Roos, your letter arrived this morning, so I am answering right away as you seem rather worried about Elwood. However, you have probably had quite a batch of letters from him by the time you get this. Elwood went away on June 28th over to France. He was in the last lot to leave here. Most of them went over three weeks before that, but a few stayed behind and Elwood was one of them. (NOTE: Critical information. Most of the 377th went over a few days after D-day. Dad being in the medical detachment doing dental work, was probably not a high priority on a Time Phased Force Deployment List).

"However, he was moved from our house and all the boys were put together in one big house so that they were all ready when the order came to go. He used to come up most days with his friend for a cup of tea or a ride in the car with my husband, because during these three weeks, they had no work to do, so I really saw just as much of him except that he did not sleep here. Since the first lot of boys went over, there was a hold up with their letters, which of course could not be avoided, and Elwood had not had any post from home since then. He said he expected it was all waiting for him in France as he thought it would all get sent there.

"None of the boys had any so it was a pretty sure guess it had all gone over there. I know Elwood wrote to you all during this time, but I expect it was held up on this end and no doubt by now you have got it. If you have not, don't worry in the least as it will be on the way, no doubt.

"As you know, a mighty army was sent over and it must be a tremendous task to sort out millions of letters, plus the organizing of the invasion. When the first boys went, Elwood was called (2 o'clock in the morning) by mistake. The officers went around to knock them up. However, there was such a voice going on outside, Elwood and I decided we would go and see what was going on. He wished a lot of his pals goodbye and they called out to him, 'We'll see you in France next week.' It was all very exciting. Everyone seemed to be out giving them all a good send off. Women and girls were out crying bitterly. In fact, some of the girls have not stopped crying yet.

"This particular morning there was a glorious sunrise, all the earth was just a bright red glow and the fields and trees on the horizon were like heaven itself. Elwood said he had never seen anything like it before. It seemed as though it had come just to give the boys a wonderful send off. This time of the year our nights are almost as light as day. It does not get real dark at all. In fact, when the boys went at 2'oclock, it was almost as light as mid-day.

"Elwood and I had a cup of tea and something to eat, then went off to bed. The next day he had to sleep with the other boys in the town. (**NOTE:** They probably stayed in The Swan Inn, right off Sturminster Newton's main town square where the cross is. The Swan was being used as a mess hall during their entire stay there.)

"Believe me, he hated the thought of leaving us all when his turn came, but as he said, it is a step nearer home and there is no place like it. He came up the night before he went with his friend, and we all had a lot of fun together. In fact, it was almost a party as I had visitors in at the time. We miss him very much, but I expect we shall see him again before long because when they have leave, they are coming here to spend it. They can get over here in 24 hours. (**NOTE:** Dad would not be able to come back until a few days before he married Mom on 1 September 1945).

"I have a letter from one of the boys that went first, it arrived today, and he says he will be coming to see me in two months. When he wrote the letter, he was expecting Elwood over anytime. That was the day he left. I am expecting a letter from Elwood any day now, as I see in today's papers that letter from now onwards should take only two days to France. They are now getting things in good order.

"Believe me, he was quite looking forward to going over. To him, it was a great adventure. What a lot he will have to tell when he comes on leave and what a lot more when he gets home to you. Believe me, it won't be long now. We have had no Doodle Bugs over here. London is the target for them, but we shall soon master them. (**NOTE:** Doodle Bugs were the German V1 Flying Bomb with wings that were mostly targeted for London.) I've no doubt.

"My kiddies send their love to yours. Here's best wishes to you all. Yours sincerely, W. Mumford."

8 July 1944: 4th ID Command Post was in Meautis, Manche, France

9 July 1944: Handwritten V-mail from somewhere in France. The 4th ID situation report mentions the 377th AAA Unit near Appeville, France this day. "I've just been talking to a French woman and managed to buy some cognac and hard cider from her. Boy, these French really go in for their hard cider. Their cognac is the most powerful drink I've ever had. Four men can get stinko on a quart."

Dad had gotten letters from many. Then he talks about the pony again: "If you want to go halves with me on the pony, I don't care. It doesn't matter to me either way. Everybody got me confused on the deal. Do as you wish."

Dad ends with: "Well, I've written six letters today and they are all different. Not bad, eh? I'm going to have a few more swigs of cognac and maybe I'll sleep better tonight. All my love, Elwood."

14 July 1944: Handwritten V-mail from somewhere in France: (**NOTE:** This letter is ripped and missing a lot of words, but is a very revealing letter). Dad opens by talking about all the mail he received and how he is trying to respond to them all, but if he did, he would be "writing all the time." He had heard from Bonnie and she's getting along fine.

"Hazel writes about every day, so far. I left my watch with her to get fixed and told her she can wear it until I write for it. She's got two big boxes of my old letters and stuff that she's going to send them home for me after the war. I'd like to see her again before I go back to the States.

"According to your letter, you and the old man are keeping busy on the farm and little John and that he and David have a lot of work taking care of the pony and lamb. I'm pleased to hear that you did so well in school, John Donald.

"It's almost time for mail call again and I hope to get a lot again. Don't work too hard and have John make me a barrel of hard cider for when I get home. All my love, Elwood."

17 July 1944: 4th ID Command Post was in a rest area at Lenauderie, Manche, France.

20 July 1944: 4th ID Command Post was in Charlemenerie, Manche, France.

20 July 1944: Handwritten V-mail from somewhere in France: "I received a package from Margie with three jars of wonderful peanut butter and a newspaper. I didn't sleep too well last night, so consequently, I'm rather tired today and after I write to Marjorie, I'm going to try to take a nap. This morning, we filled a couple teeth for some fellows.

"Hazel's father isn't a farmer by trade, but has a few acres of land, some heifers, and a horse. He works his land nights and Sundays. I helped him draw hay for the exercise which I needed very badly. Au revoir (Bye) for now. With all my love, Elwood." (NOTE: As we found out when we visited England in 1963, Grandfi worked at a farm supply house where trucks would take fertilizer and feed to surrounding farms. Grandfi also helped widows manage their gardens. He was a very hard-working man.)

26 July 1944: 4th ID Command Post was in LaCouture, Manche, France

27 July 1944: 4th ID Command Post was in Bas Marais, Manche, France

29 July 1944: 4th ID Command Post was in Le Bourg, Manche, France

30 July 1944: 4th ID Command Post was in La Chasse-Doriere, Manche, France

30 July 1944: Handwritten V-mail from France: "I received your airmail and V-mail of the 13th about four days ago and this is the first chance I've had to do much writing. (**NOTE:** This would indicate mail was getting from the U.S. to a war zone in 13 days, which was not bad. Also, it was very unusual for Dad to not write in ten days, so his unit was definitely on the move, as you can see from the multiple 4th ID Command Posts, above.)

"I wish I had some of those ox-heart cherries you were talking about." (**NOTE:** Oxheart cherries are a variety of cherries that are large in size and have a distinctive heart shape.) "They have plenty of apples over here, but it'll be another month before they're ripe enough to eat. I hope I'm headed for home by that time." (**NOTE:** Dad would not go home for another 14 months, so he was optimistic.") Of his nephews: "They'll be grown up so much when I get home. I probably won't know them. I'll get my movies out and show them when I get home and we'll compare the difference, eh? Give my regards to your old man. Be good. All my love, Elwood."

2 August 1944: 4th ID Command Post was in La Landerie, Manche, France

3 August 1944: 4th ID Command Post was in La Beltiere, Manche, France

4 August 1944: Handwritten V-mail from France: "So far, I haven't seen too many graves. There are a few scattered here and there and sometimes they use a high field for a graveyard. I'm not very crazy about looking at dead men or graves, so I doubt if I'll find Raymond's. His grave is probably close to the shoreline somewhere." (**NOTE:** Raymond was most likely a friend or someone from a church who was killed in or around Normandy). "I've seen quite a few over here. What makes me mad is that back in the States those bastards are safe and even our own people give them parties and girls dance with them. Here we shoot them, and they don't get much sympathy. These people over there ought to have their damn heads examined. Mail call is pretty soon, also chow. I still have to write to Marjorie, and then I'll take a break. All my love, Elwood."

5 August 1944: 4th ID CP was in Les Loges-sur-Brecey, Manche, France

8 August 1944: Handwritten letter from France mailed from APO #230. (**NOTE:** On the outskirts of Paris. "Here I sit in the shade of an old apple tree and believe you me, France is full of apple trees. Last night another fellow and I were over to some French woman's house drinking cider and I managed to carry on a pretty fluent conversation with her and her little daughter. Every time I asked for some cognac, they give me the same reply, 'Les baches boire tout le cognac et pris tout les pommes.' (**NOTE:** Translated: The Germans drink all the cognac and take all the apples.) "It seems as if the Germans took most of the apples every year, thus no cognac and very little cider. I haven't had any champagne yet, but when we get in the middle of France, I imagine there should be a little. That's where they make it. I slept pretty good last night and usually do when I've had anything to drink.

"This morning. we had bacon and eggs for breakfast and oatmeal cereal with coffee, of course. I haven't had any tea since I left England. All we get is coffee. The French people only get five grams of bread per person a day and you should see it. It's black bread and it smells like the cow feed you used to give your cow, Pappy. At least the English get plenty good bread, but it isn't white. When we came over here, we got white bread and the first piece of it we had looked and tasted like angel food cake, so I can imagine what the French people think when they get some bread given to them from the kitchen.

"They bring huge bouquets of flowers to us and beg bread for them. They come to us for first aid and yesterday I fixed a guy's finger up that he nearly cut off with a mowing machine. I got my laundry done one time for bandaging up some mademoiselle's leg and one other time we got some cognac for fixing some gal's leg.

"The news this morning sounded very good, and it looks like we'll be in Paris before long. By the time you get this, the Russians will be taking some village in East Prussia. On all our fronts the news looks good.

"Hazel wrote yesterday and said she received your letter, Esda, and she thinks the pictures are wonderful of you and Pappy. She said she showed it to everybody so she must be quite excited that you sent the pictures to her. She's afraid I won't come back to England to see her before I go home. It doesn't take very long for your letters to reach England now for some reason.

"Two little girls and their grandmother just came up with a pretty bouquet of flowers. We've been bandaging up her hand, the smallest girl, every day and she came back for a new dressing. When Capt. Kantrowitz finished, the little girl gave us all a kiss on the cheek.

"So far as I know, I haven't had my picture taken by any photographer, Esda, so I don't think you'll find me in the movies. Ha. Ha. Everybody has asked me in their letters if I'm at the front or near the front. Well, sometimes we're near the front but as a rule, we follow up. One of our medics broke his arm and Larry, the follow from Rochester, has been evacuated and it looks very much like I'm going to be an aid man. I'm not so keen on that but not much I can do about it.

"Well, it's chow time now and I must say Au Revoir for now. I'll write again in a few days after payday. I'll send you each a sample of the money we use over here. That is if I have any left after I pay back what I owe. All my love, Elwood."

9 August 1944: 4th ID CP was in HT Travigny, Manche, France

10 August 1944: Typed V-mail letter from France. "I've just had dinner, and we had pork chops, mashed potatoes with gravy, spinach, bread with strawberry jam, coffee, and pineapple. I didn't get up for breakfast and it's the first time this week I missed breakfast." Dad details a USO show he saw last week hosted by a Don Rice. (**NOTE:** Don Rice was an actor known for Lady Luck, the Dean Martin Show, and Perry Como's Kraft Music Hall.)

"The show lasted 90 minutes and included dancers and singers. We had to sit on a hill, which turned out to be good. It sure was good to see American women once in a while, even though I didn't get to talk with them. It lasted for an hour and a half.

"Two days ago, I received a letter from each of my sisters and THREE from Hazel. The Army Post Office people say our outfit gets more mail than any other our size. I don't believe I can trace that bracelet, Marjorie, and am terribly sorry about it. Maybe it'll get to you yet. It hasn't come back to me yet. I sent it first class mail.

"Well, I've come to the end of another page, and it looks like rain. Give my regards to all my brothers-in-laws and of course my two nephews. Be good Au revoir, with all my love, Elwood."

10 August 1944: 4th ID CP was in Buais, Manche, France

11 August 1944: 4th ID CP was in Le Teilleul, Manche France

12 August 1944: 4th ID CP was in Nantrail, Mayenne, France

14 August 1944: Typed V-mail from France: "Good morning, every-body! I don't know what's gone over me, but I've gotten up for breakfast for almost two weeks in a row. We usually get pancakes and they're really good. I'm hungry all the time. Hazel is sending me a package, but I don't know what's in it. While I think of it, I would like someone to send me a jackknife. I lost mine about a month ago and it's a very handy instru-ment. Also, I'd like some Fanny Farmers.

"Yesterday, I cleaned teeth for a few of the fellows and today I have a waiting list. This morning Capt. Kantrowitz pulled a tooth for a young Frenchman. I don't polish their teeth but just scrape off the callous. I manage to keep my teeth cleaned up pretty good. I clean them at least once a day.

"Yesterday after noon, I went swimming for the first time. We went in, in our shorts. The water was fine. It was some place where they breed fish and only fish in April.

"Last night, I went to church out here in the field. Our outfit doesn't have a Chaplain, but the Division Chaplin comes around a lot. We have rather nice services. They're not very long, but we sing, and the chap-lain gives a short sermon. This typewriter is broken, and my lines keep changing, as you've probably already noticed.

"I'd like to buy some small souvenir to send home, but by the time I get near a city, most everything is blown to hell. All towns and cities are off limits to us, and we don't get any passes, so whether I want to or not, it's an impossibility. A lot of the fellows have Germany souvenirs and have sent them home. I haven't got ahold of any yet, It's the infantry boys that get most of them.

"I had a French lady do my laundry yesterday and I should get it back today. She's going to iron them for me too! That's a job I hate, so every time I can, I get some lady to do them for me.

"I've got to write Earl and Hazel today yet and it'll have to be before chow because I have to clean teeth this afternoon. Take good care of yourselves and I'll be seeing you soon. I'm going to vote sometime soon because we have to have it in before September. Who do you think will win, Pappy? I've got a bet on Dewey with five to one odds. Dewey better win. All my love, Au Revoir, Elwood." (**NOTE:** As we all know, Roosevelt beat Republican Dewey by a lot. Dad lost his bet. Not a good one.)

16 August 1944: Typed V-mail letter from France: Dad had been receiving and answering a lot of mail! "I wrote one of these carbon jobs day before yesterday and again here I sit with my pocket full of unanswered mail. Today I received seven letters, one from Hazel, one from Mrs. Mumford, one from Ann, and the rest from home. Yesterday I received three from home and one from Hazel. Yesterday I wrote eight letters home and after I finish this, I have about a dozen more to write.

"I just had a shot of Black and White Scotch that Captain Kantrowitz gave me and I have a pint of cognac in my tent that a Frenchman gave me for pulling two teeth this morning. Yesterday we pulled some teeth for some French boy and girl and the boy's father gave Capt. Kantrowitz and I some saboutes (wooden shoes) that he made. (**NOTE:** When I was a child, we had those same shoes in our house. We always thought a Dutchman gave Dad those wooden shoes. Now I find out, the shoes were from a Frenchman.)

"Also, today I managed to get ahold of another pair of wooden shoes but they're not as fancy as the ones the Frenchman gave me. I'm sending them home to you, Pappy, and I'd like you to keep them for me. The fancy pair and you can have the other pair. Monsieur Paris wrote in the shoes, '(four or five of the first words were censored) given by Mr. Paris.' in case you don't understand what it means. I've got to find some box to send them in first. I'm trying to get some perfume to send to my sisters but so far, no got! Have patience.

"Pappy, I received your letter today and am glad that you're getting along so well. Hazel wrote and said she likes your picture very much. She sent me a package of candy bars, her ration for a month or more. Her mother wrote and said she would like to have a cup of tea with Pappy Turner in the corner sometime.

"Esda, thank you for the wonderful fudge and cookies. If you could see how fast it went, you'd appreciate it. I'll save the jam until sometime when we don't get any for chow. Happy birthday Doug, even though I am late in congratulating you. I'll have a drink tonight in your honor. (**NOTE:** Dad was still in a large compound of some type getting good food. He was in Nantrail, France which wasn't a large place, but bigger than most 4th ID locations.)

"In your letter, Lois, it sounds as if you have a night club in your house. So far, I haven't received your pictures you were going to send or did send. How is Jack? Has his business increased any? Will you send me a consolidated report on my finances? I just like to keep in mind how much I have or haven't. Thank you.

"Eunice, Hazel sent me your letter that you wrote to her today and she wants me to return it and thought I'd like to read it. It was a very nice letter, and she feels very proud to hear from you people back home. Boy you sure have a lot of crops this year. My brother-in-law is a rich bitch, eh?

"Happy birthday, Pet Sis! By the time you get this your birthday will be over. Hope you had a good time. I received the pictures of you and Pappy today, boy they're good of you both. I don't think you are fat. All the boys think you are a good dish and asked if you were married. Tell Worry Wart to be careful when he picks up the stiffs, they pull apart if they've been dead very long. It's been three days since I wrote this letter on the 16th and today's date is the 18th. (Marjorie's birthday)"

17 August 1944: 4th ID CP was in Rouairie, Orne, France

18-22 August 1944: The 377th AAA was with the 22nd Infantry Regiment on the outskirts of Paris. The 4th ID passed from the VII Corps to the V Corps, and they were prepared to move south of Paris. (Source: Dr. Boice's History of WWII)

22 August 1944: NOTE: The 4th ID Situation Report shows Dad's unit, 377th AAA: "The division was alerted and prepared for movement east to Chartres. The 4th Division Artillery and 377th Antiaircraft Artillery moved at 1350 to the vicinity of Chateauneuf en Thymerais and were alerted to rejoin the Division on its route to Chartres.

24 August 1944: 4th ID CP was located in two places. First in Ablis, Seine-et-Oise, France and second was in Bruyere near Arpajon, Seine-et-Oise, France

24 August 1944: Typed very dark V-mail from France. He hadn't been able to write in several days. (**NOTE:** Again, since he had not written in over a week, his unit was moving rapidly through France, as evidenced by SITREP data.) "I'm having a hell of a time typing this letter in my pup tent. It has been raining all morning long and I bet it won't quit. I got wet last night visiting a Frenchman for a drink. We heard last night that Paris was to be liberated, and Rumania had discussed peace.

"All along the road while enroute, the French people are lined up waving to us and of course glad to receive anything we throw at them. I threw my week's ration of candy to the pretty gals and the kids. Twenty percent of the people in Paris speak English, so if I get a chance to go there I ought to be able to get around. The farther in we get, the people look cleaner and are better dressed. There are a hell of a lot of pretty French girls also. I thought I'd be home for my next birthday, but it's almost September now and the Germans are still fighting.

"So far, I haven't decided what I'm going to do when I get home. It's quite a problem and I'm getting older every day. I'll be thinking about it. We are going to have chow pretty soon, and I'm really getting hungry.

I'm feeling okay and so far as I know, I'm in good health. Home sickness is my only trouble for the moment.

"My French is pretty good, but I'd like a French to English dictionary if one of you could manage to get one. There are a lot of words I don't know. Right now, I have two weeks washing in my barracks bag and if I can't find some lady to do it for me, I'll have a hell of a lot to do. Yesterday we had fourteen dental patients, ten fillings, two extractions, and two treatments for really sensitive teeth. It rained all day today. No worry. Be good. Au Revoir with all my love, Elwood."

25 August 1944: 4th ID CP was located in Epinay-sur-Orge, Seine-et-Oise, France

25 August 1944: 4th ID Situation Report: They were trying to cross the Seine in the vicinity of Corbeil, very close to Paris. The 4th entered Paris at 1220 and proceeded to Hotel de Ville at 1315 and "mopped up southeast Paris of scattered snipers." They were near Corbeil where they established a bridgehead across the Seine. (**NOTE:** This is probably the route Dad crossed the Seine into Paris. "The 377th AAA fired missions in support of the 2nd Battalion 22nd Infantry and materially aided in the crossing.")

27 August 1944: 4th ID CP was located in Paris (Bois de Vincennes), Seine, France

28 August 1944: 4th ID CP was located in Montfermeil (Paris), Seine-et-Oise, France

30 August 1944: 4th ID CP was located in two places: Montge (1400-1700) and Nanteuil-le-Haudoin, Oise, France

1 September 1944: 4th ID CP was located in two places: Villers-Cotterets, Aisne, France and Coeuvres-et-Valsery, Aisne, France

2 September 1944: 4th ID CP was located in Nampcel, Oise, France

2 September 1944: 4th ID Situation Report: "At 1735, Task Force was ordered to halt the advance vicinity of Landrecies and protect the right flank. The 377th AAA engaged eleven flying bombs at 0530 and one of them was heard to explode."

3 September 1944: 4th ID CP was located in Urvillers, Aisne, France

4 September 1944: Handwritten letter from Mrs. Mumford to Eunice from Sturminster Newton: "I was very pleased to hear from you again and I hope your letters from Elwood are coming in regularly. I had one from him this week. Hazel told Mary that she hears from him very often. It looks as though a romance between them is well on the way. (**NOTE:** Dad didn't propose until May 1945.) She is a very nice girl, very respectable and comes from hard working parents who think the world of Elwood.

"I hope by the time you read these few lines that we are well on the way to Berlin. It is now only a matter of weeks, perhaps only days. The news at the mid-day was wonderful. We are very near to our sweetest moment of revenge – Dunkirk. By the time you read this, it will have been over for some day, no doubt. All our men who escaped from there in 1940 have lived for the day when they could enter in triumph. Believe me, it will be their sweetest memory forever. When after the war the story of Dunkirk (1940) is told to the world, it will astound you and it will go down in history as the greatest achievement of all times.

"Churchill is a wonderful man. We have him to thank for that. If only Hitler had come on then, I should not be penning this letter now, but he was too busy counting his chickens before they were hatched and so he missed the bus, thank God. (**NOTE:** Wow, was Mrs. Mumford spot on about Hitler.)

"It looks as if Elwood will be around your X-mas table this year. If not then, soon after. (**NOTE:** Mrs. Mumford, sadly, was not accurate in this prediction.) I shall always picture him the first day he turned up at my door with that cheeky grin on his face when he introduced himself. I can see him now as I write this. He told me that he thought my home was just wonderful. When he saw white sheets and pillowcases on the bed, he nearly jumped for joy. I had a lot of good laughs with him. He takes a good joke in the right spirit. This is the last snap we took of him with a friend of his. I hope you like it. Best wishes for you all. Sincerely, Winfred Mumford."

5 September 1944: 4th ID CP was located in Tremblois, Ardennes, France

6 September 1944: 4th ID CP was located in Hargnies, Ardennes, France

7 September 1944: 4th ID CP was located in the wood in the vicinity of Graide, Luxembourg, Belgium

8 September 1944: 4th ID CP was located in Libin in a Chateau of a collaborator, Luxembourg, Belgium

8 September 1944: Small post card sized note from France: "Here I lie flat on my back in my pup tent writing this because it's raining quite hard. This stationery is a gift from some French woman. Time out while I get some new clothes (salvage). Time has gone by and now it's almost dark. Time to go to bed soon. My mail finally caught up, I have at least 15 letters. I got six yesterday and nine today. The last date was the 17 and 18 of August." One of Esda's was the 24th. (**NOTE:** That would show that the mail was still taking about three weeks to reach Dad). "Tomorrow, if I possibly can, I'm going to try to write a long carbon copy letter to you all in answer to those I received today. It's going to be a hell of a cold night tonight and my tent is like tissue paper. Good night and be careful. All my love, Elwood."

9 September 1944: 4th ID CP was located in St-Hubert, Luxembourg, Belgium

9 September 1944: Typed long letter from France on onion skin paper. "At last, I finally got ahold of a typewriter, but heaven knows how long it will be before some yo-yo comes along and asks to use it. It usually happens that way.

"Tonight, I find myself living in the woods and my pup tent is already pitched and my bed laid. It's a little chilly again so tonight I put dirt around the edges to keep the wind out. Last night I nearly froze. I haven't been digging fox holes for the last two weeks or so, but I got my fill of them back in Normandy. (I've been used to typing with all capital letters and I forget to make a capital "I" all of the time.)

Dad talks to Pappy: "Don't worry about the future. I hear you are a good dart player. I was pretty good at it in England. I didn't know they played darts in America though. I'll have to play you a game when I get home."

To Esda. "Hope you had a nice anniversary; remember the bomb I tried to put on your car when you got married? Tell me, have you let Doug put any beer in the ice box yet? Ha. Ha. You better have a few bottles of Budweiser in there for me when I come home."

"I have two letters from you Lois. I wrote that name of the perfume you want if I get a chance to get it, in my billfold so I won't forget it. I wanted to get some for you all. but I wasn't in Paris long enough and I didn't have any money at the time. If I get a chance to go back, I'll get it then or if I can find any on the way, I'll get some."

To Eunice: "I'm still working with the dentist and don't know if or when I'll be an aid man. We get pretty good meals, especially when we get fresh fruit and vegetables from the farmers. Last week we had chicken, duck, and turkey for one meal. Gifts from the French people and some we bought. Yesterday we had steak that we bought. Hazel asks about my Pappy and sisters quite often and she still has hopes that I'll go back to England to see her. I'm not going out of my way to see her on my way home, but I might get a chance someday." (**NOTE:** Very interesting that Dad thought about going back to Stur after he got home to the States. Instead, he marries Hazel in September, a year later!)

To Margie: "I hope you have a nice time on your birthday and by now you're probably home in good old Rochester with Jimmy on furlough. While I was in Paris, I met several pretty gals and had a swell time, even though I wasn't on pass. People swarmed around us, and I was so busy talking with all the gals that we didn't even do any work. We worked on one gal in Paris, and she gave me a bottle of champagne and a bottle of wine. She also came over to see me every day and night. I had my picture taken about a dozen times with the gals and Jacquiline, the one we worked on, wants me to write to her. I haven't so far, I'm waiting for her to write first. She's going to send me the pictures she took. I got so used to talking French, I started to talk it to the fellows. We had a wonderful reception there and it's a place I'm going to after the war. I'll tell you more about it later on. As far as the perfume goes, I'll try to get some when I get paid."

He closes with: "I'm froze to death and it's too dark to finish now, so I'll say good night for today and write again soon. I'm letting my hair grow in if it keeps up this kind of weather. I'll send some pictures as soon as I can. Be good and be careful. Bon nuit aved tout m'amour, Elwood." (**NOTE:** English," Good night all love, Elwood." Dad didn't write again for several weeks because his unit was on the move, as you can see from the rapid-fire 4th ID CP location changes)

10 September 1944: 4th ID CP was located in Givroulle, Liege, Belgium

11 September 1944: 4th ID CP was located in Behe (Behs), Liege, Belgium

13 September 1944: 4th ID CP was located in two locations: First, the woods east of Gruflange, Liege, Belgium and second ½ mile north of Schlierbach in Bois de St.-Vith, Liege, Belgium

15 September 1944: 4th ID CP was located in two locations: First, Auw, Rhineland, Germany and second in the woods south of Schonberg, Liege, Belgium

15 September 1944: Handwritten letter from Hazel Hatcher to Mr. and Mrs. De Roos, John and David Elwood: "I really must apologize for my long delay in answering your letter. But I am very busy and the days fly by, but at last I find time. I received a letter from Elwood's sister, and yours of course -- Mrs. Langworthy today which I will answer soon. I write to Elwood nearly every day, the days I miss are when I have any "Red Cross" duties which isn't so often." (**NOTE:** Mom knew how much dad looked forward to receiving mail. She was very good about writing and many times wrote multiple letters each day.) "I had a sweet letter from Elwood yesterday which made me very happy because he sounded very cheerful. I was worried as to how he would find this new country and its people. But he seems to be getting along very well. My dearest wish is that he will be able to come back to see us all very soon.

"My family and I were interested about your farm. My father is interested in anything concerning farming. Your farms are so much larger than ours in this country. I expect as we should like to see yours you would like to see our farms over here. Several of my uncles are farmers. The other day my father talked about taking a small farm near here. But now he thinks he'll wait and take one after this war I over. Dad is only farming on a very small scale after working hours.

"The war news sounds wonderful, and we can at last say that "Victory" is just around the corner. Maybe you have heard over your radio or in your daily papers that in certain parts of this country we are having the Black-out lifted. And just to see those streetlights once again will be wonderful. And we all look forward to it. (**NOTE:** Mom used to tell us about the blackouts and putting blankets over the windows, so the German bombers didn't see light.)

"Will you please excuse my writing material. We have been unable to buy any now for quite a while. We hope that "Pappy Turner," your husband, little boys and yourself, are in the best of health. My brother Jimmy leaves his school this X-mas so he is getting quite grown up, but we wish he would stay just like he's now always. My family and I send our good wishes to you all. Sincerely yours, Hazel."

15-17 September 1944: A WWII vet, commander in 377th Anti-Aircraft Artillery, sent the following note concerning a 4th ID Sitrep of these days: "Bob - In reading the account of WW II days Sept. 15 - 17 it brought back memories of the first time I saw flame-throwers in action, it was exciting watching the flames aimed at the front of the Pill-boxes and seeing the Krauts running out the back. I also remember well the action around and in Brandscheid. As far as I know, the 22-combat team was the first unit in Germany and the Siegfried Line."

20 September 1944: Handwritten short V-mail from Belgium, probably from Liege Region of Belgium: "I'm in Belgium now, so maybe that'll answer your question. Sorry I can't tell you where in Belgium, but that's the ruling." Dad asks about the boys and if David was able to handle the pony yet and closes with "I'm letting my hair grow in again, due to the cold weather coming on. Do you let your husband get brush cuts these days, Eunice? Remember the time he got his and John's cut that time?

Be good everybody and I'll try to write sooner next time. All my love, Elwood."

26 September 1944: Handwritten V-mail, probably still from Liege, Belgium: Dad opens with: "I have four letters from you in front of me now. After I answer my mail, I have to burn all the letters I get because I haven't the room to carry them around." (**NOTE:** They are about to go into Germany briefly and then Luxembourg so they would be on the move.)

"Sorry David and John that your lamb had to be killed. Glad it wasn't the pony, aren't you? Most of the things I need are already on the way, Eunice, but I could use some air mail stationary. It'd be a change from these V-mails.

"Hope Arnold has recovered by now, he sure had a big car buckle, didn't he?" (**NOTE:** Arnold was a helper on Johnny's farm. Dad mis-spelled "carbuncle" which means "an abscess larger than a boil.")

"Hope you canned some strawberry and pineapple jam along with all the other canning you did. I really like that jam you make. We get jam almost every day with our meals and canned fruit. I still haven't eaten any butter as you all said. Lately we haven't been getting our cigarettes ration every week. We're supposed to get 7 packs a week, a little candy, a package of gum, razor blades, toothpaste and shaving cream. All my love, Elwood. "

4 October 1944: Handwritten V-mail from 'Somewhere in Germany': "Received your air mail letter of the 18th and glad you sent me Bonnie's and her brother's picture and clipping. She looks good. That's the first time I've seen her picture in uniform. I've written and asked her for one in uniform, but she hasn't written for over a month now.

"Glad that Arnold is recuperating and I hope Johnny can find help. It must be awful hard after being used to having help. With the kids growing up as fast as they are, they will be some help to the old man. I sure would like to be able to take the kids to the zoo again, etc., soon.

"I don't know if you've been getting any bonds lately but if not, they'll be resumed again shortly. For a while we weren't able to buy them on the installment plan, but they've changed it again.

"Had an orange for breakfast this morning. Boy it was good! I guess we're having turkey for Thanksgiving. We had steak for dinner and supper yesterday. Be careful and don't work too hard. All my love, Elwood." (**NOTE:** I'm surprised they had steak for two meals while just entering Germany. Based on the 4th ID CP location, they were in Rhineland, Germany. They must have been at a very secure rear area from the battle, but they didn't know that in just a little over two months the Germans would start the Battle of the Bulge.)

4 October 1944: 4th ID CP was located in the vicinity southwest of Bullingen, Liege, Belgium

5 October 1944: Handwritten letter from Hazel Hatcher to Mr. and Mrs. DeRoos, John and David Elwood: "I have sent my picture to "Pappy Turner", Mrs. Street and Mrs. Langworthy, so I thought you would like one as well. I also hope you all like it. On the last letter I received from Elwood, he wanted to know if I had received them yet. I had them taken on my holiday and that's quite a long time ago. They were "buzz bombed" which made it so long. My mother and I have been visiting an aunt of mine, who returned home from the hospital yesterday and on our way home it seemed so nice to see the lights in the windows of the houses, after such complete darkness.

"These evenings my father is home sat by the fire instead of working on the land. He has of late been getting the crops in, and we have had a very good season. I suppose you are all very busy as well. We haven't heard anything about Boyce, we wonder if he is still in England. Hope that John and David Elwood are well. My brother Jimmy has been on

10 days holiday for "Potato Picking". He went back to school yesterday. Here's to a speedy victory and Elwood's safe return to you all soon. Our kindest regards to you all. Sincerely, Hazel."

9 October 1944: Typed letter from Belgium: "I suppose you'll notice the paper I'm using. It is nothing but wrapping paper cut up rather crudely. Well, it's the best I could find at the present time. Also, this typewriter is a German make and the "a" is where the "y" should be and the "y" is where the "z" should be. All it is, is a piece of junk.

"At the present time it is dusk and we have no electricity in this house. The houses close to the front lines were evacuated for the civilian's safety and consequently we have a house to work in and sleep in. (**NOTE:** Dad mentions being in a house for the first time in many months, and he stays in this house for several days, at least thru 20 October. The 4th ID was located near Bullingen, Liege, Belgium at this time).

"Two days ago, I had a room with a bed and clean sheets for two nights. Now I am sleeping on the floor in the hall. At least it is dry and warmer. Captain Kantrowitz and I have our office here in the house, which is a lot better than a tent out in the woods someplace. For the last month now, we have been working all day long every day in the week. Before we came over here, we had most of the men in good shape as far as their teeth went and now the work is becoming more plentiful.

"Last night I received a card from Pappy and a package from Esda with the jack knife, fountain pens, key chain, chocolate, and cookies. Oh, yes, jam and Kleenex. The knife is a beauty, and the chain is just right for my needs. The fountain pens write very good. I used them on the envelopes. Right now, the German radio we got is playing some nice music. I ate so much chocolate this afternoon that I didn't have a very good appetite tonight for chow. I'll thank you all for the package in one sentence to save time and space. Thank you!!! It was all very good.

"Thank you, Pappy, for telling me what you are going to get me for X-mas. That is awful good of you to buy me that bond, but then you are the best Pappy in the world. I had a chance to send presents home through the special service, but all the items listed that I wanted to send were too expensive for me. I'm sending most of my money home now and I just can't get it when I want it. Maybe in my travels through Germany, I can find something small to send home for souvenirs, or something. Hope you understand. Pappy, I wrote Hazel and told her about your birthday in September and she was mad at me because I didn't tell her in time so she could send your birthday card, but she said she would send you one next year.

"We are getting good chow every day, but we aren't getting very many cigarettes lately due to lack of transportation. Food and ammunition come first over here. Maybe you could send me a carton now and then until I tell you different. Pappy, it's almost dark already and we just finished chow. I'm plenty tired though because I've been standing all day. Be good and thanks again. I'll write as soon as I can. All my love, Elwood."

13 October 1944: Handwritten note, in pencil, on German paper. "Excuse the pencil please! As I explained to the others, this is the only paper I have now. German at that."

Dad had received some mail with pictures of Margie and Jim on furlough with the boys and the pony. Dad says: "Little David must have been bashful that day, his head was hanging low but they were good of him. John is going to have a TURNER smile. Note De Roos."

"Well, John Sr. I'm glad to hear that Arnold will be back to help you. You must have had it rough all alone. Especially in harvest time. I haven't had anything to drink in a good two months now. Don't miss it but I wouldn't mind a good glass of Budweiser right now. Been playing Pinochle lately. There's no show tonight so I may play some. I'm letting my hair grow back in this winter and it seems funny to have hair again. It's almost dark so I'll have to quit for the night. Be good. All my love, Elwood."

20 October 1944: Handwritten note from undisclosed location from A.P.O 230. (**NOTE:** This letter could have been written in Belgium or Germany.) "Received two V-mail letters from you since I wrote last. I've written to Pappy, Esda, and Lois so far and all I do is repeat myself it seems. But it's hard for me to write so many letters and tell you all what I've been doing and not repeat myself. So, there you have it!

"Just about got over my cold and was I glad that we have been living in a house while I have had it. The thought of my pup tent makes me shake, especially with winter setting in. In a way I feel sad for the people that were evacuated, but they must be taken care of okay.

"I went to the show tonight after chow and saw "*You Can't Ration Love*". Wednesday night I saw Diana Durbin in "*The Butler's Sister*" and "*Lady Lets Dance.*" Last night I saw a stage show with a G.I. band and yesterday afternoon I saw "*Hail the Conquering Hero.*" They were all very good. I haven't seen Bing Crosby yet. Don't' believe he came up very close to the line. At least not in this area. Glad to hear Tony making out as well as he did. I must write to Marjorie now and maybe Hazel yet. All my love. Elwood."

26 October 1944: Handwritten letter written on German stationary. "Received your letters of October 8th and 15th this week. Not bad time, eh? I'm glad to hear that silo filling is over, etc. I realize how much work it must have been for you because if all the men ate as much as your husband does, you should have had three cooks. I wish I could eat as much as he does. I'd like to be back there right now trying to eat more steak than he can. Anyway, Johnny, I hope you got all your crops harvested before the frost and that you get a good price for all your hard work. I'm smoking a cigar now and it reminds me of the time I went to that meeting at the City Hall for you and I bought some cigars to put on the act.

"I received a 1 lb. box of candy for X-mas today, but from no special person. I believe it was the compliments of Barricini candy company. It's good." (**NOTE:** Barricini is a candy store from New York City and is still in business to this day!)

"I'm glad to hear the pony is still in good shape and the kids are having some fun with it. I've got to write Marjorie now and maybe after that I'll play some Pinochle. I've been playing Pinochle quite a bit lately. Could you please send me some Pinochle cards sometime? All my love, Elwood."

1 November 1944: Handwritten V-mail from undisclosed location: "I haven't had a letter from you lately, so I'll probably get yours tomorrow night. This being your harvest season, etc., it must be trying to write letters after a hard day's work.

"I'm holding a kitten on my lap now and being a man, it's quite a difficult procedure. The kitty sleeps on my bed roll at night and it's good company. He had a crushed jaw, but it's getting better. Looks a lot like "Lucky." Pure black.

"A couple fellows helped me drink a quart of champagne last night. I had a bottle ordered but they couldn't get much so I was just SOL. Captain Kantrowitz traded a quart of his liquor ration for an extra quart of champagne and sold me one bottle, which was very nice of him. It was the first drink I had for close to three months. Really good. Last month we extracted 43 teeth and filled 161 cavities. Four times as much as the month before. We really stepped it up. Working Sundays too. Here goes another buzz bomb. Be careful. All my love, Elwood." (**NOTE:** Even though Dad was writing to the U.S., he mentions Buzz Bombs which the Germans flew into England, usually London.)

7 November 1944: 4th ID CP was located in Zweifall, Rhineland, Germany

11 November 1944: Handwritten V-mail From Germany. "This is the fourth letter I've written this afternoon, and I just realized that it's Armistice Day — Boy, I wish it was Armistice Day for this war instead of the last war.

"Received four letters from you this last week. One of them rather surprised me. Bonnie hasn't written me for two or three months. Another Surprise! I just got a nice letter from Bonnie, three from Hazel, one from Marjorie, and another from you. Glad Bonnie paid you a visit while she was home. She always did like to go to your house with me. She's getting to see the world now too.

"Glad you like Hazel's picture. She is really nice. She thinks it's wonderful to hear from my sisters. Her mother carries my picture around in her purse all the time. It sounds like I was courting her mother at one time, eh?

"I'm going to have a few hands of Pinochle tonight. Did I ask you to send me a new deck? If you will please. All my love, Elwood."

15 November 1944: Handwritten V-mail from a place not disclosed: "They are starting to lay the chow out now, but I'll start your letter and finish it after chow. You asked me if Larry was the only other fellow from Rochester. There's about a dozen fellows, but I didn't know any of them before I came in the Army. As far as I know, Larry is still in England.

"I suppose the kids are as good as they can be now with X-mas on the way. I can still remember John when he first came in our house his first X-mas and David too. Their eyes popped out; it seemed. Hope they get everything they want. All my love, Elwood." (**NOTE:** Dad did his best to provide everything we wanted as kids, even though he had six children to provide for. We each had a section of the couch or chairs with our presents Christmas morning. I'm reminded of the Reba McEntire's song lyric "Everything he gave to us, took all he had.")

20 November 1944: Handwritten note from Germany, as "Uncle Elwood" to John Jr. and David Elwood. He had received John Jr's letter. "It's been a long time since I've written to you and David separately, but

I always think about you two. I wonder what Santa Claus has in store for you and David this year? Of course, you both know that you've got to be good. I suppose he'll overlook any stunts you may have pulled on Halloween. The cops almost got me one Halloween for ringing doorbells. Some old grouch caught us on his porch and took us inside and called the cops. While he was calling, Bob Carlson, the fellow with me, and I ran through his screen door without opening it.

"Do you still get good marks in school as you used to? Your spelling is very good, and your sentence structure is marvelous. David, you're getting good at writing your name. Maybe you can write a letter to me sometime, eh?

"Have you and David taken your girlfriends for a ride with the pony as yet? You ought to have fun this winter with the pony and sleigh. Have your daddy get some jingle bells for its harness.

"I'll have to say goodbye for now. Be good and I hope you have a Merry X-mas with lots of presents. All my love, Uncle Elwood."

23 November 1944: Handwritten letter from Mrs. Mumford to Eunice written on "The Animal Infirmary and Dispensary, Sturminster Newton, Dorset letterhead: "No doubt, by the time you get this, X-mas will be very near at hand and we shall all be thinking of you this side of the great Atlantic. I shall miss Elwood and the boys this year, but I have no doubt he will somehow enjoy himself. He is not the type to sit and panic, and I am sure he can always make the best of a bad job. I do hope you all have a very Happy X-mas, this is certainly the last wartime one. All the best from Winfred Mumford."

24 November 1944: Handwritten Letter from Germany A.P.O. 230: "Thanksgiving Dinner was wonderful. They had soup, turkey, cranberry sauce, sweet potatoes, cauliflower, peas, hot buns, apple pie, coffee, candy, grapes, and nuts and White Horse Scotch "to settle our meal.

"We're having chicken for dinner, so you see we didn't do bad at all.

We'll probably have turkey for X-mas and New Years also. We usually do. We're still living in a house and consequently it made it more like home. Received your letter dated the 5th of November. I got quite a kick out of John Jr's letter. He does very well at his age.

"David is beginning to become a scholar too I see. Hope you got good prices for your crops this year, John. Do you still have trouble with your back? That's all for now. I'll write again in a few days. Don't work too hard. All my love, Elwood."

26 November 1944: Merry Christmas Card to Masters John and David De Roos: "Dear John Jr. and David Elwood, Wish I could be with you X-mas to see what you both got. But you can write me a letter and tell me, okay?"

29 November 1944: Handwritten note on a "Merry Christmas and a Victorious New Year Card from his unit, 377th AAA from Germany: "Am sleeping in a barn now; heat and electricity, no bathroom or shower, but its rent free. I've got a bed and smoke stand and six blankets. Yesterday, I put on my long johns for the first time. I slept pretty warm last night, too. I'm sorry that I asked you people back home for cigarettes now. I didn't know you were so short on them when I wrote and asked. Sorry. I got eight packs last week. Guess they're going to cut us to five per week. All my love, Elwood."

3 December 1944: Handwritten letter from "Germany": "First of all, I hope you both had a happy anniversary. I can never remember when yours or any of other's anniversary comes. I doubt if I'll even be able to remember my own, if I ever have any.

"I have a slight cold and it's bothersome. I cough quite a bit. We're sleeping in a barn now and it's fixed up pretty good. It's difficult to heat it, even with two stoves. I have a bed and about eight blankets now. The wooden slats are my springs, and I have some hay in my mattress cover for a mattress.

"I got a letter from Margie from her new address. I sent her another bracelet because she didn't get the first one I sent her. While I think of it, who's going to have Pappy for dinner on X-mas?

"Please notice my A.P.O. #4, now. Hope you're all well. Be good. All my love, Elwood. P.S. I saw Marlene Dietrich in person last week."

8 December 1944: 4th ID CP was located in Luxembourg, Luxembourg.

9 December 1944: Handwritten letter from Luxembourg, A.P.O. 4. "What a wonderful dinner you had for Pappy and Lois Thanksgiving. I sure would like some homemade pumpkin pie. We had some good meals, but they lack that home touch. Every other morning, we have hot cakes, syrup, and coffee. Other times we have dehydrated eggs, sausage, and cereal with coffee. We've been getting a lot of corned beef lately.

"I'm still battling my cold without too much success. We're living in good quarters, heat, electricity, beds, radio, and two showers in each room. I had a nice hot shower the other night and washed my hair. We have a nice office and a good chow hall. All I lack is a mattress, and I'm going to work on that this afternoon.

"I was in Aachen for a while in Germany. Most all the houses are blown up, in fact, I didn't see one that wasn't damaged in some way or another." (**NOTE:** Aachen, Germany is 124 miles from Luxembourg.) "Oh, I had a four-page V-mail letter from Bonnie last week. She likes Frisco a lot and she has a nice job. Hope you're all well, All my love, Elwood."

16 December 1944: Type written letter from Luxembourg and first day of the Battle of the Bulge. "I managed to get ahold of a typewriter tonight and if you could see all the letters I have here in front of me to answer, you'd appreciate that fact that I did get ahold of one also! I went on a two day pass three days ago and my mail got bunched up on me. I'll try to answer them all in this one letter, if you don't mind. I'll start off tell you about my pass, and then answer your letters, okay?

"Well, I had a forty-eight hour pass the other day and it was the first one since England. I didn't go to Paris, but may get a chance to go there sometime in the future. I did go to a "big city" and lived in a "chateau". (**NOTE:** If I had to guess, the city was Liege, Belgium). "It was a huge place and very pretty. They had showers and a swimming pool (inside), theater, library, reading room, card room, etc. It's a soldier's rest camp, maybe you've read about them. I didn't rest very much. In fact, just the opposite. You know me. We had good meals and plenty of beer. Everything at the chateau was free except the beer. I had quite a bit of fun with the Belgium gals, dancing and talking French with them, etc. That covers my pass. I took some pictures while I was there, I'll be sending them home next week sometime.

"My cold is still bad. I can't seem to do much for it. I've chewed aspirin, taken codeine, gargled with Listerine, rubbed Vicks on my chest before going to bed, but still no help. I'm inside most of the time too. Damn if I know, guess I need some ginger, eh Pappy?" (**NOTE:** Dad would always give us ginger ale when we were sick.)

"Pappy, Hazel thought the verse on the calendar she sent you would help you have faith that I'll soon be home, etc. She wrote and said she received the package from Lois and you. She loves the Fanny Farmers and is going to save them for X-mas, but they all had one piece. I told you she is sending me a X-mas package, didn't I? I got a X-mas package from Building 5 at Kodak today also. (**NOTE:** Dad must have worked in Building 5 in Rochester at Kodak.)

"Esda, I'm saving all my X-mas cards and X-mas wrapping paper and the ribbons from my presents and sending them to Hazel. I think she'll enjoy keeping the wrapping paper and the ribbons. I like France better than Belgium, both about the same. Most of the questions you've asked in your letters I've already answered, about the election and so forth. Some of the fellows on our front are going home for X-mas. They are going to Paris then England and then going to the States by boat. The first bunch are men who were injured and decorated for bravery, etc. Don't be expecting me right away. I sure would like to and may get a chance in a year or two, who knows.

"Lois, I'm still living inside and have a straw mattress now to sleep on. If the pictures come out good, that Capt. Kantrowitz and I took inside our office, you'll get an idea of what our home is like. We are still in the same place as I described last time I wrote.

"Eunice, some of our fellows shot a few deer in Germany and Belgium some time back. I never did care for that kind of meat much.

"Margie, I broke my camera last week, but ordinance fixed it for me and I've taken quite a few pictures this last week. So, worry Looey is still a pig and eats too fast? Lay down the law to him. Keep him busy painting the kitchen and bathroom. That'll wear down that excess fat. Put him on a beer diet. Ha. Ha. He eats it.

"Right now, I have to go down to the beer joint and get those pictures from the guy that's developed them for me and have a few beers. They have good beer here. By the way, I'm growing a mustache. Don't know how long I'll let it grow. So far, it's not very thick. I'll have my picture taken with it before I cut it off.

"Again, I want to thank you all for the presents, they are all very useful and I appreciate everything. Be good and I'll write again soon. T/5 Elwood A. Turner, 377th AAA AW BN, APO 4, U.S. Army. P.S. Received a $50 War Bond from Kodak, and I'll send it on to you soon by registered mail. You can keep it with the others, okay?"

21 December 1944: Happy New Years Post Card from Luxembourg to Eunice and family: "Dear Eunice and family, Here's to a happy and prosperous New Year for you, Love Elwood." The front of the post card shows a little girl carrying a doll with hand muffs and the card says: "Bonne Annee" or Good Year.

21 December 1944: Handwritten note still from Luxembourg: "By the time you get this, X-mas will be over, and the kids will no doubt have all their toys in the middle of the floor and in general everything will be in a hub-ub. Am I right? I hope everyone had a good X-mas and plenty presents. Hope the flowers made things cheery, too. (**NOTE:** Dad sent flowers again, his third Christmas away from home.) "It'll be just like my first X-mas to be home for X-mas again. Hope it's not any later than next X-mas.

"Had a nice package from you. The nuts were very good, candy too. Lois said you're sending me the cards I wrote and ask for, too. You can't buy good cards over here. Am enclosing a picture enlarged to postcard size. It was taken in a beer joint nearby. They have good war time beer here in Luxembourg. It's more like American beer than any I've had since I left the States. Be good and don't work too hard. All my love, Elwood." (**NOTE:** This is the letter Dad sent the picture of him and his two buddies in a beer joint).

23 December 1944: Envelope from A.P.O. 4 with a Post Card inside of a girl walking down a snow-covered street with a doll and hand mittens. It says: "Bonne Annee" "Happy New Year": "Dear Eunice and Family, Here's to a happy and prosperous New Year for you." Love, Elwood."

25 December 1944: Christmas Card from The Mumford's. Cover is a picture of Mary holding baby Jesus: "A Holy Christmas; Infinite Love; Thirst for Thy Love. Back of card: "Just the old up wish with many kind thoughts from us all."

27 December 1944: 4th ID CP was located on Highway 1 in Senningen, Luxembourg

27 December 1944: Typewritten letter from Luxembourg: "Dear everybody. Well, I finally got over X-mas with only a bump on my forehead. We had a pretty good time considering being away from home. Christmas Eve, I was down in a beer joint (Café) and while there, some lady asked me and another fellow out to her house for Christmas dinner. (**NOTE:** See picture at end of chapter of the couple who had dad and his friend over for dinner.)

"So, we accepted the invitation. Going back to Saturday night, I mean Sunday Night, we had beer, schnaps, and ended up drinking champagne. We were going out Christmas caroling, but by the time we left the café, it was too late. Another fellow and I did stop in at a house and had some Christmas pastry, cake, etc. Also, some kind of mint julip drink.

"The next morning, Christmas morning ; needless to say, I didn't wake up feeling normal because of the champagne, I believe. I had a nice hot and cold shower and shaved and put on fresh clothes. We had to meet the man that invited us out, in the same café at noon, which we did. When he took us to his home, the dinner was ready.

"I took the lady a box of candy that I got in one of my packages for Christmas. The fellow that went with me couldn't speak French, but he made out good just the same. We sat right down to eat at the table and everything was very pretty, neat and clean with a little holly in front of each plate. The people were fairly well to do.

"After we sat down, the lady asked us to make believe that we were at home with our family because they wanted to think of us as their sons. They have no children. I can't speak French too fluently and it took me quite some time, at least it seemed it, to thank her and tell her that we would and that we appreciated her kind thought.

"First, we had noodle soup. It was all very good. Next, while she was bringing on the salad course, the man opened up a quart of white wine and then we started. Every time I turned around, he was busy filling my glass up. We had two salads, a green salad, and a tuna fish salad with plenty mayonnaise all fixed up fancy. I thought that was the main course because of the shortage of food here, so I took seconds on the tuna fish salad. I was full then.

"This course was only the beginning, for she brought on another. This was rabbit, boiled potatoes, carrots and peas and bread. By this time, we had started another bottle of white wine. The man noticed by our expressions that we hadn't expected that course or anymore, so he told me that we would have some more.

"The next course was rabbit, only fried this time, with French fried potatoes and either more carrots and peas or green salad. She would not let us refuse any and we wanted to be polite and not hurt her feelings, so we proceeded to have seconds on this course and to finish up the big bowl of French fries.

"At this time, we had started on red wine. All this time he and I were having trouble being our best and showing manners that we once knew. It was a very hard job not being used to eating with such fineries. With our dessert, which was wonderful cake and pie, we had our fourth bottle of wine. So far, two white and two red. The lady practically cried because we didn't eat more than two pieces of pie plus the cake, but I just couldn't.

"All in all, it took us two hours and fifteen minutes to eat. When we finally had a cigarette, he opened up a quart of champagne and we drank it. When we left, she gave us three homemade pies and two sacks of apples to eat where we are staying. It was about four thirty when we left their house and-on-the-way home, some lady waved at us that we knew and she had us come in her house for a drink. Her husband sat two bottles on the table, one schnapps and one wine. Pretty soon another wine and another. Then came some cognac.

"This lady could speak a little English and her aunt that lives next door had been in Chicago quite a few years ago. Well, she came over and it was a circus talking to her. She used the old American expressions, and she always ended up saying, "Ain't it, mister." She told us about all her American boyfriends, real funny. Horse and Buggy days. I thought of Pappy right away.

"At eight o'clock we promised to meet the people we ate with at the café, so we did. I was having a few beers and having a good time talking to two pretty gals and one of the ladies that we know came in and asked me if I'd go and look at her husband's arm. She thought he was getting blood poison. So, I went down. I told him it wasn't and told him to soak it in hot salt water because it was an infection.

"After that he brought out a quart of red wine and she gave me some pork cheese and bread and two cups of coffee. After that I went to bed. It sounds like I had a lot to drink, and I really did, but the people wouldn't take no for an answer. I ate so much that it didn't bother me much.

"That was quite a Christmas, Eh what? The people were all so good to us that one couldn't help but have a good time. I haven't had any mail from home in the past few days. Perhaps the packages have been getting priority or something. Anyway, I think I'll get some tomorrow, Hope you all had a good Christmas and a Merry one.

"My cold is still hanging on, damn it. Can't do much about it. Most everyone has one. I saw some kids ice skating today, so you can judge how cold it is. It's very near bedtime now, so I'll say good night. Tomorrow I'll have to find a typewriter and make copies for my sisters to save all this handwriting. Good night with all my love, Elwood."

1 January 1945: Handwritten V-mail from undisclosed location: "Tis Happy New Year and I had a rough day today but am back to normal again, thank goodness. The Champaigne mixed with beer isn't too good. I had a pretty good time but nothing exceptional.

"I imagine you are pretty well covered up with all that snow you've been having. Too bad the kids couldn't take the pony out for a sleigh ride. I hope by now my mail has gotten to you. Our incoming mail is slow now that X-mas is over. It's hell when you don't get mail. I'm used to getting a lot and when none comes, it's noticeable. All my love.

Elwood." (**NOTE:** The Battle of the Bulge was on-going and the mail was delayed for all units, including Dad's. There were also cases of the Germans stealing mail and packages from back home.)

6 January 1945: Short handwritten V-mail from undisclosed location: "We had some snow here last week but not as much as what you've had back home. I imagine your driveway needed shoveling, eh? I'd like to have some skates and skis about now. You could go skating in the roads here. (**NOTE:** This tracks with the bad weather they got during the Battle of the Bulge.)

"I'm glad that you took a picture of the kids with the pony and sleigh. I'm anxious to see it. Have John Jr. write me and tell me all about the school, church program, and of course X-mas. All my love, Elwood."

6 January 1945: Handwritten letter from Mrs. Mumford to "My Dear Mrs. De Roos": Mrs. Mumford thanks Eunice for a package which was a "wonderful surprise." (**NOTE:** This letter gives excellent insight into U.S. Hospitals and how they cared for our wounded). "I had a phone message come through from an American Hospital about 12 miles from here to say that "Corporal Mattfolk", a great friend of Elwood's, was there with leg wounds and would I go see him. Half an hour later we were ready to start feeling very excited at the thought of meeting again. (**NOTE:** "Corporal Mattfolk" must have been in Stur when Dad was.)

"Well, we arrived at this tremendous place which stretches for miles and miles. First, we went to one big office and after going through hundreds of names, they sent us to another part of the place about three miles further on. Again, they went through all their patients. No one of that name, so we were sent another two miles to another part of the Hospital. After a lot of frantic searching, they told me there was no such man anywhere in the hospital.

"However, they could see I was very upset so they decided they would ring through to all the fracture wards, fortunately I knew his wounds were leg wounds. They asked the nurses to call out to all the patients and ask them if anyone knew "Corporal Mattfolk."

"At last, one man called out that "Mattfolk" was his friend, so I was sent to this ward to see him. Imagine my surprise when I found it was a mistake, but it happened to be a "unintelligible word" Ward from the same medics as Elwood. I knew him well by sight, in fact, it was Ward who brought Elwood to our house the first day he came.

"He was delighted to see us as he had only arrived three days before. He was shot on X-mas eve, was on the operating table in Paris in twenty minutes and was flown to England on Jan 2nd. Imagine his surprise when he found out he was only about 12 miles from here. He got a civilian to ring us up and he forgot his name but described him, and we took it that it was Mattfolk. However, my husband and I spent quite a nice time with him, and he was able to give us firsthand news about Elwood and the boys.

"He said they were all fine when he left them. I cannot describe how wonderful the American hospitals are. Ward says he is enjoying every minute of it. He will be there for about six months. Although I am a trained nurse, it was an amazing sight to see such a wonderful operation on each bed for the various kinds of fractures. The comfort and treatment the patients get is truly amazing.

"Believe me, you have only to visit that place, and it brings the war very close. I feel ashamed to think that we people grumble over our rations and lack of luxuries when all these men have suffered like this and still smile. From now onward, I shall count my blessings. No more grouses from me.

"I was able to call and see Hazel on my way back and give her the news. She had just received a letter from Elwood, saying he was in Luxemburg. A lot of Americans are going to have seven days leave with free travel to England, so we are hoping that Elwood will be one of the lucky ones. Some have had it and visited this place but were not Elwood's lot. They belonged to a different Battery. Time is short now so I will wish you all a Happy New Year and again, many thanks and love from the children. Very kindly yours, Winfred M." (**NOTE:** Mrs. Mumford's expressed clear sentiment that after visiting the hospital, she would "grumble" less and appreciate all that they had. We should all take this into consideration every day.)

13 January 1945: Typewritten letter from somewhere in Luxembourg. (**NOTE:** This letter was written several days after the Germans were defeated in the Battle of the Bulge. Dad's unit was just put under the Command of General Patton and his 3rd Army.) "My dear family. Good morning, everybody and how's Trices? I've just finished shaving and cleaning up so while I've got a chance, I'll use my time writing. For your information, I'm in the Third Army now, as you could probably have figured out because I put in Luxembourg on the top of my letter. We had a close call sometime back, but I've been writing to you regularly and I surely hope you've received some mail from me. (**NOTE:** This is important because Dad was only writing short handwritten V-mails since the first of the year. They were busy fighting the Germans. A month and eleven days was a long time without any mail.)

"I'm glad Hazel writes; she must be getting my mail alright. She writes me about every day. I received your letter dated the 26th, Pappy, yesterday. I'm awful glad you had such a nice Christmas and that the flowers came alright that Marjorie sent for me. I'm still living indoors and it's not bad, so don't worry about me living outdoors in the cold. It is quite cold here. Still freezing.

"I saw a movie yesterday afternoon and a G.I. show the other night. The stage show was really good. Do you still go to the movies every Saturday night? No, that's right, you work nights now, don't you? Also received your V-mail of the 26th, Esda. I read in the Stars and Stripes the other day that in the German breakthrough that they captured one freight train of our X-mas packages, but it said they didn't get any letters.

I believe they got the package that Hazel sent me for X-mas because I haven't received it as yet.

"Am pleased that you enjoyed the flowers and the center piece. I'm getting more homesick every day. Just have to sweat it out, I guess. I got a letter from Kodak telling me about all the old fellows I used to work with, where they are and what they're doing. A patient just walked in, so I must leave you now, but I'll write again soon. Until then, don't worry and be careful. All my love, Elwood."

Mid-January 1945: Postcard from Hazel to Esda: "Dear Mrs. Street: Received your letter today for which many thanks. I'm so very sorry that you aren't getting Elwood's mail. I haven't heard for a week now. About two weeks ago, I went to see one of his medical friends who is wounded and in the hospital near here. He says Elwood was quite safe and well Dec 24th. Of course, that's a long way back now. I will write you a long letter very soon and enclose one of the pictures I had taken with one of the fellows. Here's hoping you are all well and that you heard from Elwood better now. Love, Hazel."

17 January 1945: 4th ID CP was located in Heffingen, Luxembourg

22 January 1945: 4th ID CP was located in Fels, Luxembourg

25 January 1945: Handwritten V-mail from undisclosed location: "I am pleased that you all faired so well for X-mas and that Pappy could be there to watch the kids open their presents. Am surprised that Bonnie thought of sending you and the kids a card. I had a letter from her yesterday. She's more sincere now than before. (**NOTE:** Interesting how God works. If somehow Dad and Bonnie had eventually married, the Elwood Turner children as we know them, wouldn't be here. I'm sure we turned out better with our mother!!!)

"So far, I haven't received the Pinochle cards but I did receive a birthday card from John and David. It was alright. Thank them for me. I think about them often. I am pleased that you all enjoyed the pictures I sent, and I'll be glad when I get those from the home of the X-mas tree and dinner table. I'm going to take some more soon. I still have some film left. (**NOTE:** The pictures Dad sent home were from December 1945 and probably included the one taken of him and his buddies in a Luxembourg City. See end of chapter pictures.)

"My cold is a little better now, but I doubt if I'll get over it completely until summer comes. Right now, it is snowing quite hard. We already have about six inches of snow. Be good and don't work too hard. With all my love, Elwood."

28 January 1945: 4th ID CP was located in two locations: First, Trione, Luxembourg and second Durler, Liege, Belgium

29 January 1945: Handwritten V-mail from undisclosed location: "We just finished working on a patient and I got some grapefruit juice from the kitchen to make a high ball with the gin Capt. Kantrowitz gave me. (**NOTE:** Interesting how age and increased responsibilities of having a family change behavior. I never remember seeing Dad have a drink or a beer in the 19 years he was my earthly father.) It must be around three o'clock now and if no one else comes in, I'll have two hours in which to write to Lois and Marjorie.

"We have our dental office in a kitchen now and we have a cook stove and a sink. We have a fire going but the water line is frozen up, so we have to carry our water. (**NOTE:** The winter of 1944-1945 was one of the coldest and harshest in many years). I hope you're all well and not working too hard. Thanks again John and David for the card. All my love, Elwood."

31 January 1945: Handwritten V-mail from undisclosed location but he answers a question about Luxembourg from his sister's earlier letters.

(**NOTE:** I do not believe his unit was in Luxembourg on 31 Jan 1945. They were in Belgium based on the 4th ID CP locations): "Received your letter of the 11th and 12th the other day. I'm glad you got the bond okay (as far as the beneficiary goes, you can put David's name on it, like the others.) (**NOTE:** These two short sentences tell us that the mail was coming into a war zone in a matter of weeks, which is in some cases better than today! It also shows how much dad loved his nephews.)

"The people of Luxembourg are Luxembourgers. It is a country like France and Belgium, governed by the Grand Duchess of Luxembourg. The people speak a language like German to me. Luxembourg is one of the richest countries of the world. It's very noticeable, the differences between the French, Belgians, and the Luxembourg people. For instance, the people of Luxembourg wear shoes and in France they wear wooden shoes. Well, it's getting close to bedtime and I have to write Margie yet. Be good. All my love. Elwood."

2 February 1945: 4th ID CP was located in Lommersweiler, Liege, Belgium

4 February 1945: 4th ID CP was located in Amelscheid, Liege Belgium

7 February 1945: 4th ID CP was located in Bleialf, Rhineland, Germany

9 February 1945: Handwritten short note from an undisclosed location, but based on Command Post locations, his unit was now in Germany. Dad was happy to receive so many cards and letters. "I received the Pinochle cards last week. Thanks a million. They're very good cards. I'm glad you were able to take Pappy to see Aunt Nell. Too bad she wasn't home at the time. I remember how Pappy used to like to have me take him out the Ridge Road and stop off here and there to visit. I am not very close to where Clinton is located, so I doubt if I'll get a chance to meet him.

"Yes, we have a chaplain but he's a Catholic chaplain. We have a division chaplain that holds Protestant services.

"John Jr's letter came as it was written. It was stamped "blurred" so they couldn't print and develop it. I'm pleased to know that both you and David got so many presents for Xmas.

"A $1.50 is good money for potatoes, isn't it? Before the war, they were somewhere around 90 cents, I believe. My shaving water is hot now, so I must say, so long for now. After I shave, I have to write to Margie. Be good and be careful. All my love, Elwood."

16 February 1945: Typewritten long letter from somewhere in Germany. The letter was clearly censored as they had literally cut out part of the letter instead of blackening typed words out: "My dear family. Well, I'm back in Germany again and still living in a house, but will be glad to get outdoors again and live in pup tents. At least outside it's clean and plenty of fresh air. My appetite is much better when I sleep outside. These last few days, I've had a slight touch of the GI's, known to you as dysentery.

"The weather the last few days has been beautiful. The only thing, of course, to spoil it is the mud. It's good weather for washing clothes, which I have plenty to wash. Boy, I hate that job. Back in Luxembourg and Belgium, it was easy to find some lady to do it for me. Things are different here.

"I don't know about getting a furlough to England or not. I'd like to go back to see Hazel. She sent me a couple of pictures that she had taken recently, and they are very good. I think she is going to send one to Esda. I just ate chow, and it was lousy. We haven't had anything good to eat for the last week or two. Guess it's due to the bad roads. They can't bring our rations up. (**NOTE:** The next two or three sentences were completely cut out of the letter. I assume Dad must have said something that could have given away their location or future plans.)

"Glad Hazel wrote and thanked you for the candy. Her birthday is April the twelfth, I believe. I'd like to have you send her some more Fanny Farmers and silk stockings and anything else you might find that she might like, for me. Because I can't get her anything here. Pappy will give you the money. Take it out of my account. Thank you.

"So, Eunice, your old man has been driving the snowplow lately. Boy, he is everything in your district – politician, school trustee, member of the church, etc. You'll no doubt wonder why a medic shot himself, so I'd better tell you. He was looking at a pistol and thought he had it unloaded. That's something I don't mess around with but once in a while. In Aachen, I fired a few rounds just to see what it was like.

"I'm glad, Margie, you've finally received the bracelet, but I'm sorry that I couldn't have polished it for you like I did the others… I'm glad that you have quit work and taking things easy. Practically everybody I know, knows that you are going to be a mama soon. Probably the first thing your baby will say when it talks is, "Mama, why were my ears ringing when I was born." Ha. Ha.

"Jimmy, if it cries when it looks at you, don't feel bad. Ha. Ha. You eat it. You hadn't better let any farts in the same room with the baby, you're liable to gas it.

"Yes Margie, I'm still working with the dentist. We don't call in any patients over here, if they want to come in to have their teeth taken care of, then we work on them. Otherwise, it's their own tough luck. The men like the dentist and as a result, most of them come in quite often.

"In closing, I'd like to ask one or all of you to send me a pipe and a dog tag chain. Don't get me wrong. I only want one pipe and one dog tag chain. I broke my pipe the other day when we moved. Be good and take care of yourselves. All my love, Elwood."

21 February 1945: Typewritten long letter from somewhere in a field in

Germany: "My dear family. Here I am again with a pile of letters from all of you, so I'll do my best to answer all your questions, etc. All the current events I have for you aren't very interesting. In fact, the only one is that I took a shower today, and for a dressing room, an open field was it. At first, I didn't care much about taking a shower after I saw all the fellows in a field getting undressed and dressed in a muddy field, but I joined in the mob and had my shower and washed my hair. Each shower had from six to seven standing around ducking in and out like ducks drinking and the wind came blowing through the tent at about five miles per. All in all, it's quite an adventure, why don't you try it some time.

"My health is pretty good. My cold is over. My GIs was only a threat and I'm still waiting to get to go home soon.

"Pappy, I'm glad you are taking care of my bank account for me. It sure helps. I should have a little cabbage laid away by now, but still, it won't be enough once I start to get the things I want when I get out. The news is still encouraging, but not so spectacular.

"Well, Ezzie, I'd like to do some sketches for you but due to my lack of ability in that line, I'm afraid I can't. You know we've only got one artist in the Turner family. So now, you've gone to burning Doug up, eh? What did he do, put a bottle of beer in the ice box? Ha. Ha. You say that the Fifth division is going to the States? Boy, I can't understand our censorship method. They give more details over the radio and in the papers back home. Somethings I try to write which sound of less importance don't go through. Unfortunately, as it is, I'm not in the Fifth Division. Thanks for the note, Doug, also for seeing that there will be beer in the ice box for me when I get home. Ha.

"No thanks, Lois, for offering me any additional clothes because the winter is just about over and if it weren't, the army takes good care of its men. I doubt very much if I'll be home for the blessed event, but I sure would like to be. Glad Hazel and Mrs. Mumford wrote you and thanked you also.

"Eunice, can Johnny still wiggle his shoulder blades? If things get too bad when I get home, I may be his manager and put him on exhibition. Ha. Ha. Either that or offer anybody a hundred dollars who can eat as much as he can.

"Well, Margie, I suppose by now you've got plenty things on your mind and using most of your time telling that executive officer of yours to brace up. If he gets nervous and jittery, tell him you're the one that is going to have the baby, not him. I bet he has kittens while you're having the baby. Ha. Ha. It still seems strange to me that my youngest sister is going to be a mama. Not seeing you two married and being away from home so long. No matter how strange it seems, I'll still be mighty proud to have another one around like David and John. I hope you are feeling well and don't worry about Worry Looey. He may not have kittens. He may just materialize one of those farts!"

"I hope I've answered all your questions and in the meantime be very careful and see that Pappy doesn't smoke too much and drink too much when the baby is born, while he's celebrating. I'm only kidding Pappy; I know what a good Pappy I've got. All my love, Elwood."

2 March 1945: Typewritten letter from somewhere in Germany: "I managed to get ahold of another typewriter for the occasion. I've been going to church the last three times. The first two were only singing and discussions and last night the Chaplain of the division came down to give the services. All last month, Capt. Kantrowitz and I have been quite busy every day, Sundays included. Today I cleaned one of the fellow's teeth. Our meals are pretty good of late. I guess we ate up all the C-rations that were on hand. The last few mornings we've had oranges and this morning we have shredded meat for breakfast. I'm in need of another haircut and I believe I'll have another brush cut." (**NOTE:** C-rations were a U.S. military ration with canned wet foods. They were served when fresh or packaged unprepared food was not available.)

"Pappy, I'd like to have you meet me in New York and I hope it's soon. But I believe it will be quite a job because once we do get home, I don't know where we'll go from New York. When the time comes, then we'll see what we can do. Boy, it sounds good to talk about going home, but we still have a long way to go yet. The news is real good today, hope it keeps up that way.

"No, Ezzie, I don't believe we or anybody else can change the Germans. I was talking with some Belgians one night and soon discovered that they had German sympathizers. I learned an awful lot that night, even though I got so mad I could have killed them on the spot. I kept quiet and let them talk. It's only my opinion, but I believe there will be another war with Germany. Maybe not in twenty years, but perhaps in forty or fifty. However, the big three (U.S., England, and Russia) have a very stern set up and I hope it works.

"I thought I told you all that I was in the Third Army, but evidently not. Sorry. We have three overseas stripes to be worn on our left sleeve. Also, I believe I told you that we officially have three campaign stars to be worn on our ETO ribbon." (**NOTE:** ETO is European Theater of Operations. Military members received a "stripe" for their left sleeves for every six months in a war zone area.)

"I'm sending home a German rifle for a souvenir. I'm trying to get ahold of a good camera and if possible, a good guitar. One of the fellows picked up an electric guitar last week, a good one. I was playing it last night. So, your old man still eats cake. I hope he gets his new truck okay.

"Sorry I haven't got any requests right now. I'm afraid I've been asking for too much already. With X-mas and my birthday being so close together, it must have been a lot for you all. Notice that southern drawl.

"My cigarette supply is very good. I'm getting seven packs a week now and I still have plenty left that I got from home. I've got to find my wooden box to carry them in, so I won't smash them. I believe I have three cartons on hand now. I hope I didn't deprive any of you of your cigarettes. I believe that winds up everything for now. Be good and be careful. All my love, Elwood."

4 March 1945: 4th ID CP was located in Prum, Rhineland, Germany

6 March 1945: 4th ID CP was located in Schwirzheim, Rhineland, Germany

7 March 1945: Short handwritten two-page note from somewhere in Germany: "I've been writing since six o'clock this evening and I still have Margie to write to.

"Eunice, you've been quite busy these days with helping serve suppers, etc. Those steaks you told me about sound very good. I remember those steaks I had at your house when I was home on furlough. They sure were good. Yes, Eunice we're attached to a division and the division thinks a hell of a lot of our outfit. We have our own chaplain, but he's Catholic. His assistant is Protestant, and he holds services for the Protestants when the division chaplain can't come. We call this fellow deacon. I'd rather hear the deacon than I would some of the chaplains I've heard. Our division chaplain is good. I like to hear him.

"Yes, Bonnie is still writing almost regularly. Hazel still writes, but not as often as she did. We had a little misunderstanding. First time she's been mad since I've known her. She isn't actually mad, either. Oh, I almost forgot. I hope you have a happy birthday and many more to come. Sorry I can't send you a card. I'll send my love, how's that? All my love, Elwood."

9 March 1945: "Famous Fourth" Infantry Division, Friday, "From Famous Men to the "Famous Fourth": This is a typewritten letter given to the men of the 4th ID with seven different personal messages from Commanding Generals who led the 4th ID in battle. Dad included this letter in his letter written on 2 May 1945, included below. They include:

1. Maj. Gen. M.S. Eddy to Brig. Gen. Harold W. Blakeley: on transferring from the XII Corps.

2. Maj. Gen. J. Lawton Collins, VII Corp Commander, at the close of the Cherbourg Campaign.

3. General Collins after the St. Lo breakthrough: "the ability of the division to take every objective assigned to it is a remarkable achievement"

4. Lt Gen L.T. Gero, then Major General, commanding the V Corps after the division bruised its way through the Siegfried line in September.

5. General Gerow in November: "After almost continuous contact with the enemy from D-day until 23 August, the 4th ID came under the command of this Corps at the time of the attack on Paris.

6. General Collins after the Huertgen Forest Campaign: "The drive of the 4th across its sector of the Huertgen Forest required a continues display of these qualities (topnotch leadership and the highest order of individual courage)."

7. Lt. Gen George S. Patton, Jr, Command General 3rd Army in a letter to Maj. Gen Raymond O. Barton: "Your fight in the Huertgen Forest was an epic of stark infantry combat; but in my opinion, your most recent fight—from the 16th to the 26th of December—when, with a tired division, you halted the left shoulder of the German thrust into the American lines and saved the city of Luxembourg, and the supply establishments and road nets in the vicinity, is the most outstanding accomplishment of yourself and your division."

13 March 1945: 4th ID CP was located in Gerbeviller, Moselle, France on rest. (NOTE: My good friend, Mark Moe, and I visited Gerbeviller in March 2025. We met 93-year-old, Edmund, who was 13 at the time dad was in his village. Edmund still had vivid memories of the Americans. We also met the town mayor, Noel Marquis, who was very helpful and kind. Please see pictures at end of this chapter.)

16 March 1945: Long typed letter from somewhere in France: (**NOTE:** At first, I thought Dad must have done a typo because I didn't think his unit was back in France, but based on the 4th ID CP location, he was in Gerbeviller, France. Also, his letter ended with: "P.S. I just found out that I could tell you that I am now in the Seventh Army. I've got an idea why we're here, but I can't relate it to you. Sorry.")

"As you can see, I'm in France now. I can't tell you why or exactly where this time, maybe in my next letter. I already have some French lady doing my laundry and I'm getting some sewing done while I'm here. My French is still fair, but nothing extra. It seems that I can understand very good but when it comes to talking it, it is more difficult.

"I met an American last night that came over to France in thirty-two and he married a French woman. He has been a prisoner for twenty-two months and is now working for the Army. He hasn't forgotten English yet, only a few words. His wife gave me two eggs which I had for my breakfast.

"While I was in Germany, I had my hair cut off again. In fact, almost shaved off. Capt. Kantrowitz said that he'd give me permission to wear my wool knit cap all the time. Guess he doesn't like the looks of it. It does make you look rather crude at first, but after you get used to it, it isn't so bad. I've got sunburnt on the way down here and my face is chapped a little. Ever since we've been here the sun has been wonderful. Hope it doesn't change. I'll take some more pictures.

"I must tell you about the first tooth I've pulled. Well yesterday we had a patient who had a bad tooth. (**NOTE:** Dad refers to a periodontitis condition which is the reason he had to pull the tooth). Anyway, it was loose and only had the tip of the root attached to the bone. He wanted me to see if I was doing it right, etc. I've seen him pull so many teeth that it's easy to know how to go about it. I did okay, at least I got it out. Oh yes, without any pain. Of course, that's because he had a shot before. I guess that's all the news I have for you.

"Ezzie, it's infantry, not armor, what you're thinking of. I don't know where that fellow's outfit is, but I'll be on the lookout for it.

"Pappy, I hope by now you have bought a new suit and topcoat and shoes for Easter, but I'm afraid that by the time you get this letter that Easter will be very close or passed by. You'll want to be all decked out when you go see Margie. I hope the war will be over soon so I can get back and see how good you look. Let the girls help you pick out the clothes, okay?

"Eunice, tell Johnny that there will probably be plenty Jeeps for sale after the war. I don't know exactly what they will do with all the equipment, but I imagine they will save a lot here and in England. It would be nice if Johnny could get ahold of one.

"I've just had chow and lately we've been getting good chow. Tonight, we're starting our baseball teams again and I'm going out to practice."

20 March 1945: 4th ID CP was located in Batzendorf, Bas-Rhin, France

20 March 1945: Handwritten letter from Mr. Mumford to Eunice written on "The Animal Infirmary and Dispensary, Sturminster Newton, Dorset letterhead: "Elwood wrote to me last week and told me your sister, Mrs. Graham, was expecting her first baby in May. Would you very kindly send her on this little dress I bought for her today. As you will see, it's not a pure silk as that is a thing of the past in the British Isles, but this rayon is the best we can buy, but it washes very well. I would very much have liked to send her several more, but our coupons will not see to it.

"As I am not quite sure of her address, I thought you would not mind sending it on for me. Another of Elwood's friends is back here in the hospital with leg wounds. I have tried to get over to see him, but it's too far as transport here is very bad. However, I was able to ring him up on the phone and when he is well enough to walk, he will spend a few days with us. Several boys have been over here for ten day's leave, so I am hoping to see Elwood walk in one day.

"My little girl is away at boarding school, but she comes next Monday for a whole month for the Easter term. We are all looking forward to seeing her again. Our house seems very empty without little children and Michael gets very lonely since Mary went away. I hope you are having lovely weather like us, the spring flowers are lovely. Our garden is a picture. We all send our very best wishes to you all and an extra special wish that your sister has a lovely baby. Very Sincerely, Winfred Mumford."

22 March 1945: Long typed letter from somewhere in France: "Last night we played ball and we're going to play again tonight. The weather has been wonderful with the sun shining, etc. I have been living in a tent, and I like it being outdoors all the time. (**NOTE:** Edmund told us that the Americans stayed in tents south of Gerbeviller and there was a storm which flooded the tents. His dad found some identity cards left over from the storm.) My face is sunburned but is still sore. We're getting good chow. Also got two cans of good American beer yesterday. Capt. Kantrowitz sold me a quart of liquor so last night we had a party in our tent. Three other fellows in our tent got packages and one of our lieutenants gave a friend of mine and myself a quart of wine. Now to get to answering your letters.

"Thank you, Pappy, for getting the money to Esda to get Hazel a birthday present. According to your letter, you think she's pretty good., eh? I don't know about getting married to her because I haven't got anything to offer her. I may yet before it's over with, although I've never mentioned it to her. I know I wouldn't make a mistake if I did marry her. I may never get a chance to go back to England while I'm in the Army. Still haven't had a pass to Paris.

"Ezzie, your Easter card was very pretty, and the package was wonderful. Notice I'm using the stationary. I like the walnuts and the peanut butter candy. Of course, the cookies were very good. They are all gone already. My cold is over, but I always welcome Kleenex. Saves a lot of washing. I was thinking the other day how nice it would be to be back home to watch all the old Easter bonnets walk by. You ought to see mine. I've got four big red crosses painted on it, one on each side and one in front and one in back. Also, a number on top. It's a little heavier than yours, but it never seems to go out of style. You haven't seen me yet with my helmet painted up like a X-mas tree, have you?

"I went to church yesterday in our large tent. In your letter of the eighth, you mentioned the division that I'm in. I'm sending in Pappy's letter an **Ivy Leaf** talking about our feats and accomplishments. It's a damn good record. When you get through reading it, I wish you'd send it to Pet Sis and Worry Looey.

"Eunice, I can't believe that David has grown so much. He looks like a man on a mountain. Excuse me a minute. The kitchen is giving out malted milk now. I'll get fat if I drink much of that malted milk. We have some chocolate flavor and some strawberry flavor. Real rich and good. Lois can probably tell you the division I'm in. Little John has quit playing the piano, hasn't he? I think he'll regret it when he gets older. There has been a lot of times in my life that I'd give anything to be able to play well. Keep after him and maybe he'll pick it up again.

"Margie, so you weigh 135 pounds now, and Pappy wants the baby to be named Judy. I like that name too. I suppose worry Looey is still wondering why you've gained weight, and you stick out in the front. When I get back, I'll explain the facts of life to you and why pregnant women stick out in the front. Ha. Ha. Glad that you have all the baby clothes and things you need. I'll be on the lookout for something for the baby if I get a pass one of these days.

"Bonnie still writes, but I can't see any future in it. Does that answer your question? I like the pipe very much, in fact, everything was swell. I've got beaucoup cigarettes now. Thanks for the Camels. I've changed by brand to Camels and Lucky now. Hope you're not hurting for cigarettes now. You've sent me so many." (**NOTE:** Sure, do wish Dad never smoked. When he died in 1971, he smoked Marlboros. The doctor came into that ICU waiting room and asked my brother Bob and me, "Are you Elwood Turner's sons?" When Bob and I said yes, the doctor continued: "Do you smoke?" We answered, "No!" and the doctor said, "Good, don't start" and walked out of the room. Dad would die a few hours later. None of his kids ever smoked.) Tell Jimmy he'll have to eat more Wheaties if he expects to wring my neck. Hope he doesn't have to go overseas for your sake.

"Take good care of yourselves because I expect to be seeing you again soon. This damn war can't last too long now. Watch your diet, Pappy. Oh yes, will you save this *Ivy Leaf* that I'm sending for me. I'll want to keep it. If any of you haven't read Ernie Pile's book entitled "*Brave Men*", read it the first chance you got. It'll give you a clear picture of what war is like. All my love, Your overseas kid."

26 March 1945: 4th ID CP was located in Mussbach, Wurttemberg, Germany

30 March 1945: 4th ID CP was located in two locations: First, Heppenheim, Hessen, Germany and second Beerfelden, Hessen Germany

31 March 1945: Type written long letter from somewhere in Germany. (**NOTE:** This letter was postmarked 4 April which means Dad had to wait five days to mail it. His unit was on the move from France back into Germany. It took Dad two days to find the typewriter he used to type this letter): "As you can see, I'm in Germany again. We just had a few days' rest, but to me it wasn't much of a rest as far as my work went. We had quite a few patients to take care of. As we progress into Germany, the more civilians we encounter and of course we can't talk with them unless it's on business. Some of the kids smile at you and want to be around and we have to chase them away. It's hard not to smile back to some of them, but still it's a funny feeling to have them all around you.

"German soldiers, Italian, Polish are saluting every truck that passes by trying to surrender. Some walk right up to our soldiers and salute and wait for us to turn them over to the MP's (Military police). They're all around us now. Looks very much like we'll be meeting up with the Russians soon.

"Now I'm sweating out the Army of occupation. I think I'd rather go to the Pacific. Maybe then I'd get thirty days home before going there. If they ask for volunteers, I may go just to get home for a few days. I'm still in the Third Army. In fact, I was never in the Seventh, only attached. The news is really good these past few days. That offensive the Germans made last December was what I think shortens the war. (**NOTE:** Dad was 1,000 percent correct. The Battle of the Bulge was Hitler's last chance to win the war).

"It's quite nice to get letters from all my old lady friends. They are such nice letters. Wish I could save them to show you. Good old Bing Crosby is on the radio now, Ezzie. I could listen to him all day long. Still can't see what all these young girls see in the voice. None of the GI's seem to like him. When we get back, he'll probably take off. (**NOTE:** Dad was right again. Bing was a big star until his death on October 14, 1977.) I'm sorry to hear about Howard Coster, I didn't know he had been killed.

"Doug ought to be getting a pretty good bonus this year. At least enough to fill the ice box with beer. Ha. Ha. I don't believe I can tell you the date I sailed to England. I'll tell you when I get home, okay?

"I hope you made out ok at the dentist. I'd much rather have a shot for a filling. We don't give a shot for a filling in the Army, but Capt. Kantrowitz says he always used to give a shot for fillings when he was in practice. Hazel will be happy you sent her a birthday card. She always mentions my family in her letters and asks me how everybody is.

"Eunice, everyone mentioned that I'd probably be across the Rhine, but so far, I can't mention it, either way. It has been raining the last three days, but the sun is shining today. It's still chilly but we don't have any stoves in our tent. We've got them, but don't actually need them.

"How is my pet sis and the potential one. I had a V-mail from you too. It must be nice to be close enough to home to be able to talk to Pappy now and then. Remember the time you and I called them from Tenn? Everyone that I write to that I've talked about you, keeps asking about you. You must be pretty big by now.

"Tomorrow is April, in fact Easter Sunday we'll probably have some kind of services out here in the field. I too think it would be nice if the war was over with Germany before your baby is born. and it may be. I haven't got any remarks about the Worry Looey this time. I'll give him a rest. He eats it. Hope he's getting along okay with his work. Thank him for the monthly Readers Digest he sent me. I'll buy you a drink when I get home Worry Looey. All my love, your overseas kid."

1 April 1945: 4th ID CP was located in Walldurn, Baden, Germany

1 April 1945: From Dr. Boice's history: "As always, some irresponsible GI lit a cigarette, and the match flame flickered in the wind. Immediately shouts went forth, "Put out that damned cigarette." It was too late; the planes thundered down, strafing the road and lighting up the area with blue light. After a short while, the rumbling motors were gone and the column quickly moved down the road again. Each man knew the planes had only gone for a re-supply of ammunition and bombs, to return laden with their destructive missiles.

"Farther down the road, the column passed the area occupied by the 44th Field Artillery Battalion, and the planes were again heard. At once the 377th Antiaircraft Bn., protecting the field artillery, opened fire, and quick flashes of "ack-ack" burst in the sky. The column continued to move in spite of the aircraft and several hours later arrived in the prearranged assembly area. During the day the Regiment had moved over fifty miles through very hilly terrain and over poor secondary roads. (**NOTE:** This wholly corroborates Dad's last letter and him having to wait five days to mail it. His unit was supporting advancing units thru Germany at a very fast rate. Fifty miles in one day is amazing. The term "ack-ack" refers to anti-aircraft artillery or gunfire. It originated during WW II by British armed forces. The term is an abbreviation of "acknowledge", used in the phonetic alphabet of the time to signify the letters "AA". It is also used informally to refer to the repeated firing of guns at aircraft.)

2 April 1945: 4th ID CP was located in Tauberbischofsheim, Baden, Germany **NOTE:** This is a beautiful little town. I bet the Commander hated to leave it!

3 April 1945: 4th ID CP was located in Kircheim, Bavaria, Germany

3 April 1945: Handwritten, multi-colored (pink and blue) letter from "Somewhere in Germany": "Happy Birthday, My Dear Hazel Heather: I haven't had any mail for quite some time which I believe is due to the fact we're moving so fast. I found these two pencils here in the brewery where we are staying at the present time. We have plenty of beer here. I don't like the taste of this beer very good. So, I haven't indulged very much yet. I'm across the Rhine River this time and you should see all the liberated and the Germany prisoners going back. Men from all the different countries that were captured by the Krauts. Some of them even have their women with them. Your birthday is coming soon, isn't it? Hope you received that package I had Esda send on time. Also, that you have a very HAPPY BIRTHDAY!! Give my love to all and be a good two timer. Love and a Birthday Kiss."

4 April 1945: Handwritten (in pencil) letter from somewhere in Germany: "Dear Esda, Lois, Eunice, Marjorie, and their attachments. We've been moving so fast our mail still hasn't got up to us. I'm across the

Rhine now and at the present time living in a brewery. We have all the beer we want here, but I don't like the taste of it very well. I've seen Russians, Czecks, Italians, French, Belgiques, Pollocks who have been German prisoners and now are liberated. There are masses of them, also of German soldiers and they are all over.

"Yesterday, I sent a package to Pappy with two German canteens which I thought the kids would like to have. Also, a German Officer's hat for Pappy and part of a parachute that the girls could make little hankies out of, or something. That little brass button I threw in is off a Luxembourg uniform. The other medal is Kraut. There are two Third Army insignias for the kids too, unless Pappy wants them. I forgot how much silk there is to a parachute, but I just happened to think that it would be nice if one of you girls would make a dress or suit for Marjorie's baby, for me. Do you think it could be done? Please try.

"I hope you had a Happy Easter. I didn't get a chance to go to church myself because I was on the road most of the day and when we did bivouac, I went to bed about 7:30 that night. I thought about you all. (**NOTE:** Easter was the most important holiday for the Turner family. He is Risen. We took a picture by a beautiful hibiscus plant in our yard every year.)

"I took pictures when I crossed the Rhine, but we were moving and my camera isn't very good. Hope they come out. I enclosed a picture in Pappy's letter that was taken while I was in Alsace. I look like a Chinaman in it. The scene is our office in a tent. I only have the one copy and no negative. Hope you can read this okay! My love, Elwood. P.S. Received your letter of the 21st. Hazel and I are still writing each other. She's heard about Bonnie. I think I told her about Bonnie the first night I met her. I believe she's jealous of Bonnie, at least she used to be."

12 April 1945: Somewhere in Germany, "thinking of you": "I had a letter from a Roberta Miller. She's still teaching at Ontario High. She seemed quite anxious that I write to her. I wrote to her that time that her fiancée got killed in an airplane crash and she didn't answer that, not that I expected her to.

"About five days ago, another fellow and I were loading a few barrels of beer on our truck as we were moving, and we wanted to take some along. The time we were living in a brewery and there was a lot of it there. Well anyway, the other fellow dropped his side, and the barrel fell on my left foot. I'm still walking, but my toes are a little sore yet. I limped around for three days with a cane but kept on working.

"Today is Hazel's birthday, I think. I wrote to her this morning after breakfast. I don't know if she got the package yet, but hope she did. If I'm not mistaken, she's only eighteen today. Last year at her birthday she told me she was eighteen, but when her mother put the candles on her cake, I only counted seventeen!!! (**NOTE:** WOW. Our Mom was tricking our dad into thinking she was 18 a year prior! Dad was right. Hazel was 17 in 1944 and 18 in 1945!)

"I'm very happy that you're going to get a new suit, etc., Pappy. So, you think If I find a girl like mother, I'll be lucky. It's going to be hard finding one that good, but I'll try. The news still sounds good to me. I don't think it can last much longer here or in Japan. Of course, you never want to underestimate the enemy. It looks to me as if they have plenty yet, but one thing they are short of is gasoline.

"FLASH! The Ninth Army is only seventy miles from Berlin. It just came over the radio. I still think the Americans will get to Berlin before the Russians do. When we were back in Luxembourg around X-mas time, I said that they would then. I've got a chromium plated sword that I'll be sending home when I find a few more things to send with it. We can't touch a thing that belongs to the civilians, but if it belonged to the German Army, it automatically becomes the property of the US. Then, if the trophy value is greater than the military value, we can take this and that. I'm still looking for a good German camera.

"Well, folks, pretty soon we'll have an addition to our family. How do you feel, Margie? I hope you're coming through with flying colors.

According to Esda's letters of the past, she thinks she's the one that's going to have the baby. Ha. Ha. No kidding Esda, I laughed so hard when I read your letters. Maybe you are going to have a baby according to your letters. I think you'd better go to the doctor. Ha. Ha. Is Doug like Worry Looey? Or doesn't Doug go to the movies? Don't eat any beans before you go to see the baby, Jimmy, you wouldn't want to gas the poor thing. You and Johnny almost gassed me one night. Be good everybody – I'll write sooner next time. I should get some mail today. All my love, Elwood."

13 April 1945: 4th ID CP was located in Rottingen, Wurttemberg, Germany

15 April 1945: 4th ID CP was located in Creglingen, Wurttemberg, Germany

16 April 1945: A two-page typed letter on onion skin somewhere in Germany: "Thinking of You! Captain Kantrowitz and I have been busy all day today. We're living in tents, and our office is in a tent. The days are beautiful, but the nights are cold. I have four blankets and my sleeping bag, and it still doesn't seem like enough sometimes. There's plenty deer and rabbits around here and there are bullets flying all over. The other day another fellow and I took a ride in a German car that our outfit captured and while we were riding along, I saw a huge rabbit in the field. I grabbed his gun and threw off my helmet because it has red crosses on it. I took a couple of shots. So far, I haven't got one.

"Ezzie, I'm sorry if I write things to make you feel sick and to make you worry. I don't mean to, but sometimes I get in moods and I usually write what I feel. I often wonder how you're feeling about having Margie's baby. Ha. Ha.

"We've been having good meals lately, in fact the only time we get poor meals is usually when we're moving on a long trip or if it's hard to keep up our supplies. We've been having fresh eggs every morning for a week now and I see we got some more today. You and Lois both wrote about how you wish I could have some of the things you're having and sometimes I do wish I could have some of those things, but all in all, we have everything in the way of meals. I read something in the Stars and Stripes about getting ice cream soon. I'm very pleased that you got a raise, you certainly deserved one. You need that to give you encouragement for the next year.

"Lois, I'd like to ask you for a favor and this is it. Could you get me some sunglasses that I can wear on my regular glasses. I want you to get the money from Pappy and he can take it from my money. I hope you can get me a fairly decent pair.

"So, your old man is going to paint your house. When they named him Jack, they named him right. He's a jack of all trades. The day you, Pappy, and Esda went to Lake Avenue Church, I crossed the Rhine. Come to think of it, I think it was about church time. Too bad you couldn't get everything you wanted for Easter, but I don't imagine it changed the spirit of Easter in the least. I didn't get a chance to go to church on Easter this year. Maybe next year.

"I'm so glad you had such a wonderful birthday, Eunice. I hate to think of all of us getting older. I had my hair cut off two months ago and it just won't grow. I've only had one hair cut since and then it was only a trim. I hope the kids don't grow up too much before I get home. Ha. I wish I was home to take him to the zoo and fill him up with candy and ice cream.

"It would be wonderful if I could walk in to see you at the hospital, Margie, but don't count on it. I'll be thinking of you and hope you don't have any trouble. Glad you are still feeling good and that you have the car there at your convenience. Glad Ezzie will be down there with you, too. You'd better watch her though; she thinks she's the one that's going to have the baby. Ha. Ha. What do you think about Esda getting dizzy and everything?? Has Worry Looey got any dizzy spells yet? The only way he'd get dizzy is to have one too many. Or else set in a movie too long. Ha. Ha. He eats it.

"It's getting dark now, Pappy, so I must finish fast. I'll bet you look good in your new suit. I think you got it pretty reasonable, especially now with the prices the way they are. I had a couple of letters from Hazel the other day, but they were very old. I think she's still writing me, at least she said she'd never stop writing unless I told her too. Did any of your women ever tell you that? I still remember those stories you used to tell me about your horse and buggy days. Take good care of yourself, Pappy, and don't work too hard. Be careful of your meals. I'll be seeing you soon. All my love, Your overseas kid."

18 April 1945: 4th ID CP was located in Rothenburg, Bavaria, Germany: (**NOTE:** Janice and I visited Rothenburg many times with family while stationed in Germany. I only wish Dad and I talked more about his experiences. Rothenburg is a beautiful city.)

20 April 1945: 4th ID CP was located in Wettringen, Bavaria, Germany

20 April 1945: Long typewritten letter from "Somewhere thinking of you": "It's only been a few days since I've written but all my back mail is coming in now and I have a stack of it. First of all, I'm very glad that everyone had such a nice Easter and especially that Pappy had such a good time. The news sounds good, Pappy, but still a lot of ground to cover.

"I took a bath this morning and shaved, so I feel good. My hair looks like it might grow in again, although it's still quite short. The only other news is only a few minutes old and that is that a German woman just came up to a bunch of us and lifted up her dress to show that she had been stripped of her under clothes. I think she said two colored fellows had raped her and she went away crying. There have been quite a few hangings of negros for rape since we've been over here. Quite a few of the English women have married the negros in England and some of the French too.

"The picture and the Easter Sunday program were very pretty, Esda. I hope you had a good vacation. I read in the **Stars and Stripes** that Ernie Pyle got killed. Have you been reading the good write ups President Roosevelt has been getting? He sure was a good man and at this time I hate to see him go. I don't have too much confidence in Truman. He didn't have much of a background.

"Lois, I can't understand why you people got my March 16th letter before you got my March 2nd letter. It wasn't held up here unless we were on a long move at that time. It sure was a relief to get your mail from home after such a long time. The three stars are for landing on Normandy, Northern France section, and Germany around Aachen and I think it takes in the Siegfried Line. After you've read the **Ivy Leaf** I sent home, you can tell the areas we've been fighting in, although there has been several more. Those were citations.

"President Roosevelt died on David's birthday didn't he, Eunice. It's chow time now so I'll finish later. We had pretty good chow. That was nice of Mrs. Mumford to send Marjorie that baby dress. She said she was going to try to find something but that it was hard to get anything because of the Points. I think I told you she was going to send me a full-blooded German Sheppard dog when I get home and there is shipping space.

"Margie, so Jimmy met your doctor and got things mapped out as to taking you to the hospital. I'm afraid they'll have to operate on him for a baby while you're in the hospital. Ha. Ha. Between him and Esda, I get a laugh. By the time you get this you may be getting ready to go to the hospital. I sure hope you will be okay and that it won't be too hard for you. I don't like to see babies when they are first born. By the time I get home, it'll be in the cute stage. Sorry that you didn't' get a chance to drive Jimmy's car down. What would have been fun for you. This is Johnny's busy season now, anyway, isn't it. Be good. All my love, Elwood."

21 April 1945: 4th ID CP was located in Maria Kappel, Bavaria, Germany

22 April 1945: 4th ID CP was located in Jagstzell, Bavaria, Germany

23 April 1945: 4th ID CP was located in Huttlingen, Wurttemberg, Germany

24 April 1945: 4th ID CP was located in Ober Kochen, Wurttemberg, Germany

25 April 1945: 4th ID CP was located in Heidengeim, Wurttemberg, Germany .

26 April 1945: 4th ID CP was located in Aisingen, Bavaria, Germany

27 April 1945: 4th ID CP was located in Horgau, Bavaria, Germany

28 April 1945: 4th ID CP was located in Gross Aitingen, Bavaria, Germany

29 April 1945: 4th ID CP was located in Egling, Bavaria, Germany

30 April 1945: 4th ID CP was located in Ober Pfaffenhofen, Bavaria, Germany

2 May 1945: Long typewritten letter with a "Famous Fourth" Infantry Division Newsletter enclosed, somewhere in Germany "Thinking of You": "First of all I must tell you that this is a German typewriter and a hell of a one at that! Everything is different, so please excuse the mistakes! I'm sorry that I've waited so long to write but it couldn't be helped! It seems that we move all the time! (**NOTE:** Please note all the different locations of the 4th ID CP, above. Eleven different locations in only ten days! They are now in Bavaria.)

"As you probably know, Hitler and Mussolini are dead! So far, the American government hasn't confirmed Hitler's death, but if it isn't true, they'll soon get him. Things are pretty well washed up for the krauts now… so many things have happened since I last wrote that it's hard to start! It's hard to believe some of the things the German SS Troops have done to these people in Europe. The prisoners that pass by are so happy that they cry when we give them stuff! There was one today that was in a concentration camp for five years. He saw his own kid torn apart by the SS men and thrown in a grave, then he said 'that's German culture for you.'

"You hear story after story like that, yet they are true. Still the German women got the nerve to ask the American soldier to protect their houses from the Russian prisoners because they are afraid that they will steal their things. We liberated forty Russians awhile back and captured several prisoners! Before we could move into the house, we took out three kraut officers! The Russians there went out in the woods and trailed kraut soldiers then came back to get some of our boys to pick them up. While the Russians were dancing and singing for us, our boys and the Russians brought in two SS men who were trying to get across the river to reorganize them in the next town. The Russians just beat the shit out of them before they brought them in, now I wish that we let them shoot them as they wanted to do.

"We have one of those Russian fellows as our steady KP. We are trying to teach him English. He used to be in the cavalry. Oh yes, while I think of it, I'm in the 7th Army officially.

"I'm glad you like Hazel's letters, Pappy, and I enjoyed the way you wrote about them in your letter. It's been snowing here the last couple of days, guess it's because we are at such a high altitude. I may send a little money home as soon as we get paid. We should have been paid yesterday, but still haven't got it.

"Esda, I'm glad to hear that you are going to buy a house and I hope everything turns out okay with going down to see Margie and trying to settle at the same time! At least you will have enough room to store some beer for Doug!

"Lois, I'm sorry to hear that you had that mouth infection. It was probably Vincent's Infection! Tell Jack that so far, I haven't been able to send a German rifle home. They put a stop to it for some reason. I'm not in base hospital, I'm in an "ack-ack" outfit so you're all wrong in your predictions! In fact, if you people would look at the top of the *Ivy Leaf*, it's written right there. I don't know? Thank you so much for the pipe and the tobacco, Lois. I wish I could give you people some of the smokes I've got now. We're getting our rations regularly now!

"Eunice, we are going to have steak for chow tonight. Not bad, eh? If you get a chance to get David something that he wants, get it and have Pappy give you the money to buy it with for me.

"Your French is good, Margie. I'd write you in French, but I'm not allowed to. It would have to go to the base censor, comprit? So, you thought for a while that you were going to have twins. Maybe you'll have quintuplets then maybe everybody will be satisfied. Ha. Please excuse these short paragraphs. I'm tired. I'll write again as soon as possible. All my love, Elwood. (**NOTE:** Dad had included a "Famous 4th" Letter, dated 9 March 1945.)

3 May 1945: 4 Page handwritten proposal letter to Mom: "My lovely little limey, Hello again, my dear. After reading your four wonderful letters that I received this afternoon, I felt in the mood to write you again. Hope you don't mind. I love you for writing such sweet letters, me Duck. And I'm sure that we're straight on things again. I won't tease you anymore about your other boyfriends. Ha. Ha. I had a letter from Bonnie today and she says that she's going to stay in California after the war. She must like it there better than Rochester. I read Esda's letter and I'll send it back with this one. I had two letters from her today and she said that they aren't going to buy that house because it would mean selling their war bonds and that would be too unpatriotic. Guess they're going to wait and build a new house.

"I hope your mother's right in her fortune telling too. The kisses and all. Her letter was very sweet. Thank her for me and tell her that the whiskey will be better now that it's aged some. I see your dad has been keeping the Cider barrels empty. That's not hard to do I'll bet. I'm so glad you liked my two-tone letter. (**NOTE:** Dad refers to his letter dated 3 April 1945, see above.) You haven't mentioned getting my birthday package to you. Hope you get it soon. That dream you had about us going to London sounded good. That would be fun. Hope it comes true. That's cute about you not taking milk in your tea. I can well imagine how you do get kidded about it. I'm glad you know what's in store for you when I get to see you again and that you accept my challenge. You're sweet and I love you. I'll bet you're awful pretty, all tanned up. Remember when we went swimming? We really did have some nice months together.

"Yes, my dear, you do have a wonderful mother, and she has a wonderful daughter. In fact, I'm thinking very seriously of her daughter as my wife and have been for a long time. There are several things to confront her, and one is, if she does say "yes" will she want to live in America so far away from her wonderful mother. Another, the man that's asking her isn't rich. All I have is close to a thousand dollars. (**NOTE:** In 2024 currency, that is worth $17,434 which is more than I had when I got married!)

"My father is highly in favor of such a marriage and my sisters, too. That's what I want. I'm not sure as yet what job I'll take after the war. My old job is supposed to be waiting for me, but I'm going to try to get a better one. It's quite a procedure getting married in the Army, but it can be done. Your transportation to America will be free, paid by the U.S. Government. You'll have to wait your turn to get a ride on a boat and I can't tell you when I'll be home.

"If in your answer you say yes, I will tell you how it will be done and what you'll have to do. This is the first time I've ever proposed. Hope it doesn't sound too bad. Give my love to all, I love you, Elwood. **P.S. Will you marry me???"**

6 May 1945: 4TH ID CP was located in Amberg, Bavaria, Germany

7 May 1945: Long typewritten letter from somewhere thinking of you. Again, this letter wasn't mailed till almost a week after Dad wrote it, so he was on the move. Dad was still in Germany: "Today the war is supposed to be over with Germany. (**NOTE:** The Germans officially surrendered on 8 May 1945.) I'm not especially overjoyed because all week long I thought it was over. It is one consolation to know that we don't have to sweat out any German planes or shells. That's about the only noticeable change over here. Of course, now it's worse than in combat because of all the inspections and what not. I guess we start standing reveille and retreat tomorrow.

"So far, I don't know just what we'll be doing now that the war is over. It's possible that we go to the Pacific or stay here and occupy for a while. If we do go to the Pacific, we'll have to sweat out occupations over there. So, I think I'd rather stay here if I have to do either one and I'm quite sure it'll be one or the other.

"So far, we haven't heard about furlough of any kind, although if we stay here, I imagine we will have them. I doubt if there will be very many discharges before Japan is finished, so don't raise your hopes up of me being home right away until after Japan is licked. It's best that way, then you don't get disappointed so easily.

"There's some talk of some point system which states that one must have eighty points before getting home. If that's the system they are going to use to discharge the men, then I still have some to go. I only have sixty-two. One point every month in service, two points for every month overseas, and three points for every month in combat. I've had thirty-one months in service, twenty months over seas and eleven months in combat. All medals are also points such as the Purple Heart, which is five points. Well, that's the way it stands at the present time. I'll let you know if anything else comes up.

"Well Pappy, if things turn out right for me, I'll be getting married soon. So far all I've done is ask her and I have no ideas as to what the outcome will be. I haven't got any kind of a ring to give her unless I steal one off of the Germans, which I'll probably do if I get the chance. (**NOTE:** Dad raised his kids to not steal and cheat, but since he was in a wartime environment, it is clear that influenced him. He did not steal a ring, in the long run.)

"It's going to be quite a long ordeal, but it can be done. Of course, I don't know if I'll ever get a furlough to England either, so everything looks very hazy now. I've got close to fifty dollars in my pocket now and we get paid tomorrow for last month. I probably surprised the daylights out of her, but I'm sure that she's the right one. However, I don't know if she will be willing to leave her mother to go to America to live… and besides that it will be quite hard for her to get papers and with the boat ride and all she may not want to do all that. She'll have to wait her turn to get a ride on the boat too. Nothing is definite as yet, so don't broadcast it until, I'm sure. Okay? (**NOTE:** Dad had sent his proposal letter to Hazel two days prior.)

"Sorry Esda, that the house deal fell through, maybe it's a good thing. It'd be better to build your own house as Doug said. Also, you're being very patriotic. I've seen the Alps, Essie, and they are very picturesque. I didn't have any film at the time so didn't get any pictures of my own, but I'm going to get some from the other fellows. They still have a lot of snow on them. Yes, I've seen the Danube and crossed it a few times. It's just another river to me. In the Army, everything is about the same.

"Lois, I've interrupted my letter long enough to go to church. It was very good, and I really felt like singing. We have a wonderful Chaplin. He told us that we were in two army occupations. One being the Army occupation for God and one the occupation of Germany. So, for a while I'll stay here in Germany. That's official.

"Eunice, I think that was awful nice of David to wish for me when he ate his piece of birthday cake. It's going to be good to see those kids again. The more I think about the war being over, the happier I feel. I hope it isn't too long before I get home for good. It seems like ages since I've seen you all.

"Pet sis, by the time you get this, you will be well on your way. At least in the hospital. I'm glad that this war is over before your baby is born. Hope my letter cheers you up some. Your family letter was interesting, and I'm pleased that you've been feeling so well all along. Don't worry about Jimmy leaving, maybe now he won't have to leave. Thanks for your letter, Worry Looey. You eat it. Stick it out and maybe you'll get a break. Say hello to the baby for me, Margie. Hope it likes its silk dress. It's time again to say farewell. Until we meet again, be good. All my love, Your overseas Kid."

13 May 1945: Typewritten letter from somewhere in Germany "Thinking of You.": "It's a terrible hot day here today. Especially with the clothes we have to wear. We have to wear our OD's and are not allowed to take off our shirts. Today being Sunday, Capt. Kantrowitz and I are taking off now that the war is over here. We've had a hell of a lot of work all of a sudden, just like it was in England. I expect we will be busy for quite some time now. This morning, I took a good bath and changed clothes right after breakfast. I was all cleaned up by eight o'clock. I feel like I need another bath right now." (**NOTE:** Dad was in a bigger town since the 4th ID HQ was in Amberg on 6 May and in Ansbach on 14 May 45. Both cities are beautiful. My guess is they had taken over a city hall/bath/or large facility.)

"So far, I haven't had an answer from Hazel but now I'm afraid that I won't have time because according to the paper, most of the troops over here are going back to the States or to the Pacific. They're going to leave four hundred thousand over here, so I figure I'll be going to the Pacific within a year's time. I'll have to be awful lucky to get discharged within a year.

"First of all, I need 85 points and I only have 72 now. That's with the other campaign star we got for the battle of Luxembourg City. (The bulge in the Ardennes sector last Christmas). There was some talk of getting another for east of the Rhine or southern Germany, but so far nothing has come on it. If we do get the fifth star, then I'll get a silver star to wear on my ETO ribbon. Now if I had a couple of kids, I would have a good chance of getting out soon.

"If I do go to the Pacific, I hope they give me thirty-or-forty-five days home first. At least it would be something to look forward to. I filled out the form asking if we wanted to get to school while waiting shipment and I may be going to school soon. I don't know. I signed up for business, English, Psychology, and American forcing trade course of some kind. I personally don't think I'll have much time to go to school though.

"Well, Eunice, now I have five letters from you to answer. You're really on the ball. I really enjoyed your letter from John. So, David slugged Johnny on the head. You'd better watch your temper, David. I hope I get home soon so we can have that celebration. You're really going the limit, hiring a band and a hall. Don't forget the whiskey and beer. Maybe you can get ahold of an army truck after the war, although I wouldn't recommend any of these trucks that have any battle experience. They really drive the trucks around here. I'm glad you agree with me about Margie's baby not looking like worry Looey. Ha. Ha. He eats it.

"Marjorie, I hope it isn't as hot where you are as it is here, although I imagine it is. Especially now that you are uncomfortable. Too bad this war hadn't ended a few months before, then maybe I could be there with you. I think I'll blame Jimmy for not waiting. Ha. Ha. Poor Jimmy I'm always making cracks at him. He's probably worn out two pairs of shoes by now and at least one rug. Every time I think of Jimmy, I think of a movie where the guy is pacing the floor.

"Hazel says she is anxiously waiting your letter, Marjorie. I almost forgot that I got your Easter package the other day. Thank you so much. I enjoy those Fanny Farmers and that wonderful peanut butter so very much. I'm glad to get the dog tag chains too. Now I must finish up this letter and write to Hazel.

"I hope to be seeing you soon. At least hope to get home before next Christmas. I hope, I hope, I hope. Your overseas kid."

14 May 1945: The 4th ID CP was located in Ansbach, Germany

14 May-26 June 1945: The 4th ID CP was located in the vicinity of Bamberg

19 May 1945: Typewritten letter from somewhere in Germany Thinking of You (Hilpoltstein): "My dear family, Here I am again pounding a typewriter. The only time I type is when I write home and at the end of each month when I make out my monthly report. That's why I make so many mistakes. Well, tomorrow Marjorie will have her baby, and Jimmy will be all worn out from walking the floor.

"Esda, I'll send your copy to your house because Marjorie will have one too. Maybe Doug will want to read it. I imagine you're all excited and happy. Don't forget to send me pictures as soon as you can, Margie.

"Things are about the same here as far as working goes, etc. We are kept rather busy in the dental department, more so in the mornings. I've got my card with the number of points today to sign. And I still have 65, but we're waiting to hear about the fourth campaign star which will give me a grand total of 70. I can now tell you my location which is in the town of Hilpoltstein. It is close to the city of Nuremberg. I'm in the Third Army, the last I heard.

"We're living in a big building and sleeping on cots. It's rather a nice set up, but nothing elaborate. I'm still uncertain about going to the Pacific or staying here or going home. I might be able to tell in another month's time. Our outfit is an old outfit over here and we're pretty well liked. Hope we get a break. We've been spearheading ever since we've been over here. I'm speaking of the 4th Infantry Division. It took you people long enough to find out what division I was in.

"Pappy, I had two V-mails from you the other day, thank you. I've been getting a lot of mail from Hazel, but still no answer. I should get it soon, however. They really celebrated on V-E Day at her house. She'll probably write and tell you all about it. Her mother is saving up a quart of whisky for a celebration when and if I get back to see them. I hope you have a nice trip down to see Marjorie and the baby and that you'll be able to stay awhile.

"Ezzie, I have three letters from you to answer. The assembly program was quite nice, I thought. Hope you made out okay on your raise you asked for. Your letter sounds as if you'll be plenty busy taking care of Margie. I'm glad you'll be able to be with her to help her out. I got a laugh out of the part about the masks and putting the right tag on the baby. Ha. I imagine Doug will have a rest while you're gone. Maybe when you get home, the ice box will be full of beer and whisky. Ha. Ha.

"Had your letter on May 9th, Lois. It seems I have one from everybody I know that was written on V-E Day. Bonnie wrote me a real nice letter too. As you say, it will be a big responsibility coming now when everything is so uncertain, but if it's supposed to be, everything will turn out okay. That's the way I look at things. Hazel will probably give it a lot of thought and her mother will probably help her to decide if it's the right time, etc.

I am glad to hear that you are all feeling better, Eunice. How is little John's wound now? What do the kids think about having another cousin soon. I suppose they don't give it too much thought, being so young."

"Pet Sis, I received your family letter and the paper about the public toilet. That was pretty good. I've passed it around for the other fellows to read. So, you're now a mother. According to your letter, you almost had the baby on V-E Day. Ha. Glad you got so many gifts. All my love, Elwood."

27 May 1945: Typewritten letter now from Schnaittach Germany. (**NOTE:** Schnaittach is 48 kilometers northeast of the last city he was in, Hilpoltstein): "I've been trying to write to you now for the last three days and because I'm always playing ball, I let it go a day or two longer. We're supposed to have every afternoon off for athletics, but Capt. Kantrowitz said that we would work every afternoon until three o'clock because we have quite a bit of work to do.

"The place where we're at, has a wonderful swimming pool like the ones in our city parks back home, and an athletics field. This afternoon we played the officers and beat the pants off of them. When we finished, we went swimming. The water was quite cold, but it was refreshing. I'm going to spend most of my spare time at the pool and see if I can't learn how to dive.

"They're forming an orchestra for dances and shows and I'm going to try out for that sometime soon. I doubt if I will make it, but I like to try because it will be fun. I haven't heard anything about going to school yet, but I will go if I get the chance. Passes are starting for Paris next week and two out of the medics will go. I hope I'll be one of them, but I doubt it. Come pay day, I'll have a hundred dollars which I've been saving up out of the twenty-four I get every month. So, I ought to have a good time on that much.

"Pappy, I have two letters from you. It was good to hear from you again after such a long time. I'm glad you got the box okay and I hope someone can have a dress made for Margie's baby soon. Sorry to hear you have rheumatism and hope it's a thing of the past by now.

"I suppose by now you have another grandchild, although I haven't heard from Jimmy as yet. I have 75 points so far, but that's not enough to get out on. Altogether, I have five battle stars for five campaigns. We got one for Normandy, one for northern France, one for the Rhineland, one for the Ardennes, and one for Central Europe.

"I had my answer from Hazel, and even thought she feels the same way toward me, she's afraid that she will be unhappy so far away from her family. I thought that would be the thing that would decide her to say no even before I asked her. I didn't expect too much. It would have been quite difficult for her, even if she did go through with it, and I wasn't sure if I'd get to go back for a furlough. I still have a good chance to go the Pacific, and I'm expecting it will come about. Maybe I'll be lucky enough to go via the U.S. Nothing is definite yet.

"I suppose by now you two are together and by now my pet sis is a mother. I bet it looks awful red now. Ezzie, did you have a kid too while worrying about Margie? Ha. So far, I haven't got any word as to what it is, you got me guessing. I hope you are in good health now, Margie. I was almost on the borderline of Austria when the war ended officially, but naturally the war was over for us about four days before they announced it. The Germans died a slow death. (**NOTE:** The war with Germany officially ended on 8 May 1945).

"Lois, I received your cablegram yesterday and I figure by now you have heard from me talking about V-E Day, so I won't cable you back. I wish you would send me the glasses, even though I don' know when I'll be going any place, okay?

"I haven't much space left on this page, but I'm going to write very soon, maybe again tomorrow, Eunice. Hope David likes school okay. I got some glass in my eye last week when my glasses broke but it's out now and healing nicely. Some guy accidently hit me in the eye with a bullet which he threw and misjudged his throw. It hurt for a while but it's all over now and I didn't get a Purple Heart for it, darn it. Five points.

"I'll write and tell you more about Germany the next time I write. I'm enclosing a paper in Pappy's letter which you all will be interested in seeing. I'm all tired out from playing and swimming so I've got to sign off for tonight and get some needed sleep. Be good and be careful. Take good care of yourselves and Jimmy don't make the kid start working until it gets of age. All my love, Elwood."

30 May 1945: Typewritten letter from Schnaittach, Germany: "In my last letter, I promised to write again very soon, so here I am right on the job. Although I haven't much to say, I'll try to make it long enough and as interesting as possible. I've had a letter from Esda and Lois since I last wrote, and it seems that you haven't been getting my mail regularly. I can't imagine what the hold-up was, but I'm pretty sure I'll be getting a letter soon saying that you've heard from me recently.

"I'll explain further about the cablegram, Lois, in case you didn't understand. By the time I get the cablegram, I'm pretty sure that you received my letter which was written on V-E Day. At least I hope you did. No, Lois, I wasn't on any of those boats that you thought I might have been on, as you already know. That dream you had sounded okay, especially the coming home part. How much I wish I could get to go home soon, but it looks a long way off yet. Right now, I don't give a damn if I've got any money in the bank. I just want to get home.

Ezzie, Pet sis, and Worry Looey, I received your letter and I'm glad to hear that you were able to get down there before the baby was born, Ezzie. I still haven't had word as to how you're getting along, Margie. I wish I'd get word today. Hope you are okay and of course the baby. Don't forget the pictures you're going to send of you and the baby.

"Quite a few of the fellows in our outfit are getting gray hair. Ha. I wish I could walk in on you right now for a little chat. I've almost forgot what everybody looks like, it's been so long since I've seen you. The day will come. So, Ezzie got bombed by a sparrow, another one of Hitler's V weapons I suppose.

"Pappy and Eunice, I am on Charge of Quarters today and tonight so I'll get a chance to get caught up on my correspondence – I hope. I'm writing this on my noon hour and hope to finish before one o'clock because I have to go to work at one. We are busy as hell these days, but as I said before, we do get off at three in the afternoon for athletics and swimming.

"This afternoon, I must get a haircut and I think after that I'm going to play ball. Maybe I'll go swimming after I finish playing ball. Now that we are out of combat, our rations are very poor, but I guess you people are really having it tough back home according to the paper. They cut our rations 10 percent since the war has been over, and I mean that 10 percent is a hell of a lot when a guy is hungry. Sometimes I think I'll join up for the Pacific just to get something to eat. All we get are six rations now and I never seem to get filled up. But still, we are living, and I'd much rather see it go to the combat men than to have it for myself.

"It is a shame we have to give up our rations for such people. You can't trust any of these people, no matter if they are French or Germans or what they are. Another thing I don't like is the fact that these sons of bitches that we fought against, men who have killed a lot of Americans and made it miserable for those that did live through it, are getting discharged from the German Army to work on farms and run around the streets as free or freer than they used to be when Hitler was in power. That, of course, is explained by the fact that Germany must feed her own people to take the strain off of the American and British. One way to look at it, it's okay and the other way, I think we are all a bunch of fish. Let me tell you something, the American soldier is more restricted than German civilians or ex-soldiers.

"Well, the time has come for me to go to work, and I have no other alternative but to sign off. Don't pay any attention to my personal bitching, because it will all pass over. Sometime if I'm in the right mood, I'll write a letter without so many bitches. Be good and be careful, All my love, Elwood."

5 June 1945: Typewritten letter from Schnaittach, Germany: "I'm on charge of quarters tonight and as long as I have time to write I'm going to take advantage of it. It hasn't been too long ago that I wrote to Pappy and Margie in which I enclosed a booklet about the Fourth. (**NOTE:** I donated this 4th ID booklet to the museum in Bastogne in my dad's memory).

"I received two packages from you, Esda, and thank you very much. The rum candy was very good, and I needed those washcloths very much. I sent some more junk home as you will notice when you get it, Pappy. Just a little something I picked up on my travels. Most of the fellows found good cameras, but I wasn't so lucky.

"There is one thing in the package that I do want and that is that piece of cloth with the Fourth Division written on it, and I had to pay for that. I didn't do the packages up very neat because I didn't have very good wrapping paper. I'm glad the kids liked the canteens, Eunice, and hope they can use them.

"Captain Kantrowitz is on a three-day pass to Paris. He will be gone for a week or so because of the distance in traveling. I may get a pass to England for those who have wives and those who are going to get married. After all those fellows get furloughs, maybe they'll get around to the rest of us. That's liable to be in 1946 or 1947. Its's hard to tell.

"So, you see why my morale is so high. I never thought I'd be a prisoner, but that's the way it's turned out. I guess you know what I mean. I'd better shut up or I'll be writing another letter like the last one. I'm cleaning teeth this week and doing any emergency work such as treating gums and sensitive teeth. I don't work in the afternoons so that I can play ball and go swimming. We play ball about five afternoons a week, and I usually go in the pool at least six times a week. I'm starting to get a tan now. I need a bathing suit. Will you please send me one if you can buy one.

"Don't worry about my coming home and think that you ought to wait and see if I will or not. Send the damn thing because I want one and I'll no doubt be here five years after I get it. Compris????

"I'm sending a money order home which is valued at fifty dollars. Maybe in this letter if I can get it before I post it. I wanted to send a hundred, but after I got paid, I only had about ninety-some-odd dollars. So, I kept some in case I got a pass when I'm not expecting to in which case, I'll want some cash on hand. I've got fifty bucks on me now to play cards with or save up for a pass. If I don't get a pass by the end of this month, I'm liable to send some more home. Money isn't worth anything over here, in fact, I've seen guys wipe their ass with it, they've had so much.

"I have two letters from Eunice and one from Lois that I've received in the last few days and it beats me why I haven't been getting my mail. I haven't heard from Margie yet. I don't know how she is and that bothers me. I wrote a letter to Hazel today and sent her a copy of that booklet I sent you. She'll send it on to you Pappy after she reads it. She said in her letter that she was thinking about you, Margie, and hopes that you'll be alright too. I wish I'd hear from you pretty soon. Jimmie, take damn good care of my Pet Sis. You eat it.

"I suppose you all think that I'm crying my heart out because Hazel wanted to marry me and couldn't, but you're all mistaken. My letters are unusual because I feel like a trapped animal. After eleven months of combat and then they try to make toy soldiers out of us, and we can't even get a pass. That's why I'm so bitter. Be good and all my love, Elwood."

6 June 1945: Typewritten letter from Schnaittach, Germany: "Here I am again but this time I will try to do a little better. It's five minutes after seven and it looks like another one of those lonely nights. (**NOTE:** Dad was clearly homesick and was sorry for the tone of his last few letters expressing his disdain for an occupation Army.)

"This morning, we didn't have to stand reveille because it's a holiday as far as I know anyway. Pretty soon I'll have been on the continent for a year. The years go by so fast when you get older. I feel like an old man tonight because I've played ball this afternoon and it tired me out. I had a good cold shower after which helped some. I believe I've lost a little weight since I left England, although I haven't had a chance to weigh myself. I'm getting a nice tan from swimming and playing ball. My hair is awful thin on the top and I have a few gray hairs, which I can't help, so all in all you may not recognize me when I get home. I hope they get me out of this place (Germany) before I lose all of my hair.

"Our chow seems to be getting better, although we have C-rations and corn beef and hash all the time. Last Sunday we had chicken and ice cream for the first time since January, and boy was it good. I managed to get six helpings and started for sevenths, but I got a headache and had to quit. Yesterday we had ice cream again and they didn't make so much this time, so I only had seconds.

"We had a big parade the other afternoon in which I marched but didn't receive any medals. There were twenty-six men out of our battalion that go Bronze Stars and one fellow got a Soldier's Medal for Valor. He cleared a mine field for the litter bearers and amputated one fellow's leg on the same mission. The Bronze Stars were for meritorious service. None of the medics got a medal. I'll tell you something about those Bronze Stars one of these days. How some men got them. I should think some would be ashamed to wear it whereas some actually deserved them. Still, they count five points. The campaign stars are very small and are worn on the ETO ribbon. In fact, one can hardly see them at a distance.

"My dear Pet Sis. Oh, how I wish I know how you are. I can understand why you can't write me, but Esda told me how you were doing at the time. Heavens' sake, I hope they didn't have to operate on you. From your letter I think it'll be a big boy.

"Esda, I imagine Doug is having himself a time back there with all those old maid schoolteachers and the ice box full of beer. He'll probably want you to take a vacation this summer and leave him there all alone now that he knows what it is like to have beer in the ice box. Ha. Ha.

"Pappy and Lois, I'm enclosing a fifty-dollar money order in this letter to be put in the bank, unless someone needs it. Would some of you send me some homemade cookies and Fanny Farmers. Just something to eat. Be good and be careful everybody. All my love, Elwood."

11 June 1945: Typewritten letter from Schnaittach, Germany: "My dear family, nephews, and niece!! I sure was glad to hear from you about Margie and the baby. Your post card and the little card you sent was the first I got talking about the baby being born, etc. (The ones you sent, Esda). I was feeling down in the dumps that day and it sure pepped me up to hear about Judy Anne. Glad you didn't have too much trouble, Margie. Bet you are proud too, Jimmy, even though it wasn't a boy as you wished it to be. You've got to be a good man to get a boy, so they tell me.

"Anyway, I'm awful glad it's over and that you are both well. I can just see how pleased you all are, and I bet Pappy stuck his chest out another three of four inches. Bet you're pleased like you were when I was born. Ha. I know you love me, so it isn't egotism.

"Well, the latest is that the Third and Seventh Armies are going to be Army of Occupation troops. I fall under that category. Also, the points might be lowered some. I mean the critical score, and if I'm the least bit lucky, they may drop it down to seventy-five. And that will include me. There are several things to consider, one of which is the fact that all medics are essential, so if they do drop it down, I'm still the goat. I guess the baby won't be red yet by the time I get home, in fact it'll probably be going to school pretty soon, I'll be a three-year man.

"What do the kids think about having a new niece, Eunice? And how are they getting along in school? Bet they forgot what I look like by now. I'm pleased that you had a chance to fix up mother's grave. Wouldn't mother be proud of her nephews and niece now if she were living?

"Lois, say hello to Mr. Langworthy for me. Hope he's well. So, I have 750 dollars in the bank and with the fifty I sent home, that will make $800. Still isn't much, is it? Glad to hear that you finally got another letter from me.

"Ezzie, did Doug leave any empty beer bottles laying around the house? I feel sorry for him if he did. So, you don't think much of the south either. It's true of anyone from the north. I think. Glad you took such good care of Margie, bet you hated to leave her. Was Dougie glad to see you come home? Bet he was.

"I wish the hell I was home with you, Pappy. I'm getting fed up with this damn war and these Kraut headed bastards. I didn't seem to mind it so much in combat, but it sure is boresome now. Capt. Kantrowitz came back from Paris today and he had a real good time. He met a gal that he was with when we were there when we liberated Paris, which made it a lot nicer. I guess they treat you royally if they know you were one of the first ones in Paris. I hope I can run into one of my mademoiselles when I get to go. I had so many different ones that I probably won't remember any of them.

"Margie, now don't let Jimmy put the baby to work too soon. Ha. Ha. Please take good care of yourself and don't work too hard for a while. And don't tell Judy anything too bad about me. Hope she doesn't cry when she first sees me. I imagine she did when she first looked at Jimmy. Well, I believe that's all for tonight and I hope to hear more from you. My mail has been coming in rather slow and far apart. All my love and kisses, Uncle Elwood!"

19 June 1945: Typewritten letter from Schnaittach, Germany: "I haven't had any mail in so long that I forgot what a letter looks like. I'm quite sure you are still writing but they just don't have the ships to bring our mail to us. The Pacific has priority now, naturally, and because of that we are slowly forgotten.

"I'm glad I got that letter about Judy Anne being born in regular time. I wonder how you and the baby are making out now, Margie. I hope you're out of the hospital by now. Let me know as soon as she says Uncle Elwood. Ha. Ha.

"Life here is comparatively easy, not such long working hours as before the war. Capt. Kantrowitz and I work every day from nine in the morning to two or three in the afternoon, with an hour for lunch. Of course, we have Saturday afternoons and Sunday off like we did in England. That's because I run the dental section.

"I still play ball three or four afternoons a week. The swimming pool is being cleaned this week, but I think by Sunday we will be able to go in again. We have track meets, outdoor basketball court, volleyball court, weightlifting, etc. We have a battalion theater and movies three times a week. I just came back from seeing a movie entitled, *"Practically Yours"* Claudette Cobert and Fred MacMurray. Pretty good.

"We have ice cream once a week for dessert. Our meals aren't any better, but I guess we're getting used to getting less now. We have to buy our cigarettes ration now, like in England. Seven packs a week and five candy bars plus our shaving articles, etc. As I say, life is easy, but it still isn't any good because I can't be near home and you people. So, no matter how much they give us and what they do for us, I'll never like being here and I'll still bitch as much as ever. I think you can understand what I mean.

"Still, I'm thankful I'm not in the Pacific. But don't forget, I still haven't got enough points to get out and even though I expect to be home by this coming winter, I've got a good chance to go to the Pacific after I get a furlough. In the meantime, pray that the critical score will be dropped to seventy-five points. If it isn't, I'm almost sure of going to the Pacific.

I lost my fifty dollars in a crap game trying to make a couple hundred, but it didn't surprise me any. (**NOTE:** In today's money, $50 is worth $873.72). I have no need for money right now, so what's the difference. I don't owe any money out of my next month's pay, so I'm getting along alright in that respect.

"I think I'd better write Boyce's wife and Hazel tonight and Mrs. Mumford. I haven't heard from Hazel for quite some time, which I believe is due to the fact of shipping too. I haven't written anybody for a week because I didn't get any mail all last week. Of course, I had to write to you.

"I wish I knew how you all are. I hope none of you are ill and that you're not working too hard. If everything goes well, I may be seeing you sometime this year. I hope. I have two maps that I'll be sending home as soon as I can get them wrapped. They show in detail just where we fought and gives some details. I think it's an enlargement of the one in that little pamphlet. It's something I want to keep.

"Pappy, now be careful and don't work too hard. Remember, watch your health and eat properly. What do you think of your new niece? Hope you liked your trip down to see Margie. All my love and take care of yourselves. Your overseas kid…"

24 June 1945: Typewritten letter from Schnaittach, Germany: "I'm getting caught up on my letter writing today while I'm on charge of quarters. Today is Sunday, supposedly my day off, but besides my regular job, I have to pull charge of quarters.

"Today, being Sunday, we had ice cream for dessert, and we had chicken which wasn't too bad. I've got a half a case of beer handy and a guitar that I borrowed so I guess I'll be happy for the day. I wanted to go swimming this afternoon, but I can't find anyone to take my place for a while. Everybody is either sleeping or out somewhere for a walk. I played ball last night and hit my first home run this year. I was up five times and got a hit every time. We had to go out for track too, and I did better than I thought. I could do hundred-yard dash in 11 seconds; running broad jump, 16 and a half feet; and standing broad jump, eight feet. Pretty good for an old man. I'm getting a good tan too.

"Pappy, I had another letter from Hazel, and she loves me too much to say no, so now she says I will. I'm getting the papers made out but can't tell just exactly when it'll take place. I haven't got her a ring. I'm broke but I will get twenty-four dollars this coming pay day. I haven't any idea how much money it will take so I'll see if I can't borrow some and then write home for what I need. It hadn't ought to cost too much just to get married, had it?

"The fellows that are going to get married to their English gals have already left on furlough and some more are going soon. If I can get my license soon, I'll probably get to go sometime next month. I guess Hazel wrote to Esda telling her about her saying no to my request and she wants me to explain it to you. Ha. I'll give you further details as they progress. Me thinks you'll think a hell of a lot of her as a daughter in law.

"Ezzie, I don't believe they will lower the score any lower than 80 myself which means I'll miss it by five points. Guess we'll soon find out. I may get to stay as Army of Occupation, but there's still that remote possibility that I might go to the Pacific. I never count my chickens before they hatch. If I could only get five more points, a Bronze Star or another campaign star. They're trying to get one for England because we fired on enemy aircraft while we were there. It looks kind of doubtful though.

"Lois, Hazel is pretty young, but she is very sensible and sincere. You'll find out when you meet her. I'm glad you were trying to get the sunglasses for me. I sure do need them, and I don't care what they cost. I can't imagine you having to pay 52 cents for a head of cabbage. Prices really are high, aren't they?

"So, David is shy just like his uncle used to be, Eunice. I'll bet he says his piece about me when I get home. Glad John Jr. does so well. I saw a little fellow about Johnny's size last night and he reminded me of him.

"How is my pet sis and her baby? Eunice wrote and said that you were coming along nicely. Sure am glad to hear it. Jimmy hasn't tried to get you to send her out to work yet, has he? I'll be glad to get a letter from you as soon as you are able to type and as soon as you have the time. Does she look like you? How about that dress someone was supposed to make for her, is it done? Did you tell her about Uncle Elwood yet or isn't she old enough to understand? Ha. Ha Boy, I'd like to get to see her soon. Please take good care of yourself and don't work too hard.

"I'm enclosing some pictures and some negatives in Pappy's letter and some in Margie's letter. They aren't very good, but I may as well send them home." All my love, Your overseas Kid."

26 June-2 July 1945: 4th ID CP was in Le Havre, France

2July-10 July 1945: 4th ID CP was aboard the U.S.S. Hermitage headed home to the Port of New York.

3 July 1945: Typewritten letter from Schnaittach, Germany near Nuremburg "Raining": "Right now it's raining, as usual. What terrible weather we've had this past week. No swimming or ball playing, darn it. The swimming pool is the only thing I like about this place. I've taken some pictures of the pool and I'm enclosing them in this letter. Oh, I just thought, I sent them to Hazel and I'm having some more prints made. I'll send the negatives to you as soon as I get them back. (**NOTE:** The pool is Olympic sized and still in use today. I took my own pictures of the pool on two trips to Schnaittach. See pictures at end of chapter.)

"Boyce sent the pictures we took back in England to Hazel and she sent me a copy. I wrote and told her to send you people some or to send you the negatives, okay? I sent a group picture home the other day of the medical detachment, taken in front of our barracks. Also, two maps showing our travels in combat. Pappy don't forget to save them for me, will you? I made the enlargements from Capt. Rheas negatives for each one of the fellows. Please notice the good work. Ha. I've been developing my own negatives, but we haven't got much paper, so that's why I don't make a copy for all of you. Hope you understand.

"Well, Pappy, I finally got two letters from you and was I glad to hear from you. I got a good laugh out of the one. Instead of Jimmie wiggling his ears like a rabbit, he ought to wiggle his toes. Don't you think. Ha. Ha. Pappy I'm going to enclose one of the letters Hazel wrote me because I want to keep it. If you read it, you'll understand why she was confused at first. Don't read it to everybody, just the immediate family. Ha.

"I've sent her the papers to sign and as soon as she sends them back, I'll turn them in for the colonel to sign. I've already signed mine and Capt. Rhea has signed some. It won't take effect until August 25th. Now I'll have to sweat out getting a furlough and, first of all, staying here long enough to go. (**NOTE:** This late August date matches to their wedding day of 1 September. Travel time to England would have taken that long so his furlough must have started around 25 August 1945).

"Today things are really coming out as to our destination. They keep changing it though. First, it's one thing and then they change it again in an hour. The critical score is supposed to come out today. I should know pretty soon just what I'll be doing and just about when I'll be getting discharged. There are so many rumors floating around now, I don't know what to believe. I do think I'll be stationed in France soon, but don't know how long or anything. That's the way the Army is. (**NOTE:** He ended up in Antwerp, Belgium).

"I've received a lot of mail these past few days. It does seem good to hear from you people again. I'm on charge of quarters tomorrow night and I'll have beaucoup time to write you another letter in which I'll be able to answer all of your letters in detail. Today I'll just give you the current events and make it short because it's almost chow time now.

"This morning Capt. Kantrowitz didn't come in and I took care of the emergency cases. We've got a lot of trench mouth now that the war is over, and the fellows get to go out drinking beer out of a common drinking vessel. So far, I've been fortunate in not getting it, but then I take special care of my teeth and mouth, whereas a lot of them don't. I never have kissed a girl with a filthy mouth or bad teeth and never will. That's the way a lot of them get it.

"Well, my dear family, I must go to chow, even though it's nothing to look forward to. Only on Sundays do we get a real good meal. Chicken and ice cream every Sunday. I hope to be seeing you all soon, at least by next year at this time and if everything goes well, I'll be married to a sweet little gal. So far, I don't know what I'll do for a job, if I'll go back to Kodak, or something else. Well, I'll have to wait and see how things turn out. All my love, Elwood."

4 July 1945: Typewritten letter from Schnaittach, Germany: "My dear family, I told you yesterday that I would write again today, so here I am right on the job. Today is a holiday for most of us here except me, because I'm on charge of quarters. But then there isn't much of anything to do even if I did have the time off. Jack Benny is at Nuremburg in a stage show today and I'd like to go, but I imagine it will be awful crowded and beside that it's raining again today which is according to schedule.

"A bunch of the old timers in our outfit are leaving this afternoon and are scheduled to go to the States for discharges. I've been bidding everybody goodbye and it's hard to do after living with them for three years, especially during combat. Two fellows from the medics are going home and two are being transferred to category one outfits. Outfits that are going to be deployed. My first sergeant is one of them going home. He has 99 points. Damn nice guy.

"I'll remain with the outfit for a while, so far as I know. If they take another count in October, I'll have eighty-five points. I don't believe they will lower the critical score from 85 but I think they will count up the points every so often. I think it's the fairest way. Hope it works out that way. We officially have five campaign stars now and my score is 75 at the present time. October will be five more months overseas time at two points a month. I will have ten more points. Compris??

"Esda, I think you've been misunderstanding my letters or seeing too many movies. I won't have a chest full of decorations as you're thinking I will. All I have is an ETO ribbon with five tiny bronze stars on it and a good conduct ribbon. They don't look like much, but it took a lot of sweating to get each of the stars. Most of the fellows with a log of decorations are the Air Corps men, but the Infantry men are the men you want to look up to. The ones with the Combat Infantry Badge on and the infantry medics with the Combat Medic's Badge on. They are the boys that did the job. Don't take me wrong about the Air Corps men, they did a good job but anyone of them will tell you that the infantry boys are the real heroes. I never did think they talked the infantry boys up enough.

"My job isn't the kind of a job where one can make a lot of decorations, and I've thanked the Lord night after night that I had the job I did have. I'd rather be alive than to be a dead hero. I can explain it better when I see you. Bet you're glad that school is over. Did I tell you that I finally got the cablegram day before yesterday. Sure took a long time.

"That price is okay about the sunglasses, Lois. I'll just have to be extra careful with them. I'm sorry that I've been sending your letters to your home instead of the office. I'll correct the mistake. Glad that you've received my money order okay. I got paid the first of the month and I won five dollars on a ball game the other night so that made me thirty dollars. I let some fellow take it so I wouldn't spend it because I'll need all I can get by the end of August in case I get to go to England and get married. I haven't even got a ring yet and haven't the slightest idea where I'll get one. Oh well, I'll make out some way or other.

"Glad that Johnny's boils are better, Eunice. Yes, I can get glasses quite easily here. I bust a pair every month or so. I think that's awful nice of you to make Judy's dress for me. I'm quite honored that David and John haven't forgotten me and that they mention me in their prayers. I am surprised that little John will be in the sixth-grade next year. Boy, the time does fly.

"Was I glad to hear from you, Pet Sis. It's been such a long time that I didn't hear. I'm glad that you too are satisfied in my marrying Hazel and even though she is very young. I'm sure she'll accustom herself to being an American. I'm glad to hear that you're getting stronger, and that Judy is growing so nicely. Please be awful careful and take things gradual. All my love, Elwood." (**NOTE:** This is Dad's last letter in Germany, and it would be 13 days before he writes another letter).

July 10 1945-13 July 1945: 4th ID CP moves from New York to Camp Butner, North Carolina, U.S.A. The 4th ID was sent there for the demobilization and inactivation of their unit.

Dad's remaining letters from Europe came from the port of Antwerp, Belgium.

17 July 1945: Typed letter from Antwerp, Belgium: "My dear family, first of all, you will notice that my APO number has changed again and that's because I have moved and I'm not in the Third Army anymore. I'm in an AAA group and at the present time am sitting in my office and only about a quarter of a mile away from beaucoup ships sitting in harbor. You'd think with all the ships I can see from my window that there would be ample shipping space for little me, but as far as I know, we'll be here for some time. However, nothing is ever definite. We could be here for a year and yet again we could be here for two weeks, get what I mean?

"It took us three days to get here and I'm telling you it was a damn rough trip in the back end of a 2 ½ ton truck. We crossed the Rhine at Mainz this time, but I was sleeping at the time and didn't get to see it again. Didn't miss too much. On the way to Antwerp, we passed through Brussels. I like Brussels very much from what I saw of it. Oh yes, we also went through Luxembourg city again, but I didn't get a chance to get out to see any of my old friends there.

"Antwerp is also a very pretty city, but it's a rough place being a great seaport. I went into town last Sunday to see the President come in. I didn't have to stand guard of course, because I am a medic, but our battalion was lined up on both sides of the street from seven o'clock in the morning till noon when the President came through. We took a jeep with a litter in case of any of our men falling out because of the heat and I rode along with the jeep. We parked right on a corner and had a damn good place to see. He and his party came through about thirty-five miles an hour, so consequently I didn't get a very good look at him. In fact, I'm not sure which car he was in, so actually it was a waste of time in a sense of the word.

"Well after that we drove all over the city trying to get a good look at him and a picture but never could find him, so we ended up going out to dinner. I had steak with two fried eggs and French-fried potatoes and orange pop. Everything you buy in this town is out of the black market so consequently it's very dear. Yet it was well worth the money. I went back to camp which, by the way, was out in tents in the sand and it was so hot there you could hardly stay alive. I took a shower and went out and got a shave and went back up to Antwerp.

"Talking about a shave, for the five or six days we lived out there in tents, I went out to a civilian barber and got a shave because it was so hot. The coolest place in Europe was the barber shop. So now, I'm shaved and then two other fellows and I hop a truck and beat it back to Antwerp. First thing before you get into town is a tunnel about a mile long, it's cool there too, by the way.

"I loaned out all my pay last payday so consequently I had to borrow a little. I loaned it out so I wouldn't spend it and now I'm afraid these beer joints, dances, movies, stores, etc. have given me the urge to go out and let loose a little. It's been a hell of a long time that I've had such an opportunity as you can imagine, so until I get tired of going out, I will be on the go day and night.

"You can buy ice cream, sodas, well just anything you know just like back home before the war. There's only one catch in the whole set up, it costs like hell. I could spend a hundred bucks a month just on ice cream alone, the way I love the stuff. The trouble is, the damn ice cream isn't any good but still it's something I haven't done for a long time and boy I'm telling you; I've gone hog wild.

"Practically all the people here in town can speak English, which is a good thing because I can't speak Flemish. That's what they speak here. It is a cross between English, German, and French. Mostly German. Just like in Holland. The last week I was in Germany I got to know a pretty fraulein in one of the cafes where I used to go quite often to get a beer and play billiards. I used to play her guitar and sing for her, and I snowed her under. Well, she taught me Dutch, and I got to where I could speak it almost as good as I can French. You know, just enough to get by on.

"I had a laundry lady there too that I had to talk Dutch to so it came in handy. I interpreted a lot of times for my friends and for some of the civilians that came to the dispensary for medical treatment. I told you that Capt. Kantrowitz and I worked on the SS prisoners of war there in Schnaittach, didn't I? I'll tell you the details of that some other time.

"When I left Schnaittach, I left at one o'clock in the morning and we had already packed up in the afternoon, so I spent my last evening down at the café drinking beer and dancing with my fraulein. Well, she kept crying practically all the night while I was there because I was going, and she wanted to know if I would come back to marry her and if I would write to her. When I told her I couldn't, she really started to cry. She was a darn nice gal, even though she was Dutch. I called her my prisoner.

"I haven't written in such a long time that I'd better keep going and make up for the last time, okay. Actually, why I didn't write a carbon copy last time was because it was so darn hot and living in the desert, the conditions weren't too good. Hope you will understand.

"You are probably wondering how I managed to go out and drink beer in Germany. Well, it wasn't too difficult to sneak in a beer joint and if any officers came, they warned me, and I hid until they left. We only have a few officers that would actually make any trouble about it, so I didn't worry too much. I suppose you've read that they have lifted the non-fraternization policy, and I believe it's because we left. The people of Schnaittach really treated us decent while we were there. The little kids would walk down the street with us all the time and I used to go to church there in one of the churches (**NOTE:** I went to all churches in Schnaittach since I knew Dad would go to church) and there would always be little kids sitting in the back. Of course, the services were for the soldiers, but we let them come in if they wanted to. Did I tell you that I used to lead the singing on Wednesday nights when we had Bible class? Well, I did.

"Now to get back to Antwerp on last Sunday while I was on pass. I'm sorry I got off the subject, but I thought I'd tell you about Else, my fraulein. Well, the only thing to do on a pass on a Sunday is to go out and drink beer, so that's what we did. We got two quarts of cognac and a few beers under our belts in a matter of three or four hours and then went out to supper. I had the same thing for supper that I had for dinner because it was so good. We walked around town window shopping and ended up in one of those sidewalk cafes where your table is right out on the sidewalk where you can watch the crowd, etc. Drank some more beer and went to another place and ate again. All together for the day, it costs me around six dollars just to eat. Then we hit the road for home.

"Now we have moved from our sandy home to a large building with I think is an ex-school house. In this building where I sleep and have my dental office, there is a swimming pool, two large shower rooms, a theatre, gym, and dance hall. There is also an American Red Cross that serves hot coffee and doughnuts. It has game rooms, lounges, libraries, etc. In another large building right close by, they have a large beer hall where they sell beer and Coco Cola.

"It is without a doubt the best set up we have ever had in the Army. Dance two nights a week and movies three nights a week. **(NOTE:** During Mark and my visit to Antwerp in March 2025, we found the building dad was housed in! It fits his description perfectly. It is now a cultural center and is being refurbished to celebrate its 100th anniversary! Please see pictures at end of the chapter.)

"It's getting so dark that I can't see. We haven't any electric light bulbs here as yet, and it's already ten minutes after ten. Although I haven't answered any of your letters that I've received these last two weeks, I think I'd better sign off for the night and mail this the first thing in the morning because you will be anxious to hear from me. So, I will write again in the next day or so and answer all your letters then, Okay?

"Please be very careful and good. Lots of love to you all, Your overseas Kid.

"P.S. Dear John Jr. Even though I'm late with my wishes for your past birthday, I want you to know, I was thinking of you, and I hope you had a good time. As I told your Aunt Lois, I was on the road both on your birthday and hers, but I was thinking of you. Lots of love, Uncle Elwood."

21 July 1945: Typewritten letter from Antwerp, Belgium: "My dear family, here it is almost seven o'clock and I just finished work for the day. It took me all the afternoon just to bring my battalion roster up to date and to type out some dental appointments. So, I thought to myself while I have the typewriter right here, I'd better write to my family. As I said in my last letter, I'm going to answer your letters of which I have seven, from all.

First of all, I'll start out with Pappy's letter of the 28th of May. I haven't had any mail for about a week now, so actually I'm answering real old letters. Every damn time we change APOs, we don't get any mail for a week or longer. Pappy, your letter is a very old one and I think I've answered it before and didn't throw it away when I finished. I wonder if you have gone down to see Judy Ann and Margie as yet. When my mail catches up with me, I suppose I'll hear all about it.

"I've been asking around town how much it would cost me for a ring for Hazel and all the answers I've got so far are very steep. I've also been window shopping and I've seen a lot of pretty souvenirs. They too are very expensive, but still, I want to get you all a little souvenir sometime before I have to leave. The real good perfume, about the best in the world, costs somewhere around twenty dollars an ounce over here. I guess it's a dram instead of an ounce. Anyway, if I got any, I'd have to get four bottles, which is eighty dollars. So, you see prices are pretty rough here. I'd like to get Hazel some too. Boy I wish I was a millionaire.

"Esda, I have three letters from you dated the 21, 26, and the 28th of June. While I was in Schnaittach, there was an artist there who did paintings in oil for thirty-five bucks and of course I was broke so I didn't get my picture painted. I wanted to get it done to send home as a lot of the other fellows did, but maybe I'll run across another one when I've got the money. He did darn good work.

"No, I didn't get the orchestra because we left before they had try outs for it. So glad you helped Pappy clean up his new room and get him settled again. I too will be glad when I get home, and Pappy and I can have a big place. Because even if I do get married, which I probably will in the near future, I want Pappy to live with me. I haven't mentioned it to Hazel yet, but what I want, she will want.

"I have two letters of the 26th and the 29th of June, Lois. Right now, I'm attached to some port instead of a division or a group. Our outfit, I mean. I don't know the number of the port, as yet. I saw in the Stars and Stripes a picture of the boat with the 4th Infantry Division arriving in New York. I sure would have liked to have been with them. All the old men of the division are either killed or gone home. We lost a lot of men in our division. I don't know just how many, but the number would probably stagger you if you heard.

"Our rations seem to be a lot better here now and I'm thankful for that. According to your letter, you should be on your vacation now and maybe down to see Margie. Hope you are and that you have a good time. I'm a long way from the Seventh Army area now, so I don't think I can look up that fellow. Too bad, eh?

Eunice, I haven't any letter from you now, but when I do hear from you, I'll probably get beaucoup of them. I'm going to the show tonight after I finish this. So far this week, I've seen two shows and tonight makes a third. Sunday I'm supposed to have a date with a gal I met here in town. I don't know yet what we're going to do. Probably go for a walk and take pictures because I don't have any money. Oh dear, what a life when a guy's broke.

"So glad to hear you and Judy are getting along so fast and so well, Margie. I got a V-mail from you, but it wasn't dated. Sorry to hear that Worry Looey had to go to the hospital right after you got out. Things happen that way though, don't they? I figured he'd have a baby or get something out of it. Ha. Ha.

"I've heard rumors around here lately that they might lower the critical score down to 75 points and according to the Stars and Stripes, the score should be out soon. One reason why I think they might lower it to 75, is the fact that men with 75 or more points were asked if they wanted to volunteer for the Pacific or the Army of Occupation, and if you don't have 75 points, they would send you or keep you here at their own will. I didn't volunteer myself. I'm going to sweat it out and hope I get the breaks. I sure hope they do lower it to 75, but even if they do, it'll be sometime before I'd get to go home. There are a lot of men still here with 90 points. See what I mean.

"Well, my dear family, again I have come to the end of the page and I'm just about typed out. It's also time for the show to start. Be good and be careful. I'll write again soon and hope that I hear from you soon. Have you got my money on the way? The more I think of it, the more I think I'll need but I'm going to try to do it with 200 bucks. Boy, I've got a lot of nerve trying to get out of it that cheap, eh? With all my love and kisses, Elwood."

24 July 1945: Typewritten letter from Antwerp, Belgium: My dearest family, "I'm writing this rather late in the evening but I'm going to stick with it until I finish what I have to say. It's already nine thirty and I've just come back from the Red Cross where I had a cup of coffee and a couple of sinkers. I started writing to Hazel about six o'clock and just finished her letter about nine o'clock. I wrote her a twelve-page letter because there is so much to talk about, our plans, etc. Our mail has been traveling around these past few weeks and consequently I got it all at once. Believe me it was all at once.

"Yesterday I got thirty-three letters and today I got two more. And just tonight I got the package with the sunglasses, Lois, they are wonderful. I'm really pleased over them. The only trouble now is that I'm afraid of breaking them, but believe me, I'm going to be extra careful with them. I hope they keep me from squinting all the time because if I'm not careful, I'll have a forehead like a washboard.

Well, I have twenty letters in all from home and I had fifteen from Hazel. She writes almost every day. First of all, I want to tell you people how far our plans have advanced as to our marriage. Hazel has signed the papers, and I have already turned them in to the office. They will be signed the twenty fifth of August and if I'm still here or in England by September, I'll get my furlough then. That is of course if they give furloughs in September. Boy, there are a lot of ifs in my life, aren't they?

"According to her letters, she has already taken over. Ha. She's already told me that I should cut down on my drinking because it cost too much, and I wrote back and promised her I wasn't a drunkard, but I did like my beer and would only drink it moderately. I did promise her that I'd cut down on what I usually drink or quit entirely. She's having a hell of a time getting enough coupons to buy her wedding gown and her bridesmaids are too.

"She mentioned in her letter that she would like to be able to wear Pet Sis's wedding gown because of it being so hard to get a gown. I told her that it's a little late in the game to write to Pet Sis and ask her to do the best she could. She did manage to get Judy Anne a little wool dress and it should be on its way now. She really was worried for a while that she couldn't get it because of the coupons or something. Anyway, I think it was awful sweet of her to do it.

"She said that I'd probably need 50 pounds which is equivalent to 200 dollars for the occasion but I heard of a fellow that just came back from England who got married and he spent about 350 dollars and he got the ring with that too. He also went to London on his honeymoon and that's where we're going on our honeymoon. So, I have a faint idea that I'll need some more cash on the line. Send me two hundred more right away. What I don't spend, I can send back or give to her to keep. Gee, this is an expensive deal, you know it? Ho hum, why wasn't I a rich guy?

"Tomorrow I'm going into town and look around the stores because I have to buy the bridesmaid presents, three in all. I think I have to buy my best man a present, although I don't know who he will be as yet. Young Mary Mumford is going to be the flower girl or something, which will please Mrs. Mumford, I think. I forgot to tell you it's going to be a church wedding. If it's alright with young Jimmie, Hazel's brother, I think he will be the best man, because I can't just walk out in the street and pick one up. She did mention her cousin but he's still in the army and I don't know if he'll be able to make it. I've met him three or four times and he's a real guy.

"She also sent me her ring size and she sounded as if she was hoping I'd send home and get them but, it's too late to do that. Now I've got to go around the black market and see what kind of a deal I can promote. Black market is expensive, but that's the only way you can buy a ring or gold of any kind over here. I'm going to talk with that fellow that has already done this and find out where he got his ring, etc. I suppose I could get it in England, too.

"I don't know anything about getting married. If it wasn't for Hazel and her letters telling me what I had to do, I don't believe I could manage such a deal. Also, in one of her letters, she mentioned how she and Pappy would go shopping together while I was at work. I hadn't mentioned to her about how I wanted Pappy to live with us and she wrote and told me about it. So, it looks like we're going to get along alright, we three.

"As far as I know, I don't know where we will live, but I do want a place sometime or other that is in the outskirts of the city or just outside with ten or twenty acres of land which I thought would be good for

Pappy and I to grow our own grub. There's a depression coming one of these days and you've got to prepare for it ahead of time. (**NOTE:** There was no depression, instead a post-war boom).

"I'll probably have to go back to work at Kodak or where Doug works, which also means I'm going to need a car one of these days. That problem along with the others is going to be tough. Now I wish I hadn't sold my old car. Not that I want it back, but I'll have to manage to get a jalopy of some kind. Maybe Harland can dig me up another one sometime and keep his eye on it for me. Before I had planned to get married, I had pictured in my mind a brand-new car when I got home, but I've got to get settled down before I get too old or I never will be married.

"So, my dear peoples, if any of you find a place like I described just outside of the city with a little land, try to line it up for me and find out prices, etc. Hope you are all well. I'll answer your letters tomorrow because it's terrible late now. All my love, Elwood."

26 July 1945: Typewritten letter from Antwerp, Belgium: "My dear family, this afternoon I didn't have to work and as usual, I'm catching up on my letter writing. I wrote Hazel and Mr. and Mrs. Hatcher right after dinner. I'm going to try to answer your letters this afternoon. Yesterday afternoon, I went up town and priced some diamonds and wedding rings. Well, the first diamond I priced was 30,000 francs or in American dollars, it was 660 dollars. I went in several different places and the cheapest one I could find was around 80 dollars. I would like to go to Amsterdam, Holland and price a few there because it's the diamond center of the world. I'm not too far from Holland from here so I think I will try to go.

"I'm actually lost trying to buy a ring because I don't have any idea as to how much I should pay, however, I think a fair price is in the vicinity between a hundred and two hundred dollars. Wish I could get your opinion before I buy it, but then I'm afraid it'll be too late to wait for an answer from you telling me. I'll ask several of the fellows that have already been married and get some idea from them. I'll let you know more about it later, but right now, I'm sweating out getting the money on time, so I won't have to do everything at the last minute.

"Pappy, I heard today that Japan is talking peace terms to its people over the radio. Hope they decide to give up now. I received a letter from that girl that works at Elko's. She sounds okay to me, even though I'm not looking around for anyone. I'll write and thank her for the letter. Too bad your plans didn't work out to go down to see Margie. Glad you had a good time on the Fourth of July with Ezzie and Doug.

"Hazel won't be able to come to New York the same time as I do. I'll come home on a troop ship. She's going to stay with her mother until I get home and then she is coming over. That will give me time to get things settled before she comes. But eventually, we'll all be together.

"Ezzie, Hazel wrote and said that we'd cable you when I arrive in England and tell you just when we were to be married. Every letter she writes, she says how I wish that your family could be at our wedding. Glad you're taking care of my clothes. Do you know that I've forgotten what clothes I do have and what they look like. The only piece I can remember is my tweed suit. Glad to hear that I have a box on the way, even though we are getting better food here.

"My hair seems to be in pretty good shape so far but as I said it's a little thin on the top. It should grow now that the shells and bullets have quit going over my head, don't you think?

"Lois, again, I want to thank you for the glasses. I wore them yesterday practically all day. So glad you had such a nice birthday and such nice presents. Nothing but the best for the best. I would like to see your home now. It must seem like new, all painted up. Hope Hazel and I can get a fairly decent place too.

"Yes, it will be quite an affair when Judy and Margie and Hazel and I get home, won't it? Pleased that you are all looking forward to our homecoming. You can't be any more anxious than I am. Hope you have a nice time in New England States on your vacation.

"Eunice, I think John Jr. did marvelous in school. I can imagine what a help he is around the farm too. He must be quite the young man now, 11 years old. It hardly seems possible to me, that he's so old. Little David must be quite grown up now, too. When I went to the zoo last Sunday here in Antwerp, I thought of them and wished I had them with me. I gave one of the monkeys a lighted cigarette and you should have seen him batting the air trying to put it out. Ha. He'd put some tobacco in his mouth and spit it out, funniest damn thing you ever saw. (**NOTE:** Years later when dad took his family to Busch Gardens in Tampa, a monkey swooped down from a tree and took his Marlboro's out of his shirt pocket.)

"Glad to hear that you have some pineapple and strawberry jam made up and that you are saving some for me. You'll have to teach Hazel how you make it, okay? I'll be able to tell you better about my experiences when I get home, okay?

"Pet Sis, I sure am glad to hear that you and Judy are getting along so well. I hope they hurry up and send me home so I can see her. I imagine she's over the red stage by now. Boy she sure is growing, isn't she? I'm hoping you and Jimmie get to go home in August for a while. You know how anxious everybody is to see her.

"I enjoyed your family letter very much and thankful that you are getting your strength back so fast and being able to go out once in a while. I'd like to get something for Judy, but so far haven't found anything. I'll keep trying. Worry Looey hasn't sent Judy out to work yet, has he? Ha. He eats it and I'm glad he didn't have it in him to have a boy. Better luck next time Jimmie. How about it Jimmie, don't you eat the right things? (Followed by five long sentences of French)

"Pappy, if you don't understand that, I was just signing off and it's just a lot of words. All my love, Your overseas kid."

1 August 1945: Typewritten letter from Antwerp, Belgium: "Good evening my dear family, I just finished cleaning up my office for the day and before I got settled down somewhere I thought I'd better write to you. I'm in need of a shave, shower, shampoo, and change of clothes, but I think I'll wait until I go to the show, then if I have time, I'll clean up. I'm not in much of a mood to write tonight, but I'll try my best to make it interesting.

"First of all; I've decided to wait until I get home to buy Hazel's rings and to buy a cheap wedding band just to serve the purpose because these over here are too expensive and from the advertisements, I've seen the papers you've sent, Esda, I like the ones I've seen in it.

"Also not being a critic of diamonds, I'm afraid I'll but a lemon and I could get Jack, one of the fellows I graduated with, to get me one at the store where he works and probably at a discount. I hope. I wrote and told her it was the wisest thing to do. She'll probably understand.

"Nothing has come up about my furlough as yet. I'm still sweating it out. I'm going to try to get a plane ride to England when I do get to go, that would give me a little more time. One of the fellows I know out of HQS Battery said he would be my best man because he expects to get a furlough at the same time. He's a nice fellow and comes from Virginia. (**NOTE:** The best man's name was never revealed).

"Yesterday I got paid and now I'm broke again. I borrowed too much last month. I'll have to be careful this month though. I'm not going to cash the money orders when I get them but am going to wait until I get ready to leave. I may have to cash one to get some presents for the bridesmaids and best man. I wish I knew what to get them. Boy, I'm really ignorant when it comes to buying people presents.

"Yes, Pappy, I'll let Hazel handle the money and see if she can't do better than I do. She wouldn't have to do much better to make an improvement, would she? I told you that we wouldn't be able to come home together in my last letter, I think. She's planning on staying with her mother and working until I get home. Or she may have to take the boat when the American embassy tells her to go, and heaven knows when that will be. I hope you have a good time with Judy when she comes home to see you. Should be sometime this month, right?

"Ezzie, thank you so much for the cookies, walnuts, candy, washcloths, and the glasses. I got the package today along with a newspaper. The cookies are marvelous. Everybody likes them. I hope my clothes fit me too, Ezzie, because I'll probably have to wear them for heaven knows how many years. Ha. Did I tell you how good your pictures are, and Capt. Kantrowitz wouldn't believe you were as old as you are. I told him how well you always kept yourself. The artwork in the background is very good. I sent them to Hazel, and she will send them to you. I thought she would like to see them.

"Your airmail letter was very sweet and am pleased you like Hazel and want to help her do things the American way. She'll need a lot of mothering when she gets there because of being away from her mother and I'm sure that with the four of you and Pappy, she'll feel at home. Thanks for the advice, but I imagine that all comes naturally. I'm sorry you people won't be able to be here, but it can't be helped.

"Lois, that's awful considerate of Jack to say you could send his suit and I appreciate it. How I could get along without such a wonderful family, I don't know. I too wish you could stay at home all the time and just take care of your house. You'll have something to look forward to when you do decide to quit, won't you? So, you had a ride in the cart and even drove the pony. You mean the kids let you drive it? Ha. It sure would be fun for me to get back and see them with the pony. I've got a lot to look forward to when I come home, haven't I?

"Next time you write, let me know how Jack is making out with his business, etc. It has been a long time since you've mentioned it. Of course, it's probably due to the fact that everybody was so excited with the coming of little Judy, eh?

"Eunice, I have three wonderful letters from you and I'm glad that the kids still remember me. That was awful cute of David to mention that he wished I were there to take him to the zoo. Tell him I miss taking him and John to the zoo. Sorry to hear that you are getting so much rain there and hope it doesn't spoil too many of your crops. Thanks for telling me that Leon was wounded. She hasn't written me in over a month and I imagine that's the reason.

"I still haven't told her about Hazel and I but will get around to it someday. I've got the feeling she's going to be surprised. What do you think?

"Thank you, my dear Pet Sis, for your two long air mails. Am so glad your little infant is growing so much and that her daddy hasn't sent her out to work as yet. Ha. Ha. She must take after you, Margie, if she is getting prettier every day. I'm glad too that Worry Looey is so contented that it's a girl instead of a boy. Also pleased to hear that Pat is home. I enjoyed the way you can account of your baby and she really must be a sweet little baby. I am anxious to see her picture now after I've had such a full description. Love, Elwood."

6 August 1945: Typewritten letter from Antwerp, Belgium: "My dear family. It's very close to supper time but I'll get this started now and maybe by the time I get finished; I will have time to go to the show. I wrote to Hazel in between our dental patients today because Capt. Kantrowitz takes a smoke, and it gives me a little time in which I'm not doing anything.

"Nothing new has come up about my furlough to England. I'm still sweating it out. I did get your letter, Lois, with the two one-hundred-dollar money orders and I was surprised at the short time it actually took getting here. I think it was eight days in all. I had to have one cashed in order to buy the gifts for the bridesmaids and the wedding band. I'm planning on going to town tomorrow afternoon to get them. Thanks, an awful lot for sending it as soon as you possibly could.

"I've talked with some more fellows that just came back from England that got married and it sounds rather reasonable to me. I guess if

I'm careful it won't cost as much as I thought. However, I'd like to have enough on hand just in case. Also, when I wrote for the additional two hundred, I was planning on buying the diamond here. So, I'll hang onto the rest that I don't spend and probably send it home again.

"I haven't mentioned it to Hazel yet, but I don't think London is too good a place to go on our honeymoon. I think that Brighton or Bournemouth would be a better place. They are two summer resorts and spoken very highly of. Hope she will change her mind. Then too, I think they are closer to Stur, and it'll mean less travelling and more honeymooning. Get me.

"Now to answer some of your letters. Pappy, I received your letter of the 25th. Glad that you got the maps okay and that they aren't too badly beat up. I didn't wrap them too good. I suppose you've read that they didn't lower the critical score, and it looks like I'll be in this damn Army for quite a while yet. I didn't expect it to be lowered and the way I look at it is that when they swore me in, it was for the duration plus six months. I'd probably be more satisfied in combat, but now that I'm getting married, it'll take up my mind enough so that I won't be too dissatisfied.

"In fact, now, I'm in hopes of staying here instead of going to the Pacific. It would be nice if we could be married on your birthday, but I'm afraid it's at the discretion of the Army and can't make it just when I want it. I see you're planning on giving me some money for my wedding and I'm very grateful because I'm going to need beaucoup of the stuff.

"Ezzie, I have two from you and one was with the clippings. Very good. So, Pappy thinks that when you and Doug build, Hazel and I can move into your place. Well, I was thinking today that if I couldn't manage to get a place like I previously explained, I'd like to get a home under this federal housing program. I think it's about the only way I could manage to buy a place. What do you think? I guess I'll just have to wait and figure it out when I get home.

"Lois, I got your card and two letters. So glad that you enjoyed yourself on your vacation. So, you've read my love letter and realize why she was mixed up at first. I thought it would explain to you better than I could write. She's awful sweet and I'm sure you will all love her, and she couldn't help but love you. That was very nice of you all to write her and welcome her to our happy little family.

"Eunice, I don't have any of your letters to be answered, but I expect to get a few from home by tomorrow or the next day. Most of your letters are only three days apart but when I answer your mail, sometimes I answer six or seven in one letter. I'm going to play a little pinochle tonight just for the hell of it. I can't afford to gamble.

"Pet Sis, I got one letter from you since I last wrote. Always glad to hear about my niece and get all the latest dope about her. Did I tell you I got the snaps of you and her? She's a pretty little baby I think, but I don't see where you get the idea she looks like her old man. Ha. It seems strange to see you holding a baby because I didn't see you get married for one thing and also, it's been so long since I've seen you. I remember you from away back when you were single and you used to get our meals for us, etc. Then too you used to have more than one caller. Boy Jimmie used to get mad, eh?

"I sent your letter on to Hazel after I read it. It was written okay. I laughed when you said you wanted me to censor it. So, you've already taken Judy in a beer joint. Now when Jimmie is told to stay home and watch the baby, he's liable to take her down to the nearest beer joint and think it's alright because you've already done it. Ha. I can tell by your letters that she means an awful lot to you both and that she's increases your happiness a hundred percent.

"I'm glad to know that even though I've never heard of you two having any spats. I'm glad Jimmie is a good sport because I like to kid him. I'm glad Jimmie has a chance to stay where he's at for a while. You really need him while the baby is so young. So long for now and I hope you're all in the best of health. Lots of love, Your overseas kid."

12 August 1945: Typewritten two-page letter from Antwerp, Belgium:

"My dear family. It's now two thirty Sunday afternoon and I've just finished reading the paper and the paper I got from home. This morning,
I slept until ten thirty and got up to go to church at eleven o'clock. We
had a nice service, also communion. We have chicken for dinner every
Sunday and today I had a leg and part of the breast, very good. I don't
know just what's the matter with me today. I don't feel just right. I seem
to ache all over. The only thing I can think of is that I have a cold coming
on. I'm going to have Capt. Rhea look me over sometime today. I'm not
running a temperature right now either. I don't believe it's much, but I
never could stand to feel sick. Nothing to worry about.

"Well, there is a lot of good news in the papers these last few days.
I sure hope they decide to accept the answer to their peace proposal.
(**NOTE:** Emperor Hirohito announced the surrender of Japan on 15
August and formal papers were signed on 2 September. Atomic bombs
were dropped on Japan on 6 and 9 August). It'll mean that I'll get home
that much sooner, I believe.

"I kind of celebrated the good news last night because I didn't do any
celebrating when the war with Germany was over. We have a bar room
in the building where we are living, and we can get scotch, gin, highballs,
and beer. It's for the noncoms and we get the scotch from the officers. I
had a few highballs before I went to bed. They're quite reasonable here
in our club, about thirty cents a glass.

"Pappy, as far as I know, I'm leaving on furlough the 22nd of this
month to England. The colonel will have to sign my papers three days
in advance as of the 25th. I probably won't get there until the 25th so it
may work out okay. I wrote and told Hazel to plan everything for that
date but told her there's a possibility that I can't make it. I figure we will
probably get married around the 26th or 27th if I get to go this time.
(**NOTE:** There was a delay in Dad's departure and the wedding would
be on 1 September.) Maybe a little later than that, I don't know.

"Now I have ten days to sort out getting my other money orders. I
think I'll need one of them anyway. I bought Hazel a two-ounce bottle

of Worth perfume for a wedding present, and I bought the two brides-maids both compacts. One is white leather and one a robin egg blue leather. They are very nice. I have to get something for little Mary Mumford yet and I think I'll get her some pretty handkerchiefs. My best man said he would be satisfied with a quart of scotch. I want to get Mrs. Hatcher a little something too if I can find something reasonable. I also have to buy the wedding ring yet; I plan on doing it some afternoon this week.

"Capt. Rhea just listened to my chest, and he says it's okay. Hazel had my civilian shoes mended and Capt. Kantrowitz is going to let me take his Kahiki shirt for the wedding. I'll wear my Eisenhower Jacket with OD (olive drab) pants of the same material which looks darn good for an Army issued uniform. You'll have a better idea when you get the pictures. Hazel and I are going to have a portrait taken while we are on our honeymoon, just the heads and shoulder for you people and her people.

"She had difficulty getting a gown but seems quite sure she'll have one by the time I get there. I told her I'd rather go to Brighton or Bournemouth on our honeymoon instead of London. They have some summer resorts in England, and I've heard they are quite nice. I'll tell you more about that later. She's in favor of living on the outskirts of Rochester, the garden, etc. Now all I've got to do is to find such a place. I got a letter from her today saying that she wrote you, Pappy. She's counting on you to take the place of her mother and father. Cute et? I received your letter of the 2nd and I'm heeding your advice, aren't I? Sorry you had to tell me.

"Ezzie, I have your long letter of the 31st. I see you and Doug are buying land now. It's high priced, isn't it? You people back home sure are getting a lot of rain. So, you've been showing people my wife's pictures and getting compliments on them. She's prettier than her pictures. Glad you liked my pictures and the maps. I do want them framed and I'll have it done when I get home. My acquaintance with the Germans was only for educational purposes. I just wanted to study them and see why they do things as they do. You know the more acquaintances you make the more you learn. That German girl taught me German inside of two weeks so that I could carry on a conversation in German. I figure that to my advantage, don't you?

"I'm sorry to hear that you have been having some trouble again, Lois, but only now it's worse. Hope by now, you're feeling normal again!! Good thing you weren't troubled on your vacation. Your boss sounds like some of our officers, lame brained fools. I will be very glad when you will be able to quit your job and get to housekeeping. You deserve it.

"It looks much like I'll have to start another page in order to answer Eunice's and Pet Sis's letter. By trying to get it all on one page, sometimes I omit a few things. I guess it's due to laziness. I have beaucoup time today, so I'll use it to a good advantage.

"Eunice, I have two letters from you to answer this time, the 30th and the 31st. I imagine you are very busy, and I knew you didn't forget me. Ha. Now we have a certain job to do here and as far as I know, our shipping orders haven't come through. I figure that if the Japan war is over this month, that we will be coming home soon because we are a category four outfit, and they are the ones scheduled to be shipped to the States. I believe we'll get priority on the shipping list as soon as the war is over. I'm just crossing my fingers that they'll come to some terms soon so that it will be over.

"I was thinking how nice it would be if the war was over this month and as soon as I get back from my furlough to England, we would get our shipping orders to sail for the States. That would be a miracle. (**NOTE:** Dad' dream would come true for him, but Hazel would not come to the States until April 1946). I'm waiting patiently for the Fanny Farmers and thank you so much.

"Hazel wrote and said how nice she thinks it'll be to be an aunt. I think the kids will like her. Yes, Eunice, perfume is very expensive here. I got a two-ounce bottle for Hazel and even though it was very good perfume, I could've bought more expensive stuff. The bottle I got her cost me around twenty-some-odd dollars. That's a lot for such a small parcel, I think. I know she'll like it because she always wanted some and I thought it'd be just the thing to get her at this time. As soon as I get married and when I come home, I'll count up and see what I can get. Okay? More about it later.

"Your baby is getting prettier every day according to her photos. Who's that ugly man holding her in the picture? Ha. Ha. You've heard that story about, all the monkeys aren't in the zoo, or would you rather be a fish. Ha Ha. Do you know, I always laughed to myself when I think these crazy things to say about Worry Looey. It breaks up the monotony of writing.

"I sent them on to Hazel, after I showed all the fellows my niece. You look very good after going through such an ordeal. Jimmie looks thin and pale anybody would think he was the mother. I got a kick out of your letter, Margie, and I will heed your advice as you did mine. Ha. Ha. She's rather young yet and we'll have beaucoup time for kids later on. I think.

"Well, I've spent all afternoon writing this letter trying to answer your questions. I was going to take a sunbath but didn't realize it's taken so long to write this. I still don't feel normal but am feeling a little bit better. I will try to let you all know as soon as we are going to get married and if it's at all possible to make a phone call from England and I have the time. I'll call Eunice's because her number is the one I can remember. Fairport 920F5. I hear it's awful expensive and I may not have the money. I'll call on a Sunday, it'll either be on the 26th and the 2nd of September. So, if you all could manage to be at Eunice's on the 26th and 2nd I may talk to you for a few minutes. I'll do my upmost to make the call at seven o'clock British time. Don't be too disappointed if I can't make it. It all depends on if I get the furlough and if I get there before the 26th.

"Hazel said I could call America from England in one of her letters and she's already more or less planned it because she wants to talk to you too. I don't care how much it will cost, as long as I can hear your voices again. So, count on it and hope that I get there and that I'll be able to make connections. I have a feeling I will be talking with you in a short time after you get this letter. Lots of love and be careful.

Margie your birthday is coming up next Saturday and I'll be thinking of you all day. I hope you have a happy, happy birthday with all my love, Your overseas kid."

15 August 1945: Typed letter from Antwerp, Belgium: The Day Japan Surrenders: "Happy V-J Day! Last night I went to bed at twelve o'clock and at one thirty some of the fellows came in and woke me up to tell me the war was over. To tell you the truth, I was so sleepy that I tried to go back to sleep right away but couldn't because there was so much noise around. I just couldn't. I thought the war was just beginning there was so much shooting going on around here. All the guards emptied their guns, I believe. I didn't realize there were so many ships in harbor until last night. They blew their whistles for two solid hours. They spelled out victory from their whistles, shot off rockets, flares, and did everything imaginable. Sirens blew, machine guns fired, I thought I was up on the front for a while. When a bomb is falling, there is an awful whistling which no one could mistake for anything else but that and they even had some kind of a whistle that sounded just as if we were being bombed. Automatically, I held my breath and waited for the explosion, but there was none.

"I sleep in the aid station in my dental office because I couldn't get any sleep up in the barracks because everybody comes in drunk and keeps one awake. Last night several of our fellows came in to be sewed up. They'd been drunk and got in fights. One guy tried to kill another fellow. Boy, I'm telling you it wasn't safe around here. If one of the guys gets drunk and gets mad at somebody, the first thing he does is to get his gun and try to take after him. A fellow in my room, when I was sleeping upstairs, came in drunk and woke everybody up trying to find his 32 because some car owner slammed a door in his face and he was going out to get him.

"Some one of the fellows got the gun away from him and we finally persuaded him to go to bed by telling him we'd go and get him in the morning. It was a hard job, but we finally talked him out of going.

"I don't know how you celebrated back home, but I think I'd be safe in saying that there were more people killed last night than in any major battle of the war. It seems a shame that it happens like that. Anyway, I'm awful glad the damn thing is over and all I hope now is to get home quick after I'm married. The paper said something about the points being lowered to fifty right after V-J-Day. Now we will see what the score is. It will be sometime yet before I get discharged, I think. However, I'm in a category four outfit at the present time and hope to stay in this outfit. If so, I think they will give category four outfits priority in shipment.

"I imagine I'll get a thirty-day furlough before being discharged from the Army and I'll like that better. I believe they will give thirty-day furloughs as soon as we hit the States, I hope. I had a letter from Boyce's wife, and he was home for thirty days and is now in South Dakota. He probably won't have to go to the Pacific now so all in all he got a break. He's got ninety-three points and has a good chance of getting out soon, I think. I don't see how he got so many, but then the Air Corps get a lot.

"I got your letter today, Lois, but minus the other two money orders, I'm afraid I'm going to need one more or part of it. As far as I know, I'm leaving the 22nd and after talking with some of the fellows that just came back, I don't think I'll get there before the 28th or 29th which means I won't be able to call you on the 26th. If possible, I'll try to call you on the 2d then. I'm still not sure if I can do it or not, but I'll try. By getting there the 29th, I think we be able to get married on the first or second of September. I'll have seven full days in England and on the eighth day, I'll have to go down to get my boat back.

"I bought my cigarettes, candy, and toilette rations yesterday for two weeks and I also bought a box of cigars for the wedding which cost me ten dollars in all. We used to get all our rations free in combat and now when we have to pay for them, you can really tell the difference. The cigars cost about seven dollars; I think. Not having any money left from my last pay, I had to spend some out of one of my money orders for my rations and my laundry. I'm going to make it up out of my next month's pay, but won't get paid until I get back. That's why I'm going to need at least part of another money order.

"I guess I can't have a home right off the bat when I get home so will have to be satisfied with what I can get until I can afford one of my own. It's going to be harder for me than it was for all of you girls, because you didn't have to buy your own diamond rings, or your homes, even though you have helped your husbands an awful lot. Even though I'm not well off to start, I will do the best I can with what I've got. I know we will be happy and that's all that counts in my books.

"I must write Hazel now, so I'll write again soon and answer your latest letters. Until then be happy and be good. I hope to see you soon, if not sooner. I'm enclosing some pictures and negatives. I'll explain them on the backs. Beau coups of love, Elwood."

19 August 1945: Typed letter from Antwerp, Belgium: Dad's last letter from Antwerp and from the war that I have. "My dear family, I've just finished dinner, and it was unusually lousy compared to the meals we've been getting. We always have chicken on Sunday and it's usually good. Some joker has decided that he has to make out some reports now and he wants the typewriter immediately, so he says. I'll finish this a little later on.

"I went to church this morning at ten thirty and we had a very nice service. The chaplain we have now is a pretty good speaker. This afternoon after I finish this, I may go to the dance in the Red Cross building.

"I had two letters from Hazel this morning and one from Mrs. Mumford. Hazel is very excited and I'm getting a little nervous as time progresses. She has the dresses, and everything is supposed to be ready when I get there, except that I'll have to get the license and the ring in Salisbury and make a trip to Blandford. My best man wants to go to Scotland right after we get married, and he wants me to hurry and get married as soon as I can. I also want to get it over with as soon as possible, but can't tell much until I get there. As far as I know I'm still going to leave on the 22nd of this month and I think I'll have to go through Paris both ways. I believe we get a day in Paris going and coming while waiting for the trains. I'm still going to try to call you on the 2d of September, but if I can't make it, I expect to be coming home soon thereafter. Don't count on that either. I won't believe it till I'm on the boat.

"I don't know how all of you people got married on so little money, but then the times have changed considerably since then and I can assure you that it costs much more now. You say that I'm not supposed to buy the gifts for the bridesmaids and you're probably right for all I know. But when two people get married, they are married as one and it doesn't matter to me who gets the presents because it all comes out of our money in the end. You people don't seem to realize things in every respect, do you?

"I'm not saying that to make you feel bad or that I don't listen to you in what you tell me to help me, but you must remember that you are girls and I am a man. I've already got all the gifts for the bridesmaids and also some cigars for her father, a teapot cover for her mother with souvenir from Antwerp on it. It's real pretty and I'm going to take her brother my candy rations for the last two or three weeks, just more or less a gift of good will or whatever you want to call it.

"If I told you what I paid for everything I bought so far, you'd be surprised and shocked to say the least, but in the position I'm in, it just couldn't be any different. You ought to be a soldier in the US Army and then maybe you would understand what I mean. I figure the wedding itself will cost me around 77 dollars alone, not counting the honeymoon or the gifts I've already bought. I'm still got to buy a wedding ring for the wedding, which will cost 20 or 30 dollars.

"Maybe you should have been men instead of ladies, I'm sure you would be in a hell of a spot. Anyway, you shouldn't get too upset over me because I'm only planning on getting married once. I'll take your advice as often as possible but don't forget I have to have a mind of my own at times too. I don't like to write to you people like this and I know I have an awful lot to learn so don't think wrong of me for doing it. I'm glad you are all trying to help me and wouldn't want you to be otherwise. (**NOTE:** Dad was dealing with the opinions of four different sisters who wanted the best for him!)

"I got the other two money orders from you yesterday, Lois, and it took a lot of worry off my mind. I was afraid I wouldn't get it before I left and that I'd have to borrow some until I got back. If I have any left over, which I think I should, and if Hazel doesn't need it, I'll send it back. I'm planning on sending home most of my next month's pay to make up for some that I've spent for my rations and laundry, etc.

"You see, I'll have another allotment made out to Hazel, which will be 22 dollars out of my pay, and then the government will add 28 dollars to it and in all Hazel will get fifty dollars a month. So, actually I'll be drawing more money, which is okay with me.

"I have a few letters from you all, except Pappy, but I did get your picture and yours Ezzie and Doug. They are very good, but I didn't realize Pappy had gotten just a few more grey hairs. Boy Pappy, I won't hardly recognize you when I get home, it's been so long since I've seen you. I think you look very good, and I notice you have some flashy ties.

"Ezzie, Capt. Kantrowitz and I think that the one picture of you sitting on the steps doesn't do you justice. I get a kick out of Capt. Kantrowitz. He knows all of your names and every once in a while, he'll name you all off just to show me he hasn't forgotten you. He says he thinks he knows you people already. Ha.

"Page two starts: I'll make this a long letter because I don't know when I'll have the time to write again until after I get back from my furlough." (**NOTE:** In fact, this is his last letter. I think once he got back from England he had to pack and get on a boat back to the US).

"I don't know of anything else I should say about my wedding except that I wish you were there, but as Margie said in her family letter that when we get home, we'll have a mock wedding just for you people and Margie you can be maid of honor. I've heard an old saying that a mock wedding brings bad luck so I'm not too sure of having one. We could dress up for you though and give you a life picture of it, couldn't we?

"I'm not sure Lois if I have to pay Hazel's passage to America because I read in the Stars and Stripes awhile back that all the English and other foreign brides transportation would be free. Anyway, I wasn't counting on having to pay for it. I'll find out from the embassy in London about her getting to America and all the particulars before I come back. We'll have to sign a lot of papers, etc. I wrote and told her about that already and told her what it will be like at first until she'll have time to change her mind. A lot will be decided when I get there to talk to her. You know you can't do everything in letters.

"I'm sure she will understand everything the way it stands when I give her some more of the low down. I've already told her a lot of things not to expect and by no means have disillusioned her.

To Pappy: "So Margie has said that I can't have you with us all the time, Pappy, but I'm glad to know that I can have you with us some of the time. I'm afraid your daughter-in-law to be is counting on having you with us most of the time. Boy, it must be wonderful to be so popular as you are. So, you can count on having a home with us whenever you want it and know that you will be welcome at all times. I can't promise you what it'll be like, because I don't even know myself. I hope I get a letter from you before I leave because I won't get any over there.

To Ezzie: "So glad you and Doug had such a grand time on your little trip, Ezzie. I got the post card of Lake George, also the long letter telling me what you both did on the trip. You really did lots of things and it sounded good. Glad you had the chance to do it.

"Oh, I went shopping last Friday and ended up sightseeing the city of Antwerp and we ran into a guide in front of the town hall and statue which is in front of it. I saw some artwork that was wonderful and beyond words of expression. I really enjoyed it. We also went thought the cathedral which was built in 1350 and the old castle that was built in the 800s. The guide explained to us how Antwerp got its name, which was illustrated by the statue of the sailor and the giant in front of the town hall. The cathedral was positively beautiful, even though some of the stained windows were blown out. The town hall council room is the most beautiful room I've ever seen. Paintings all over the ceiling and walls. There were rooms with all marble carvings, floors, and fireplaces.

"Well, I just can't explain at all, you'll have to come to Antwerp to see it. If you ever do come here, I'll tell you where to go, okay? I thought I'd been all over Antwerp until I'd seen those places Friday. I wish now I had taken notes on the tour so I could tell you in detail all about the place. I do remember how they got the name of Antwerp; I'll tell you later. (**NOTE:** Mark and I visited all the Antwerp sites Dad mentions in his letter during our March 2025 visit. Beautiful indeed.)

Eunice, I'd like to go to Holland before I leave Europe because they really do treat the Americans good there. I'll keep the addresses you sent and if I do get to go, I'll try my best to look them up. Also, if I could get a good diamond there reasonable enough, I might do it. Some of our fellows have been there and they said the people go crazy over there when they see an American. They gawk at you and make a fuss over you, so they say. Instead of streets, they have canals and boats are their main transportation. It sounds very interesting, and I do want to go when I get a chance.

Margie, I got your long family letter, and your daughter must be very sweet, like her mother. I enjoy your letters telling your daily routine about her, etc. Too bad we couldn't have made arrangements so that Hazel could have worn your dress in time, but thanks anyway. Why don't you go home for a while now and get rested up some. You could have someone help you there and make things easier for you. I'm sure Jimmie wouldn't want you to get rundown and sick in bed just to have you there with him. You must look out for your health first. I don't believe it'll be too long before Jimmie will get discharged now that the war is over. (**NOTE:** Jimmy stayed in the Army and retired as a Colonel.) I'm sure he'd much rather have you alive than not to have you at all. Don't think harsh of me for mentioning it, but think it over anyway. With all my love and be careful, Elwood."

4 September 1945: Handwritten letter from Hazel to Eunice, John, John Jr. and David Elwood: From Mrs. E. A. Turner, Marley 2, Church Street, Sturminster Newton, Dorset, England: "Dear Eunice, John, John Jr. and David Elwood, I should have written you before, but I've been very busy. So, I hope you will forgive me. Today, I just wandered around and can't seem to settle to do all the jobs I still have to do. Elwood left at 0930 this morning. (That's the reason). I was very brave and saw him off at the station. But I'm in hopes that he'll be back again tonight as he has an awful sore throat and stiff neck. At least we've both had it. So, he was going to see a medical officer at Southampton and see if he could get a few more days leave.

"Last night we took pictures of the wedding group because our wedding day was wet, so we were unable to take many. As soon as I've had them developed, I'll be sending you some. Elwood and I thought about John and David starting school and by now I guess they are settled back into the routine again. Elwood wrote you a long letter on Wednesday telling you all the things he's been doing. I'll be writing a letter myself with all details later. I'm going to try and send the two tiers of our wedding cake—which was made especially to send out to you all. But I understand it's rather a hard job to send cakes, so if it's impossible I'll bring it myself when I come. I hope that you are all well. All my family sends their kindest regards. And I hope it isn't so very far away my coming to meet you all. Fondest Love, (Aunty) Hazel.

7 October 1945: Army Separation Record from Fort Dix, New Jersey: WD AGO Form 100 has Dad's serial Number, Grade (Tech 5); Entry into service date: October 1942 and date of birth 3 Feb 1920. Military Specialties show one month as a Private with principal duty "Basic Training Med with Army Code 657. It shows 2 years 11 months service as a Tech 5 Dental Technician and Army Code 855. The summary of military occupation reads, "DENTAL TECHNICIAN: Assisted dental officer in routine dental service. Mixed dental cements and amalgams for fillings. Scaled and polished teeth with dental instruments. Dad signed on 7 October 1945 as the soldier and the Separation Classification Officer was W. W. Von Schlichten, Major (**NOTE:** It's ironic that the separation officer's name appears to be of German descent).

7 October 1945: Army of the United States Honorable Discharge wallet size given at the Separation Center, Fort Dix, New Jersey.

12 March 1946: The 4th ID is officially inactivated after serving and fighting in the following battle campaigns: Normandy, Northern France, Rhineland, Ardennes-Alsace, Central Europe

12 March 1946: Subject: Orders To: Civilian Named from Headquarters London Area Office, Western Base and Section, US Forces, European Theater, APO 413 US ARMY. "Under the provisions of WD Circular 345, dated 11 August 1945, the following named dependents of US Servicemen, are, subject to passport and diplomatic clearance, authorized and invited to proceed from points indicated in the United Kingdom to destinations in the United States: Mrs. Hazel Turner (priority 2) wife of T/5 Elwood Turner 32547801, from 2 Church Street, Sturminster Newton, Dorset, to Rochester, New York. (**NOTE:** Mom was authorized 200 lbs. baggage allowance for adults and travel by Army or Naval transport, rail and/or motor transportation it authorized. She was given a cost code to charge costs to. Each wife received ten copies of this document. Mom still had six of the ten copies of her orders when she died in April 1984. She waited seven months to receive the approval to go to Rochester).

15 April 1946: Hazel Turner's Area Transportation Office Personnel Movement Division Papers: Here are some interesting extracts from this two-page 8 ½ x 14" document: "Arrangements are now complete for your passage to the United States. It is VITAL that you follow these instructions implicitly. Your failure to arrive at the designated points on time may forfeit your early passage. Your cooperation is requested." "If you are late in arriving you risk being returned to your home." "There are no facilities for changing pounds sterling to dollars in the Reception Area. DO NOT BRING ANY 5 POIUND NOTES TO THE RECEPTION AREA." "In order to facilitate handling the large numbers of dependents, each ADULT is being assigned a "group number". THIS NUMBER MUST BE PRINTED IN LARGE LETTERS ON EACH LUGGAGE LABEL. Mom's group number was 31-N-5. (**NOTE:** This document shows Mom left Sturminster Newton, 8: 14 am and arrived Andover Junction 10:20 am on 15 April. She was going to Southampton, England to travel to New York Harbor aboard the Saturnia. She arrived at noon, 27 April 1946. I still have the "trunk" she used to carry all her earthly belongings to the states. Her group number, 31-N-5, is prominently labeled on the inside of the trunk and on a label on the outside. Mom had just turned 19. She was married on 1 September 1945 at the age of 18. She had to be scared but I know she was brave. She would not see her mom or dad for another 6 years).

Antwerp, Belgium

August 15, 1945

My dear family

Happy V-J day! Last night I went to bed at twelve o'clock and at one thirty some of the fellows came in and woke me up to tell me the war was over. To tell you the truth, I was so sleepy that I tried to go back to sleep right away but couldn't because there was so much noise around here, I just couldn't. I thought the war was just beginning there was so much shooting going on around here. All the guards emptied their guns, I believe. I didn't realize there were so many ships in harbor until last night. They blew their whistle --s for two solid hours. They spelled out victory on there whistles, shot off rockets, flares and did everything imaginable. Sirens blew, machine guns fired, I thought I was up on the front for awhile. When a bomb is falling, there is an awful whistling which no one could mistake for anything else but that and they even had some kind of a whistle that sounded just as if we were being bombed. Automatically, I held my breath and waited for the explosion but there was none. I sleep in the aid station in my dental office because I couldn't get any sleep up in the barracks because everybody comes in drunk and keeps one awake, and last night several of our fellows came in to be sewed up. They'd been drunk and got in fights. One guy tried to kill another last night, boy, I'm telling you it wasn't safe around here. If one of the guys get drunk and gets mad at somebody, the first thing he does is to get his gun and try to take after him. A fellow in my room, when I was sleeping upstairs, came in drunk and woke everybody up trying to find his 32 because some cafe owner slammed a door in his face and he was going out to get him. Some one of the fellows got the gun away from him and we finnally persuaded him to go to bed by telling him, we'd go and get him in the morning. It was a hard job but we finnally talked him out of going.

I don't know how you celebrated back home, but I think I'd be safe in saying that there were more people killed last night than in any major battle of the war. It seems a shame that it happens like that. Anyway I'm awful glad the damn thing is over and all I hope now is to get home quick after I'm married. The paper said something about the points being lowered to fifty right after v-j day. Now we will see what the score is. It will be sometime yet before I get dischagged I think. However I'm in a catagory four outfit at the present time and hope to stay in this outfit. If so, I think they will give catagory four outfits priority in shipment. I imagine I'll get a thirty day furlough before being discharged from the army and I'll like that better. I believe they will give thirty day furloughs as soon as we hit the states, I hope. I had a letter from Royce's wife and he was home for thirty days and is now in South Dakota. He probably won't have to go to the Pacific now so all in all he got a break. He's got ninety three points and has a good chance of getting out soon, I think. I don't see how he got so many but then the air corps gets a lot of medals.

I got your letter today Lois but minns the other two money orders, I'm afraid I'm going to need one more or part of it. As far as I know, I'm leaving the 22nd and after talking with some of the fellows that just came back, I don't think I'll get there before the 28th or 29th which means I won't be able to call you on the 26th. If possible I'll try to call you on the 2nd then. I'm still not sure if I can do it or not, but I'll try. By getting there the 29th, I think we be able to get married on the first or second of September. I'll have seven full days in England and on the eighth day, I'll have to go down to get my boat back.

I bought my cigarette, candy, and toilette rations yesterday for two weeks and I also bought a box of cigars for the wedding which cost me ten dollars in all. We used to get all our rations free in combat and now when we have to pay for them you can really tell the difference. The cigars cost about seven dollars, I think. Not having any money left from my last pay, I hadto spend some out of one of my money orders for my rations and my laundry. I'm going to make it up out of my next months pay but won't get payed until I get back. That's why I'm going to need at least part of another money order.

I guess I won't have a home right off the batt when I get home so will have to be satisfied with what I can get until I can afford one of my own. It's going to be harder for me than it was for all of you girls because you didn't have to buy your own diamond rings or your homes, even though you have helped your husbands an awful lot. Even though I'm not well off to start, I will do the best I can with what I've got. I know we will be happy and that's all that counts in my books.

I must write Hazel now so I'll write again soon and answer your latest letters. Until then be happy and be good. I hope to see you soon, if not sooner. I'm enclosing some pictures and some negatives. I'll explain them on the backs.

Beaucoups of love, Elwood

Elwood A. Turner 15 August 1945 Letter from Antwerp Belgium

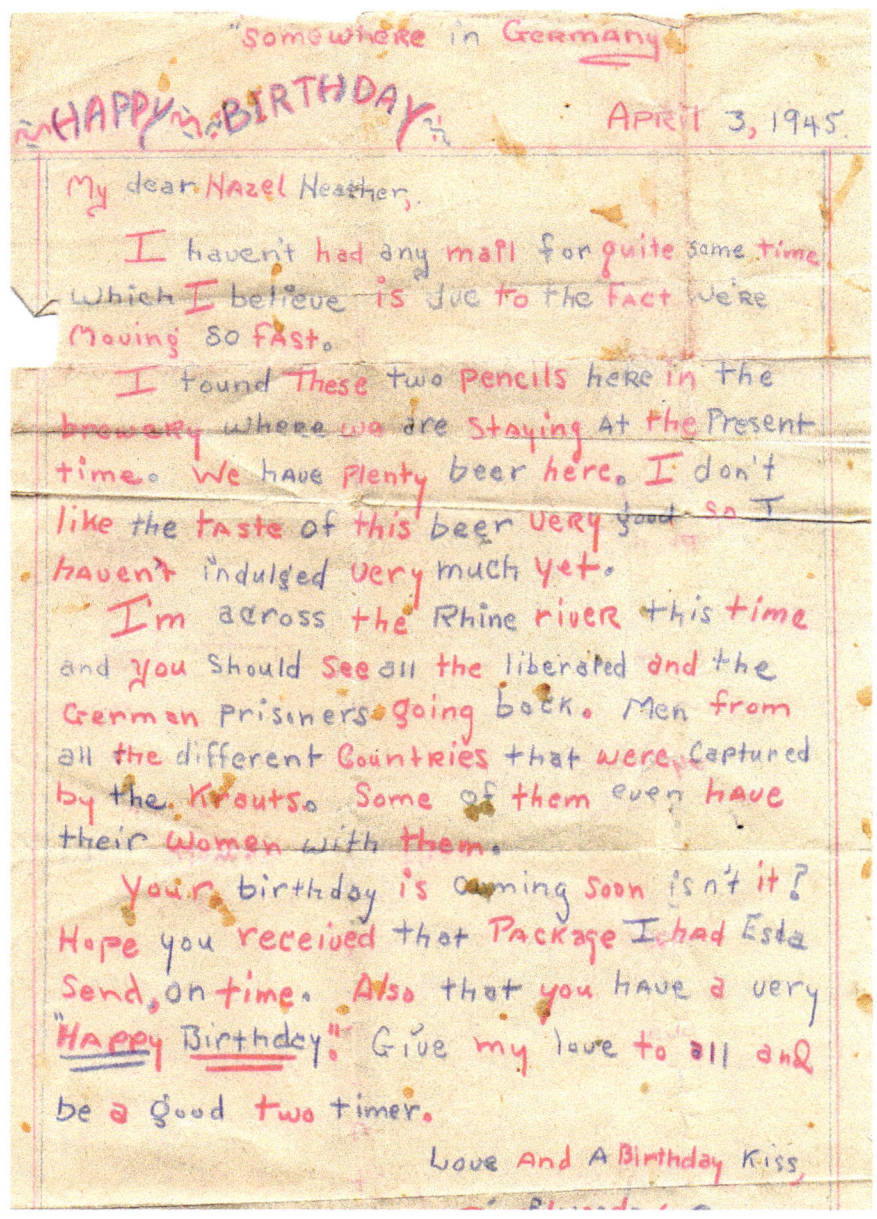

"somewhere in Germany"

HAPPY BIRTHDAY   APRIL 3, 1945.

My dear Hazel Heather,

I haven't had any mail for quite some time which I believe is due to the fact we're moving so fast.

I found these two pencils here in the brewery where we are staying at the present time. We have plenty beer here. I don't like the taste of this beer very good so I haven't indulged very much yet.

I'm across the Rhine river this time and you should see all the liberated and the German prisoners going back. Men from all the different countries that were captured by the Krauts. Some of them even have their women with them.

Your birthday is coming soon isn't it? Hope you received that package I had Esta send, on time. Also that you have a very "Happy Birthday." Give my love to all and be a good two timer.

Love And A Birthday Kiss,

April 3, 1945 letter from somewhere in Germany to Hazel

218

From left: Belgium, seated in woods by tree,
Luxembourg Couple who hosted Dad for Christmas dinner 1944

Dad and his buddies in a Luxembourg City beer joint

Dad in Belgium with Red Cross Doughnut girl

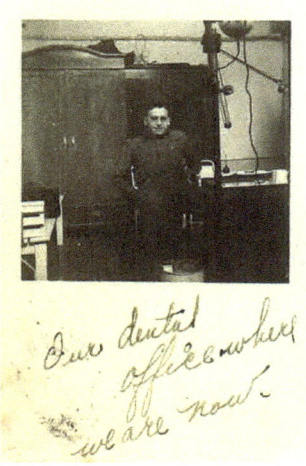

Our kitchen - chow line -

Our dental office where we are now -

From left: Dad in the chow line, Dad in a dental office in Germany,
Dad in a Luxembourg City window

Chateau de Gerbeviller France

From left: Rick with the Mayor of Gerbeviller Noel Marguis March 2025, Rick with traveling companion Mark Moe and Edmond (93 years old) who lived in Gerbeviller when 4th ID was in town

Village of Gerbeviller France 2025

Clockwise from top: Brussels 2025, building in Antwerp 2025,
building in Antwerp 1940s

Top: Swimming Pool in Antwerp 2025,
bottom: Olympic pool at Schnaittach Germany

Top: Waterloo statue in the 1940s, bottom: Waterloo statue in March, 2025

People

Elwood Almy Turner: Born in 1920. "Dad" Father of Susan Almena, Catherine Anita, Richard Elwood, Robert Steven, Barbara Ann and Jennifer March. Married to Hazel Heather Hatcher.

Hazel: Our mother. Dad courted her in Sturminster Newton and married her on 1 September 1945. She left her family at age 19 to move to America.

Almy "Pappy": Elwood's dad. Our Grandfather (First wife, Almena, died when Dad was 5 years. Almy re-married to Grace and lived on a street called Albemarle. Jobs: Elevator operator, security guard).

Esda or "Essie": Elwood's oldest sister born in 1903. (Married to Doug. Job: Art teacher). Esda helped raise Elwood and the other kids when their mother, Almena, died when Dad was five years old. She was a huge influence on the lives of Elwood, Margie and even Margie's daughter, Judy. Doug and Esda had no children.

Lois: Elwood's sister was born in 1905. (Married to Jack: Job: Western Union and helped Jack with his trailer business. Lived on Canandaigua Lake. The couple had no children.)

Eunice or "June": Elwood's sister born in 1913. (Married to Johnny: Job: Worked on the family farm. They had two boys: John Jr. and David Elwood.)

Marjorie/Margie/Pet Sis: Elwood's youngest sister born in 1917. (Married to Jimmy: Job: Western Union and later helped Jimmy with Holiday Inn ownership. They had one daughter, Judy.)

Doug: Our uncle. Esda's husband.

Johnny: Our uncle. Eunice's husband. Farmer and later worked at Kodak.

Jimmy: Our uncle. Margie's husband. Referred to as "Worry Looney"

Jack: Our uncle. Lois' husband. Owned a trailer business.

Jim Hatcher: Our uncle. Hazel's brother. Later became an electrician.

Walter Hatcher "Grandfi": Our Grandfather Hazel's Dad. Worked in a feed store in Sturminster Newton

Susan Hatcher: Our grandmother. Hazel's Mom.

John Jr.: Eunice and Johnny's eldest son. Elwood's nephew. John Jr. married Lanora and has five daughters: Vickie, Diane, Leslie, Julie and Kristina. John is 92 years-old.

David Elwood: Eunice and Johnny's youngest son. Elwood's nephew. David Elwood later passed away with a brain tumor

Judy Norton "Jud": Margie and Jimmy's daughter born in May 1945. Elwood's niece born while he was deployed. Judy is married to Jim.

Bonnie: Dad's girlfriend from Rochester prior to going into the Army. Bonnie is mentioned 43 times in his letters, first appearing in a 30 November 1942. The last time she was mentioned in his 19 May 1945 letter. Her address was 2613 Titus Avenue, Rochester.

Mrs. Bellis: She sent Dad 2 dozen cookies to Camp Stewart. (30 November 1942 letter).

Boyce: Dad's good friend serving in England in the Air Corps. Referred to him as "Gooche" one time. First appearance was in a 30 November 1942 letter and last reference was in a 15 August 1945 letter. He appears 29 times in Dad's letters.

Jane Dunk: Elwood's friend who wrote letters to him (7 December 1942 Letter).

First Lieutenant Doctor Blum: Elwood's first Lieutenant (7 December 1942 Letter).

The "Cook": Dad bandaged a wound for "the cook" and from then on, he would get a steak sandwich anytime he asked. (7 December 1942 Letter).

Capt. Hoffman: Dad's Commanding Officer at Camp Stewart was from Albany, N.Y. (11 December 1942 Letter).

John Foley: Friend at Camp Stewart (17 December 1942 Letter).

Aunt Nora and Uncle Allen (Almy's side): Dad mentions them from Camp Stewart (26 December 1942 letter).

Mrs. DeRoos and Uncle Ike: Johnny's parents mentioned in 1 February 1943 from Camp Carrabelle. John Jr. updated us on his grandmother. Here name was Rica. Her Dutch name was Rensca. Her first husband died and later when she cooked for Isaac Herman, on the Turner side, on a farm north of their farm on Ridge Road. Rica and Isaac later married.

Arnold: Dad mentions him from Camp Carrabelle. Arnold helped out on Johnny's farm. (1 February 1943 letter and 26 September 1944 letters)

Lt. Guilaiano: Dentist at Camp Carrabelle and Camp Stewart (27 February 1943 Letter).

Stan Marshall: Friend from Rochester he saw at Camp Carrabelle. He knew Jimmy and Margie (8 March 1943 Letter).

Larry: Dad mentions him often because he was from Rochester and they were friends: 8 March 43 from Camp Gordon-Johnston; 25 April 1943 from Camp Stewart (going to show); 28 May 1943 from Camp Stewart; 8 August 1944 from France (Larry had been injured and evacuated to England): 15 November 1944 from Germany (Larry was still in England hospital).

Janet Hummel: Friend who wrote to Elwood while at Camp Stewart (21 April 1943 Letter).

Nelson Eddie and Jeanette McDonald: Dad said his Chaplin and the Chaplin's wife sounded better than Nelson and Jeanette! (25 April 1943 Letter).

Frank: Friend of Dad's at Camp Stewart (28 May 1943 letter).

Matty: Dad went to Nashville with him (20 June 1943 letter).

Aunt Lucy: Had recently passed away while Dad was at Camp Forrest. (28 June 1943 letter).

COL Ackerman: Dad mentions from Camp Forrest. (26 July 1943 letter).

Lt. Anders: Dad mentions from Camp Forrest (26 July 1943 letter).

Earl: Wrote letters to Dad at Camp Forrest (26 July 1943 letter).

Captain Kantrowitz: His Commanding Officer and Dentist first mentioned in a 29 February 1944 letter. He was Dad's CO until he left Antwerp in August 1945.

Lillian: Friend of Margie's who was going to write to Dad (29 October 1943 letter).

Dr. Watkins: Pastor of Dad's home church, Lake Avenue Baptist Church, Rochester, New York. Dad wrote a letter to the church family in mid-Dec 1943 and mentions Dr. Watkins in a 19 February 1944 letter.

Mr. and Mrs. Mumford: Dad stayed with them in Sturminster Newton. Dad alludes to them in December 1943 letters, but first mentions them by name in a 14 March 1944 letter. Mentioned over 10 times in letters.

Nier family: Wrote Dad a Christmas card. (26 January 1944 V-mail).

Mrs. Bonfield brother: Dad mentions him as someone he was looking for in London. I believe this is Bonnie's mother's brother in England. (10 February 1944 letter).

Norm: Friend of Boyce who traveled to Sturminster Newton in March 1944 to see Dad. (14 March 1944 letter).

Mary Mumford: Flower girl in Mom and Dad's wedding. The Mumford's daughter. First mentioned in May 1944.

Michael Mumford: Son of the Mumford's where Dad stayed while in Stur. (25 May 1944 letter).

Raymond: Friend of family killed in the war near the beaches. (4 August 1944 Letter)

Don Rice: Don Rice was an actor known for Lady Luck, the Dean Martin Show and Perry Como's Kraft Music Hall. Dad saw him in a U.S.O. show in France in August 1944. (10 August 1944 letter).

Wilbur Buyck: Wilbur helped Pappy on a farm (non-dairy) in Walsworth, New York where Pappy had a house and some land. Dad tells Pappy since Wilbur is helping on a farm, he probably would not have to go into the Army. (24 August 1944 V-mail).

Jacquiline: Parisian girl dad helped when he was in Paris. Jacquiline wanted him to write her after he got home. (9 September 1944 letter).

Tony: "Glad to hear Tony making out as well as he did." (20 October 1944 letter)

Bing Crosby: Dad mentions listening to him on the radio. He never saw him in person. (20 October 1944 and 31 March 1945 letters).

Bob Carlson: Dad's friend in Rochester who played pranks on Halloween. (20 November 1944 letter).

Marlene Dietrich: German-American actress and singer. Dad saw her in person late November 1944. (3 December 1944 letter).

Corporal Mattfolk: Injured friend of Dad's in hospital 12 miles from Sturminster. Ironically, they were given the wrong name. A different soldier had in fact suffered a leg injury by shooting himself in the leg. (Mrs. Mumford's 6 January 1945 letter).

Trices: Dad uses this unknown name and asks: "and how's Trices?" (13 January 1945 letter).

Aunt Nell: Pappy's sister. Pappy had visited with her. (9 February 1945 letter).

Clinton: Dad mentions him and regrets he could not visit him. (9 February 1945 letter).

Howard Coster: Family friend (Esda) who was killed in action. (31 March 1945 letter).

Roberta Miller: A teacher at Ontario High (12 April 1945 letter).

Ernie Pyle: Dad mentions that Ernie Pyle was killed in action. Ernie was killed on 18 April 1945 in the Pacific. (20 April 1945 letter).

President Roosevelt: Dad mentions what a good man he was upon his death, 12 April 1945. (20 April 1945 letter).

President Harry Truman: Dad first mentions him on 20 April 1945 when he became President upon Roosevelt's death. Dad saw him in Antwerp, Belgium and mentions him in a 17 July 1945 letter.

Pretty Fraulein Else: German girl he met in Schnaittach, Germany the last two weeks in Germany. (17 July 1945 letter).

Dad's Best Man: He never gave a name. Mentions him in 1 Aug and 19 August 1945 letters.

Places & Things

Rochester, New York: Where Dad grew up and went to High School.

Ft. Niagara, New York: Where Dad was inducted into Army. One of the oldest Forts in America. Established by the French in 1679. (1 and 4 November 1942).

Niagara Falls: On trip to Camp Stewart (4 November 1942).

Buffalo, New York: On trip to Camp Stewart (4 November 1942).

Chicago, Illinois: On trip to Camp Stewart (4 November 1942).

Cincinnati, Ohio: On trip to Camp Stewart (4 November 1942).

Kentucky: On trip to Camp Stewart (4 November 1942).

Tennessee: On trip to Camp Stewart (4 November 1942).

Camp Stewart, Georgia: Basic Training (4 November 1942).

Savannah, Georgia: Rest and Relaxation near Camp Stewart. Hotel Savannah (8 November 1942).

Jesup, Georgia: City near Camp Stewart. Dad went on a date and to a show (30 November 1942).

Hindsville, Georgia: City near Camp Stewart. Dad had pictures made there (17 December 1942).

Syracuse, New York: Dad described swamps as "Manazumas" similar to Montezumas near Syracuse. (7 January 1943 letter).

Tallahassee, Florida: Near Camp Gordon Johnston (Florida Agricultural and Mechanical College) (17 January 1943).

Camp Carrabelle, Florida: Dad had maneuvers/Training there. Camp Carrabelle became Camp Gordon Johnston. (17 January 1943 letter).

Camp Gordon Johnston, Florida: Maneuvers/Training (1 February 1943-April 1943).

Carrabelle, Florida: Near Camp Carrabelle Amphibious Training Center (8 March 1943).

Crawfordville, Florida: City near Carrabelle. (8 March 1943).

Glenville, Georgia: City near Camp Stewart. Dad went to Church there on 18 April 1943 (25 April 1943).

Camp Forrest, Tennessee: Training near Tullahoma, Tennessee (First mentioned 30 May 1943. Dad had training there from 20 June 1943-1 September 1943)).

Lake Avenue Baptist Church: Dad's home church in Rochester, New York. Dad mentions the church 14 times. He loved his home church. (11 August 1943).

Nashville, Tennessee: R & R near Camp Forrest (20 June 1943).

Lookout Mountain, Georgia and Inn and Wander's Park: Dad went there with Aunt Margie (1 August 1943).

Sturminster Newton (Stur), England: Dad lived there with the Mumford's from Dec 1943-June 1944. Pop Cluettes Tea House. Dad mentions Stur directly only one time in his letters after he went to Normandy as he was honoring censorship rules. (2 July 1944).

Portsmouth, England: U.S. troops departed from there to go to France. No direct reference.

Weymouth, England: U.S. troops departed from there to go to France. No direct reference.

Dorchester, England (Dorset): 36 miles from Stur. And possible first stop after entering England. No direct reference, however, there were pictures of Dorchester in his photos.

London, England: R & R from Stur: Madam Tussaud's Wax Museum; American Bar; Houses of Parliament; St. Paul's Cathedral; Tower of London; Tower Bridge; Big Ben (11 October 1943).

Hospital 12 miles from Stur: Mrs. Mumford visits a wounded friend of Dad's: Sherborne, England the old Coldharbour in Sherborne (6 January 1945).

Paris, France: 4th ID liberated Paris and Dad and his unit marched thru the city. (25 August 1944).

Luxembourg City, Luxembourg: Dad was stationed here for weeks in December 1944 and had Christmas here. Also, Dad passed thru here again on his way to Antwerp in August 1945.

Gerbeviller France: This is the town the 4th had a few days of rest. First referred to in 4th ID SITREP of 13 March 1945. Dad refers to being in France in his 16 March 1945 letter.

Puttelandge France: This is the town the 4th had a few days rest referred to in 4th ID SITREP

Hilpoltstein. Germany: Dad was stationed there before going to Schnaittach. First mentioned in 19 May 1945 letter.

Schnaittach, Germany: Dad lived there after the war ended. He visited at least two churches in this town and a café with a pool table.

Antwerp: Dad was stationed there the last few weeks in August and September 1945 only a quarter mile from the port. He specifically mentions: Townhall (council room most beautiful room he saw in Europe), a mile-long tunnel, old castle from the 800s, cathedral from the year 1350, a barber shop, statue in front of town hall, old school house where he stayed, the zoo, diamond shopping in diamond district.

Brussels, Belgium: Dad stopped here on way to Antwerp and visited from Antwerp

Holland: Dad mentions wanting to go there, but I don't believe he ever did

Barricini Candy: Dad had received free candy from this business in N.Y.C. Mentioned in 26 October 1944 letter.

Bleialf, Germany

Aachen, Germany: Nov/Dec 1944 and February 16, 1945 letters.

Alsace Lorraine (Strasbourg, Nancy, Colmar, Metz): 8-25 March 1945

Batzendorf: 20 March 1945

Bad Durkheim, Germany: 26-27 March

Danube River, Germany: 4th crosses the Danube on 25 April 1945

Worms, Germany: 4th I.D. crosses the Rhine River

Kodak building 5: Dad mentions in a letter. He must have worked in that building in Rochester.

Mainz, Germany: Dad crossed the Rhine on his way to Antwerp for last time

Near Austria: Bad Tolz is the probably location furthest south Dad made it in Germany

Southampton, England: Mom departed there on 19 April 1945 to go to U.S. on the Saturnia.

Salisbury, England: Dad probably bought the wedding rings here 31 miles from Stur

Blandford, England: Dad probably got the wedding license from this town

Brighton, England: Possible honeymoon town 116 miles from Stur.

Bournemouth, England: Most probable honeymoon town 53 miles from Stur.

New York Harbor: Mom arrived in the U.S. there on 27 April 1945 on the Saturnia.

Postlude: The Final Story of Elwood Almy Turner & Hazel Heather Hatcher Turner

Dad was honorably discharged from the Army on 7 October 1945. He returned to Rochester to work at Kodak. Dad and Mom lived and worked on a Chicken Farm when their first child, Susan Almena Turner, was born in August 1947. They moved to Tamarac Drive in Rochester in 1948. Their second daughter, Catherine Anita Turner, was born in October 1948; Rick was born in June, 1952; Bob was born in April 1955; and the first one of the "Little Girls", Barbie, was born in May 1957. The Tamarac Drive location was perfect for a young family. We walked to school and even had a zoo close by! There was also a "Suicide Hill" nearby that we sledded down, with Dad and Mom's help. Mom sold Avon door to door to help ends meet. We attended Irondequoit Presbyterian Church where we were all baptized.

In June, 1958, the family moved to Cocoa, Florida. Dad went to work for RCA at Patrick Air Force Base where he processed film for NASA and the Mercury, Gemini, and Apollo programs. The family first settled into a rented house in River Heights, before moving to 13 Burlington Avenue, Rockledge, Florida. This would be Mom and Dad's last house. The second "Little Girl", Jennifer March Turner, arrived in Mar, 1960. Dad was laid off in December, 1968 but found a job at Eckerd Drugs Photo Lab where he worked until he passed away on 9 July 1971. He made a 110-mile daily round trip to work. It was tough on him, but he never complained.

Mom and Dad had their hands full with six kids. Between work, church activities, baseball, house and yard maintenance, they did their best to make ends meet. Mom and Dad had no quiet time for themselves. They continued to dedicate their lives to their children. Here are just a few examples of what they did to provide for the family:

- Part time work on paper routes driving an old French made Peugeot!!
- Part time work selling pavement repair products.
- Part time work at Church
- Part time work at flea markets
- Raising Chinchillas in our house
- Giving haircuts, using a bowl, for the boys and neighbors
- They never went out on a date unless an uncle paid for it and we never ate out as a family except the one time a realtor paid for it
- To be sure, Mom and Dad were far from perfect, but they set the example for us:
- They never left us "Home Alone"
- They were always there for us when we needed them
- They led us to Sunday School, Church, and to Christ
- They taught us the importance of hard work and education
- They instilled a sense of urgency (get up early to study)
- They instilled the importance of earning what we received and not expecting a handout
- They tolerated our fake diarrhea attacks and smoke bombs tricks. What a sense of humor they both had! They showed us the importance of laughter.
- They always had something for us at Christmas, even if it was only one section of the old white couch.
- They praised and encouraged us and never picked at us about little things.

- They took us to as many places as they could afford (Key West, St. Augustine, Ocala, Church Camp)
- Dad served as Cub Scout Master, coached baseball, was in the choir, served as a deacon and much more. He modeled the behavior he expected of us. He used the Army Values he learned while serving in the Army.

Dad had a massive heart attack on the 4th of July 1971. He struggled to live for five days, until his death on 9 July 1971.

One of the most memorable things about Dad's funeral was when Uncle Jimmy, "Worry Looey" greeted people at the funeral home with his loud, booming voice. "Hi. I'm Jim Graham, Fredericksburg, Virginia. God, this is awful, but you know, Elwood left quite a legacy. Look at these beautiful kids!"

At Mom's funeral, after her long battle with bone cancer ended in May 1984, another funeral home memory comes to mind. There was a tremendous outpouring of love, flowers, and mourners. She too had touched so many lives along the long, winding road from England. It's no accident in God's eyes that she is buried within feet of the children's section at Memorial Gardens.

Elwood and Hazel's legacy live on in the lives of their children, grandchildren, and great grandchildren. We thank God every day that we had Elwood and Hazel as our earthly parents. The grandchildren and great grandchildren are a testimony to the wonderful and unconditional love Elwood and Hazel had for their children.

From left: Elwood holding Rick with Mom and Grandfi and Grandma Sue Pappy Eunice Lois Doug (1954), Dad on a pony bought for John Jr. and David Elwood (1945), Mom and Dad wedding cake September (1945)

From left: Elwood and Hazel Rockledge Florida (1967),
Hazel and Esda at Elwood's Gravesite

Top: Mom and Dad (3 September 1945), bottom left: Mom and Dad wedding cake (September 1945), bottom right: Mom and Dad Wedding Picture at Church in Sturminster Newton (September 1945)

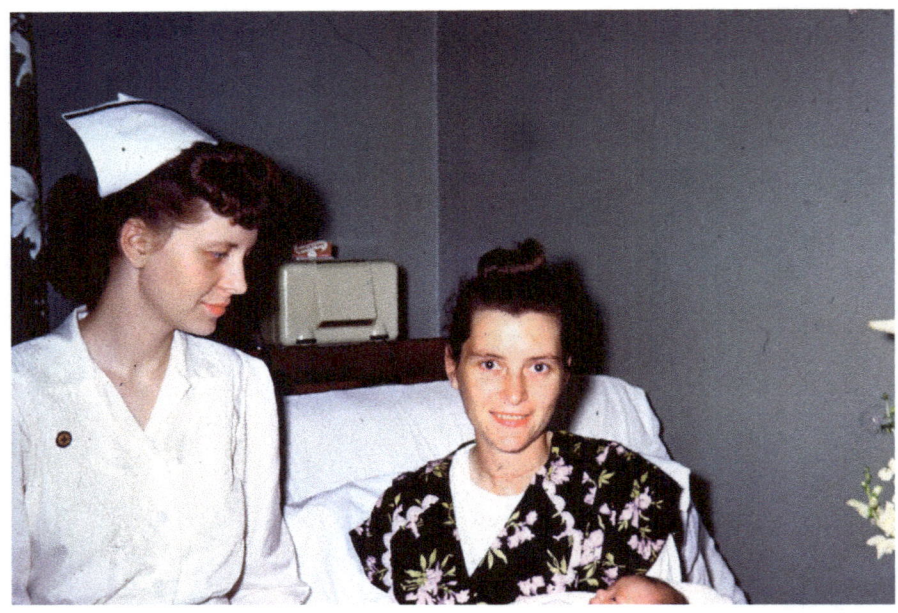

Hazel holding Rick June 1952

Mom in Rochester

The four youngest Turners (1963)

Pappy in Florida (1963)

Rick with Grandfi (1976)

The Turner girls, Margie, Eunice, Lois, and Esda

Rick with Elwood's great grandkids, Brooke, Ace, Beckett, and Brielle

Richard "Rick" Turner

Rick is a first-time author with a passion to preserve the legacy and selfless military service of his father, Elwood Turner, for his family and others to enjoy. In the late 1990s, Rick was given over 160 of his dad's letters dating from his entry into the Army in 1942 and ending in post war Germany in August 1945. His first book captures all 160 letters and traces Elwood's steps from New York, South Carolina, Florida, Tennessee, England, France, Belgium, Luxembourg, Germany and return to the United States.

Rick retired as a Department of Army Civilian (DAC) in November 2009 after over 33 years of service. He transitioned to local industry in 2010 to continue supporting military customers worldwide until his retirement in April 2021 to become a full-time "Papa" for Brooke, Richard "Ace," Beckett and Brielle.

A native of Rochester, New York, Rick earned a Bachelor of Science Degree in Business Management (Summa Cum Laude) from the University of Central Florida in 1974 and a Master's Degree in Systems Management from the University of Southern California, European Division in 1982.

Rick began his career with the Army in 1976 as a DAC in Logistics. He served in multiple locations including a 5-year tour of duty in Germany (1979-1984) with the 200th Theater Army Materiel Management Center, where we supported wartime planning, Operational Projects and served as Deputy Director, Readiness, Plans and Operations. Rick was aware of his father's wartime service; however, his dad never discussed details. As a result, Rick visited many of the same locations his dad served, without realizing until decades later their paths had crossed.

Rick continued to serve in over 19 positions as an Army logistician with responsibilities supporting Army Missile and Aviation systems around the globe. Rick was appointed to the Senior Executive Service in 2006 as the Executive Director, US Army Test, Measurement, and Diagnostic Equipment Activity, where he was responsible for leading over 620 professionals responsible for the US Army's calibration, metrology, and repair mission at over 61 sites worldwide and a presence in 11 countries and 26 states.

Rick is the recipient of several performance awards, a Commander's Award in 1993, the 1994 Ernest A. Young Logistician of the Year Award, the Superior Civilian Performance Award in 2003, and the Secretary of the Army Exceptional Civilian Service Award in 2007. He was selected as one of Army Materiel Command's Ten Outstanding Personnel of the Year in 2001. In 2009, Rick was named the Department of the Army Civilian of the Year by the Association of the US Army.

Rick is very active in his Church where he teaches Sunday School Connection Groups, serves as a Deacon, and is on multiple committees. Rick enjoys mentoring and coaching others on their careers and helping careerists prepare for leadership positions of greater responsibility and authority.

Rick is married to the former Janice James of Russellville, Alabama. Their son Bradley is an electrical engineer, and their daughter Angela Turner Crawford is a Foreign Military Sales Analyst supporting the Army. Rick and his wife Janice greatly enjoy caring for their Grandchildren: Brooke, Richard "Ace," Beckett and Brielle.

www.ingramcontent.com/pod-product-compliance
Lightning Source LLC
Chambersburg PA
CBHW051302120626
46547CB00015B/2055